Full and Productive Employment in Developing Economies

The United Nation's Sustainable Development Goals include a specific target for full and productive employment. However, what constitutes full employment in developing countries is not yet clearly understood. And likewise, there is no clear direction for developing strategies and policies to address this challenge.

Drawing on the author's deep knowledge of employment and inclusive development, this book presents a broad framework which could enable us to pursue the challenging goal of full, productive employment in developing countries. It re-visits the conceptual foundations of full employment and carefully examines the issue of suitable indicators for monitoring progress. It also examines the challenges created by globalized production chains and labour market fluctuations caused by economic crises. This book throws light on a major lacuna in development thinking on how the challenge of creating productive employment for all in developing countries needs to be addressed. It provides a solution by re-examining relevant theories and empirical evidence, and by bringing out their implications for development strategies and policies. Finally, the focus falls on the effective implementation of employment strategies and policies.

This authoritative work will appeal to a diverse readership of academic researchers, think-tanks, international organizations, and development partners.

Rizwanul Islam is former Special Adviser in the Employment Sector at the International Labour Organization, Switzerland.

T0371833

Routledge Studies in Development Economics

Global Commodity Markets and Development Economics
Edited by Stephan Pfaffenzeller

The Service Sector and Economic Development in Africa
Edited by Evelyn F. Wamboye and Peter J. Nyaronga

Macroeconomic Policy for Emerging Markets
Lessons from Thailand
Bhanupong Nidhiprabha

Law and Development
Theory and Practice
Yong-Shik Lee

Institutions, Technology and Development in Africa
Jeffrey James

Urban Policy in Latin America
Towards the Sustainable Development Goals?
Edited by Michael Cohen, Maria Carrizosa and Margarita Gutman

Unlocking SME Finance in Asia
Roles of Credit Rating and Credit Guarantee Schemes
Edited by Naoyuki Yoshino and Farhad Taghizadeh-Hesary

Full and Productive Employment in Developing Economies
Towards the Sustainable Development Goals
Rizwanul Islam

For more information about this series, please visit www.routledge.com/series/SE0266

Full and Productive Employment in Developing Economies

Towards the Sustainable Development Goals

Rizwanul Islam

LONDON AND NEW YORK

First published 2020
by Routledge
2 Park Square, Milton Park, Abingdon, Oxon OX14 4RN

and by Routledge
605 Third Avenue, New York, NY 10017

First issued in paperback 2021

Routledge is an imprint of the Taylor & Francis Group, an informa business

British Library Cataloguing-in-Publication Data
A catalogue record for this book is available from the British Library

Library of Congress Cataloging-in-Publication Data
A catalog record has been requested for this book

ISBN 13: 978-0-367-78462-1 (pbk)
ISBN 13: 978-0-8153-6786-4 (hbk)

Typeset in Bembo
by codeMantra

To **Professor Amartya Sen**
Who supervised my doctoral research

And **Professor Azizur Rahman Khan**
Who supervised my doctoral research for a short period but has been my mentor since then

Contents

Preface

Although the international development agenda articulated in the Sustainable Development Goals (SDGs) includes full productive employment and decent work as one of the goals, and a number of indicators have been proposed for monitoring progress in attaining the goal, it is not clear how the goal should be conceptualized for and pursued in developing countries. The challenge of productive employment faced by developing countries is in many ways different from that in the developed world. And hence a nuanced approach at both conceptual and operational levels is essential if real progress is to be made. The motivation for writing the present book came from this difference, the interest shown by the publisher, and the strong support expressed by the reviewers of the proposal.

While there has been some work (including by the present author) on the link between economic growth, employment, and poverty reduction, the framework for an employment strategy has not yet been fully articulated. Likewise, indicators that would be appropriate for monitoring the progress in attaining full employment in developing countries need to be formulated carefully. Gaps also exist in the analysis of issues relating to the strategy for employment and decent work in a world where production chain is globalized, labour markets are vulnerable to periodic economic fluctuations, and the pursuit of competitiveness often exposes labour to the danger of falling off the cliff. There is thus a gap in the existing literature on the challenge of employment, and the present volume intends to address that gap.

This book starts by arguing that for developing countries, structural transformation of the economy is critical for transferring workers from jobs characterized by low productivity to those with higher productivity. And the challenge of full employment in such economies needs to be looked at in that framework. It presents a conceptualization of the notion of full employment for such economies where open unemployment is not the only or even the main issue for many. An expanded framework is suggested for monitoring progress in boosting productive employment. Whether labour market outcomes observed in developing countries are indicating progress towards inclusive development and the goal of full employment is examined. The issues of job quality are examined in the context of globalization, supply chains, and the danger of a race to the bottom.

As for employment strategies and policies, questions are raised about the conventional approach of focussing only on output growth and of blaming labour market rigidities for slow employment growth. A multi-pronged strategy for addressing the employment challenge in developing countries is outlined, and practical aspects of implementing such a strategy are discussed.

A good deal of the material presented in this volume emerged out of papers I presented at conferences organized by academic and research institutions. They include annual conferences of the Indian Society of Labour Economics and seminars at the Giri Institute of Development Studies, Lucknow, India, and the National Institute of Rural Development, Hyderabad, India. Lectures delivered at various universities and research institutes also helped in shaping up the contents of some of the chapters. Specific mention may be made of the Institute of Human Development, Delhi, India, and BRAC University, Dhaka, Bangladesh. I am grateful to all those institutions and the organizers of the conferences for the opportunities they provided to introduce the various ideas that eventually took the shape of this volume. Thanks are due to the participants at the seminars and lectures for very useful discussions on the issues.

Several friends and professional colleagues read and commented upon earlier drafts of the various chapters of the book. They include Kaushik Basu Iyanatul Islam, Selim Jahan, Muhammad Muqtada, Atiqur Rahman, Ashwani Saith. While I am thankful to them, I take full responsibility for what is presented in this volume.

Mention must be made of my wife, Gitasree, whose continued support and encouragement have been critical in completing the work on the volume.

Finally, thanks are due to Routledge for the interest they expressed in publishing this volume, the speed with which they processed the initial proposal, and the care they have taken throughout the process of publication. I would like to particularly mention Natalie Tomlinson, Emily Kindleysides, Laura Johnson, and Lisa Lavelle, who have been very helpful at various stages of the work.

RI

Acknowledgements

The author would like to thank the following organizations for permission to reproduce texts and figures from the publications listed below:

1   **Indian Society of Labour Economics**: For permission to use material from Islam, Rizwanul (2016): "Pursuing the Employment Goal: Need for Re-Thinking Development Strategies", *The Indian Journal of Labour Economics*, Vol. 58, No. 2, pp. 196–216.
2   **International Labour Office**: For permission to use Figures 4.1 a through 4.1 d from Islam, Rizwanul (2011): "The Employment Challenge in Developing Countries during Economic Downturn and Recovery" in Islam, Iyanatul and Sher Verick (eds.): *From the Great Recession to Labour Market Recovery: Issues, Evidence and Policy Options*. ILO and Palgrave Macmillan, Geneva and London.
3   **International Labour Office**: For permission to use parts of Islam, Rizwanul (2014): "Employment Policy Implementation Mechanisms: A Synthesis Based on Country Experiences". Employment Working Paper No. 161, Employment Policy Department, ILO, Geneva.
4   **Springer**: For permission to use Islam, Rizwanul (2019): "Labour Market Outcomes and Inclusive Development: Experiences of South Asian Countries" in Mamgain, Rajendra P. (ed.): *Growth, Disparities and Inclusive Development in India*, pp. 75–102. Springer, Singapore.
5   **UNDP**: For permission to use Islam, Rizwanul (2015): "Globalization of Production, Work and Human Development: Is a Race to the Bottom Inevitable?" Think Piece, Human Development Report Office, UNDP, New York. http://hdr.undp.org/sites/default/files/islam_hdr_2015_final.pdf.

1 Introduction

The background and purpose of the book

As labour power is often the only productive asset possessed by the poor, productive employment that provides them with a decent living can be an effective means of getting out of poverty. Hence such employment has to be the cornerstone of the process of inclusive development. So, it is not surprising that the post-MDG development agenda articulated in the Sustainable Development Goals (SDGs) includes full, productive employment and decent work as one of the 17 goals.

However, it is far from clear how full employment should be conceptualized in the context of developing countries, in many of which open unemployment by standard definition is very low, and yet many who work continue to struggle with a living below poverty. Moreover, the question whether economic growth would automatically lead to the required growth of employment or whether development strategies and policies need to be geared towards more job-rich growth remains unsettled. Slow growth of employment is often blamed on rigidities in the functioning of labour markets, and making the latter flexible is regarded as "employment policy". But the disappointing record of employment in situations where sustained high growth has been attained clearly demonstrates the need for a re-thinking in this regard.

Despite the recognition of the issue of employment in formulating the SDGs, the debate surrounding the issue of jobs, especially on why economic growth often does not lead to job creation at an expected rate, has not been resolved. At one extreme, there is still a tendency to deny the existence of the problem of slow growth of jobs in relation to economic growth. For example, the World Bank's World Development Report on jobs (World Bank, 2012) attempts to dispel the notion of jobless growth by pointing out that economic growth is always accompanied by some growth in employment (pp. 98–99). There is, however, empirical evidence to show that there have been cases of zero growth of employment when economic growth has been positive (Islam, 2010; Islam and Islam, 2015). Moreover, the term "jobless growth" need not be interpreted in a literal sense of zero employment growth; when employment growth remains low, despite substantial output growth, the situation may be termed as one of jobless growth.

A more important point to note is the approach adopted to explain the slow growth of jobs. In this respect, the conventional wisdom is to argue that distortions in the labour market and its imperfect functioning act as constraints on employment creation. This view equates employment policy with labour market policies – i.e., policies for making labour markets flexible. Influential studies like the report of the Commission on Growth (2008) and the IMF's report on job growth (IMF, 2013) are examples of this strand of work, although there are differences in details. In addition to labour market flexibility, the Growth Commission's report does talk about the need for measures to jump-start the process of job creation by encouraging the growth of new industries. Likewise, IMF (2013) talks about "selected policy interventions" that might lift barriers to private sector job creation. However, the debate on employment still seems to fall short of recognizing that economic growth and labour market flexibility alone cannot solve the problem of slow employment growth.

Although there has been some work (including by the present author) on the link between economic growth, employment, and poverty reduction, the framework for an employment strategy has not yet been fully articulated. Likewise, indicators that would be appropriate for monitoring the progress in attaining full employment in developing countries need to be formulated carefully. Gaps also exist in the analysis of issues relating to the strategy for employment in a world where production chain is globalized, labour markets are vulnerable to periodic economic fluctuations, and the pursuit of competitiveness often exposes labour to the danger of falling off the cliff. There is thus a gap in the existing literature on the challenge of employment, and the present volume intends to address that gap.

This book presents a broad framework within which the challenge of the goal of full productive employment in developing countries could be pursued and argues that a re-thinking of development strategies and policies is needed to attain this goal. In doing so, it re-visits the conceptual aspects of full employment as well as indicators for monitoring progress in attaining this goal in developing countries. In addition, challenges created by the pursuit of competitiveness in the globalized system of production, economic fluctuations and crises, and concerns about conditions in which work is carried out are examined. The challenge of implementing employment strategies and policies is also addressed.

A readers' guide to the book

Chapter 2: Structural transformation and employment

This chapter addresses the issue of the type of structural transformation of an economy that would be effective from the point of productive employment.

The process of economic growth and development involves transformation of the structure of economies in a way that is characterized by a reduction in the share of agriculture and a rise in the share of industries and services in total output. An important aspect of this process in economies with surplus labour is transfer of workers from sectors characterized by low productivity to sectors/activities with higher levels of productivity and a rise in the incomes of workers. Theoretical explanations of structural transformation of economies have been provided by a number of scholars – both in the context of economic growth in general and in the context of dualistic economies of developing countries. And they postulate that the process of development involves a transfer of labour from traditional sectors (e.g., agriculture) to modern sectors (e.g., industry). In the received economic theories, manufacturing plays the role of the engine of economic growth and is expected to play a major role in absorbing surplus labour.

The experience of countries (especially of East and South East Asia [ESEA], e.g., Republic of Korea, Malaysia, Taiwan-China) that have been successful in achieving economic growth shows that the process of development was indeed characterized by a transfer of labour from agriculture to industry and the attainment of the so-called "Lewis turning point" – the stage where surplus labour was fully absorbed and expansion of employment beyond that point involved rise in real wage rates.

But the process described above has not been the universal experience; in many developing countries, even respectable rates of economic growth have not been accompanied by similar rates of employment growth and transfer of workers to sectors with higher productivity. In fact, countries of South Asia, e.g., Bangladesh, India, and Nepal have been less successful than those in ESEA in absorbing surplus labour. Such divergence in experience raises the question as to whether there are alternative approaches to structural transformation and generation of productive employment. The present chapter attempts to address this issue. In doing so, it adopts a comparative approach and provides an overview of the experience of selected countries of Asia. For addressing the question of alternative pathways to structural transformation, the main focus is on selected countries of South Asia, viz., Bangladesh, India, and Nepal.

Chapter 3: Conceptualizing the goal of full employment and the SDG framework

The post-MDG development agenda (viz., SDGs – adopted in 2015, with 2030 as the terminal year for attaining the goals) includes full and productive employment and decent work as a goal in addition to the goal of economic growth. If this goal is to be pursued seriously by developing countries, it is important to start from how the notion of full and productive employment can be conceptualized from a practical point of view. Once the goal is defined in a concrete and realistic manner, the next task is to identify a set of indicators that can be used to monitor progress towards attaining the goal. Both are areas where work needs to be undertaken at the conceptual as well as empirical level.

This chapter addresses the question how the notion of full and productive employment can be conceptualized for economies with surplus labour where open unemployment does not capture the challenge of employment. Given the limitations of the concept of non-accelerating inflation rate of unemployment (NAIRU) from the perspective of developing countries, an expanded framework and a few indicators are suggested for examining the progress being made with regard to the growth of productive employment. Possible application of the proposed alternatives is illustrated with particular reference to selected countries of South Asia.

Chapter 4: Labour market outcomes and inclusive development

In this chapter, an attempt is made to examine whether labour market outcomes like employment, wages, returns to self-employment, and social protection are contributing to make economic growth inclusive in developing countries. Although the term inclusion may be conceptualized in different ways, it is important to focus on both the process and outcome. While the process of inclusion can be captured through measures relating to employment, the outcomes can be assessed in terms of poverty, inequality, or other dimensions of human development like education and health. Another important element of inclusion is the degree of social protection provided by a society. Characterized this way, labour market outcomes are of direct relevance for inclusive growth. A number of questions are raised in this context.

- Is economic growth leading to the growth of productive employment that is needed for absorbing the new members of the labour force and for transferring workers from sectors characterized by low productivity to those with higher productivity?
- Is sector composition of employment changing in a way that contributes to poverty reduction (through higher incomes of workers)?
- Is access to social protection expanding along with economic growth?
- Is economic growth associated with growth of labour productivity and rise in real wages?
- Are real wages rising to contribute to reduction in poverty and inequality?

The present chapter attempts to address some of the above questions with particular focus on the experience of the countries of South Asia. The concept of employment elasticity with respect to output growth is used to examine the labour absorptive capacity of various countries and how that has evolved over time. Challenges faced by these countries in the area of social protection are pointed out. What has happened to real wages and the share of wages in value added is also be examined. Based on the above-mentioned analysis, an attempt is made to assess whether labour market outcomes have helped make economic growth inclusive.

Chapter 5: Economic fluctuations and vulnerability of labour markets

Central planning has by and large been abandoned as a tool for pursuing economic growth, and dependence on markets has become the rule. In such situations, periodic economic fluctuations are quite common, and in some instances, such fluctuations turn into economic crises. Apart from periodic fluctuations arising out of business cycles, economic crises also occur due to a variety of factors. Labour markets face risks and vulnerabilities arising out of economic fluctuations and crises, and are often adversely affected by crises. Moreover, recovery in labour markets may take longer than economic recovery. Unless an economy builds resilience to face such crises and to protect their labour markets from their adverse effects, lives, and livelihoods of workers are likely to be affected seriously. The present chapter deals with this issue.

The chapter starts by providing an understanding of the risks and vulnerabilities faced by labour markets in the face of economic fluctuations and crises, and reviews the experience of how labour markets were affected by a few major crises, e.g., the Asian economic crisis of 1997–98 and the global economic crisis of 2008–09. Labour market instruments that can help build resilience and address the adverse effects of crises are outlined.

Chapter 6: Has employment-intensive growth become history?

As mentioned already, economic development in countries with surplus labour is often characterized as a process of structural transformation through which the surplus labour is absorbed in modern sectors – first in manufacturing, followed by services. As several countries of ESEA attained success by pursuing such a growth path, other developing countries were also advised to pursue the same through open (or export-oriented) economic and trade-policies – the expectation being that such strategies would enable them to achieve growth, absorb their surplus labour, and reduce poverty. It may, therefore, be quite legitimate to raise the question about the degree to which such countries with surplus labour have been able to achieve the kind of development that was attained by the initial set of countries mentioned above.

The analysis and discussion in Chapters 2–4 show that the countries of South Asia have not been able to attain the same degree of success attained by countries of ESEA in terms of the level or pattern of growth required for absorbing surplus labour and reaching the Lewis turning point. And that was despite their shift from inward-looking economic policies towards outward-looking and export-oriented policies. Such experiences, in turn, raise the question whether a repeat of the type of employment-intensive economic growth through industrialization achieved by the countries of ESEA is at all possible. This question becomes even more pertinent in the context of two recent strands of discussions. The first concerns the possibility of premature de-industrialization while the second is a concern arising out of the availability of new technology that is regarded as the hallmark of the fourth industrial revolution. If de-industrialization starts before a country's economy has absorbed all its surplus labour, the task of further labour absorption would become correspondingly difficult. Likewise, a premature spread of new labour-saving technologies may make it difficult to attain the Lewis turning point.

The purpose of the present chapter is to address the two issues mentioned above. It starts with a brief outline of the notion of employment-intensive growth and the role of industrialization in achieving such growth. That is followed by a recapitulation of the East Asian experience from the perspective of the employment-intensity of economic growth that was achieved. Then the issues of de-industrialization and of new technology acting as a brake on employment growth are examined with particular focus on countries of South Asia. The concluding section points out the difficulties faced by contemporary developing countries of Asia in achieving development and employment through labour-intensive industrialization.

Chapter 7: Globalization of production and the world of work: is a race to the bottom inevitable?

Globalization of production has influenced the world of work in ways not seen before. While some impacts have been positive from the point of view of workers, others have given rise to serious concerns. On the positive side, new employment opportunities hitherto unknown in many developing countries have opened. On the other hand, serious pressure on the working class has come through the stagnation of real wages and adverse workplace conditions. The term "race to the bottom" has come into circulation in that context. But this does not have to be the only way forward because there are useful positive aspects from which workers could benefit alongside the rest of the global community. This chapter explores possible paths to such outcomes.

The chapter starts by providing a brief overview of the picture of the world of work in a globalized system of production which gives rise to the danger of a race to the bottom. It is argued that a static view of competitiveness is inadequate even from the point of view of profitability and of benefiting from advantages opened by the globalization of production. This argument is illustrated with practical examples. How the global supply chain creates pressure on workers is illustrated with the specific example of the ready-made garment industry of Bangladesh. The broader question of how the alternative path of a "high road to development" (as opposed to the race to the bottom approach) can be pursued and what role public policy can play in this regard is addressed.

Chapter 8: Re-thinking development strategies and policies for productive employment

This chapter addresses the issue of slow growth of employment, particularly in the formal sector, and outlines development strategies needed for attaining the SDG of full and productive employment by 2030.

The conventional wisdom often leads one to argue that if economic growth is not associated with employment growth, it must be due to distortions in the labour market and its imperfect functioning. This view equates employment policy with labour market policies, i.e., policies for making labour markets flexible. Although some recent work by influential institutions (e.g., the IMF and the World Bank) does concede the need for measures to "jump-start the process of job creation through encouraging the growth of new industries" and the importance of "selected policy interventions" for lifting barriers to private sector job creation, the debate on employment still seems to fall short of recognizing that economic growth and labour market flexibility alone cannot solve the problem of slow employment growth.

The present chapter starts by questioning this conventional approach and then goes on to outline a broader alternative approach combining economic and labour market policies that would be needed to attain the goal of full employment. To be specific, questions are raised about three conventional wisdoms in this area: (i) economic growth always leads to job creation; (ii) when growth is not accompanied by job creation, that is primarily due to rigidities in the labour market; and (iii) a large part of the unemployment problem must be due to lack of education and skills of the labour force. Empirical evidence is used to examine and dispel these conventional notions. And on that basis, it is argued that a re-thinking in development strategies is needed in order to effectively address the employment goal in developing countries. Outlines are provided of macroeconomic and sector-level policies, and appropriate labour market policies that are needed to achieve economic transformation and diversification that are critical for making growth more job-rich. How the task of formulating and implementing employment policies could be mainstreamed into the policymaking framework is also be discussed.

Chapter 9: Implementation of employment strategies and policies

In order to address the employment challenge, it would be important not merely to formulate strategies and policies for making economic growth more job-rich but also to implement such policies in an efficient and effective manner. Unless appropriate institutional arrangements can be put in place for coordinating policies, monitoring performance, and evaluating results, even sound policies may not produce the desired results. The other challenge is that of finding resources, especially when the question of allocating resources for active policies to be pursued by the government itself arises.

The purpose of the present chapter is to illustrate, with examples from selected countries, different approaches to the formulation and implementation of strategies and policies for employment. In doing so, attention is given to alternative institutional approaches and modalities that can be adopted.

In reality, different countries have adopted a variety of approaches to the formulation and implementation of employment policies. They range from adoption of specific quantitative targets for the number of additional jobs to be created within a specified period to target rate of open unemployment. The institutional mechanisms for implementation also vary a great deal. Some countries like China and Republic of Korea have well-specified mechanisms to monitor and coordinate the process of implementation, others (e.g., the countries of South Asia) may simply have periodic labour force and employment surveys that can be used to monitor the employment situation.

Chapter 10: Concluding observations

The concluding chapter summarizes some key findings of the book and highlights policy options for promoting durable, productive, and broad-based employment creation in a developing country context. In doing so, specific attention is given to how countries can pursue the SDG of full and productive employment by 2030.

References

Commission on Growth and Development (2008): *The Growth Report: Strategies for Sustainable Growth and Inclusive Development.* The World Bank, Washington, D.C.

International Monetary Fund (2013): *Jobs and Growth: Analytical and Operational Conditions for the Fund.* IMF, Washington, D.C. www.imf.org/external/np/pp/eng/2013/031413.pdf (Accessed on 14 July 2014).

Islam, Rizwanul (2010): "The Challenge of Jobless Growth in Developing Countries: An Analysis with Cross-Country Data". Occasional Paper Series No. 01. Bangladesh Institute of Development Studies, Dhaka.

Islam, Rizwanul and Iyanatul Islam (2015): *Employment and Inclusive Development.* Routledge, London.

World Bank (2012): *World Development Report 2013 Jobs.* The World Bank, Washington, D.C.

2 Structural transformation and employment

Introduction

The process of economic growth and development involves transformation of the structure of economies in a way that is characterized by a reduction in the share of agriculture and a rise in the share of industries and services in total output. Productive employment is also generated through this process. An important aspect of this process in economies with surplus labour is transfer of workers from sectors characterized by low productivity (e.g., agriculture) to sectors/activities with higher levels of productivity (e.g., industry) and a rise in the incomes of workers.

The experience of countries (especially of East and South East Asia [ESEA], e.g., Republic of Korea, Malaysia, Taiwan-China) that have been successful in combining economic growth with productive employment and the absorption of surplus labour shows that the process was indeed characterized by a transfer of labour from agriculture to industry and the attainment of the so-called "Lewis turning point" – the stage where surplus labour was fully absorbed and expansion of employment beyond that point involved rise in real wage rates.

But the process described above has not been the universal experience; in many developing countries, even respectable rates of economic growth have not been accompanied by similar rates of employment growth and transfer of workers to sectors with higher productivity. In fact, countries of South Asia, e.g., Bangladesh, India, and Nepal have been less successful than those in ESEA in absorbing surplus labour. Such divergence in experience raises the question as to whether there are alternative approaches to structural transformation, employment generation, and absorption of surplus labour. For example,

- Does the "modern sector" mentioned in dual economy models have to mean manufacturing, or can it be interpreted more flexibly to include other sectors like trade, services, etc.?
- Is transfer of surplus labour from traditional to modern sector synonymous with migration from rural to urban areas or workers may be able to

find higher productivity employment in rural (or semi-urban) non-farm activities?

• If answers to the above questions indicate the existence of alternative ways of attaining structural transformation and of reaching the Lewis turning point in dual economies, the question of their speed and effectiveness would remain.

This chapter addresses the above questions. In doing so, it adopts a comparative approach and starts with an overview of the experience of selected countries of Asia. For addressing the question of alternative pathways to structural transformation, the focus is particularly on Bangladesh, India, and Nepal. The chapter is organized as follows. It begins with a brief discussion on some theoretical underpinnings of structural transformation and goes on to provide some empirical evidence on the issue, drawing on data from both developed and developing countries. How the major drivers of structural transformation through industrialization (viz., external and domestic demand and policy environment) has worked for South Asia is examined. That is followed by an empirical analysis of some alternative pathways to structural transformation with illustrations from Bangladesh, India, and Nepal. The chapter concludes by providing a brief assessment of the possibilities of attaining structural transformation in countries of South Asia through alternative pathways other than industrialization.

Structural transformation: some theoretical underpinnings

The early theories

While Clark (1951), Fisher (1939), Kuznets (1966, 1971), and Kaldor (1966, 1967) have provided the theoretical explanations of structural transformation of economies, models of dual economy (*à la* Lewis, 1954 and Ranis–Fei, 1961) postulate that the process of development involves a transfer of labour from traditional sectors (e.g., agriculture) to modern sectors (e.g., industry). In Kaldor's framework, manufacturing plays the role of the engine of economic growth, and the dual economy models consider this to be the modern sector that should play a major role in absorbing surplus labour.

Clark, Fisher, and Kuznets explained structural transformation from demand side. In that regard, they refer to Engel's law postulating that with increases in incomes, demand for food (and hence, agricultural commodities) increases less than proportionately while that for industrial goods like clothing, consumer durables, etc., increases more than proportionately. Again, at a higher level of income, demand for services like financial and personal services tends to increase at higher rates. As the pattern of demand changes, the structure of production also changes accordingly – thus creating conditions for a decline in the share of agriculture and a rise in the share of manufacturing at the early stage of growth and then a decline in the share of manufacturing and a rise in the share of services at the subsequent stage of growth. As the structure of production changes, the structure of employment should also change accordingly.

Kaldor, on the other hand, looks at the issue from both demand and supply sides. His framework starts by recognizing the standard classification of an economy into broad sectors like agriculture, industry, and services, and by focussing on their respective characteristics. Since agriculture is more dependent on land and the latter is subject to diminishing returns to investment, there is a limit to increase in productivity (and hence, production) in the sector. But this limitation of agriculture does not usually apply to manufacturing, and hence, growth in the latter can be much higher than in the former. As a result of the operation of these forces, manufacturing usually plays the role of the engine of growth in developing economies.

Like in Lewis's model, Kaldor's framework also features transfer of workers from agriculture to industry without an adverse effect on the output of the latter. As a result of this as well as the use of modern technology, productivity increases in agriculture. Productivity increases in industry also because the sector can reap the benefits of economies of scale and technical progress. However, productivity growth in manufacturing is expected to be higher than in agriculture. And from that follows three hypotheses:

- Overall economic growth is influenced more strongly by manufacturing growth than growth of agriculture.
- In manufacturing, productivity growth drives growth of production.
- Given the spillover effects of manufacturing – through backward and forward linkages – expansion of the sector helps raise productivity growth in the economy.

Whether it is a demand-driven framework, as provided by the explanations of Clark, Fisher, and Kuznets, or a combination of demand- and supply-side forces, as in Kaldor's framework, structural change in a growing economy is expected to follow the pattern depicted in a stylized manner in Figure 2.1.

To sum up the above discussion, as an economy grows over time, the share of agriculture in GDP is expected to register a secular decline while that of services a secular rise. But the share of manufacturing is expected to rise to a point and then decline. A critical issue in this regard is the point at which the share of manufacturing starts declining. The timing and level of development (per capita GDP could be taken as an indicator of the latter) at which this happens may vary from country to country (Islam and Islam, 2015). And that can happen due to a variety of reasons.

The employment issue

Structural transformation of an economy along conventional paths, i.e., shift from agriculture to manufacturing followed by services would depend critically on the sectoral pattern of growth that unfolds in an economy.

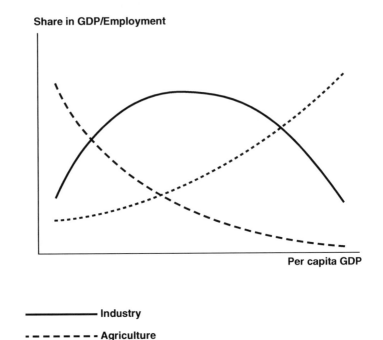

Figure 2.1 A Stylized Description Changes in the Share of Different Sectors in GDP/
Employment.

However, neither the theoretical frameworks of Clark, Fisher, and Kaldor nor
the dual economy models of Lewis and Ranis–Fei mentioned anything about
the composition of the manufacturing sector and its possible implication for
employment. But from the point of view of engendering a process of quick
transfer of labour from low productivity sectors like agriculture to industry,
it is important not only to have high growth of manufacturing but also to
have high growth of employment in that sector. That would be possible when
labour-intensive industries grow at high rates and have a higher weight in
the growth of the manufacturing sector. The experience of the countries of
ESEA (e.g., Republic of Korea, Taiwan-China, and Malaysia) who succeeded
in attaining high rates of employment growth alongside economic growth
and were able to fully absorb their surplus labour clearly demonstrates this.

The pattern of growth mentioned above would, of course, depend on a
variety of factors like the pattern of demand in the domestic as well as the
external market or the policy environment prevailing in an economy – an
issue to which we shall return later in this chapter.

As for the demand-based explanation mentioned earlier, given the possibility of imports in an open economy, a part of the growing demand for

manufactured goods can be met through that channel. In a country following that strategy, manufacturing industries may not grow in tandem with the growth of demand for products of that kind. On the other hand, demand for the products of the service sector does not have to remain confined to the domestic market alone. Although services are generally considered to be non-tradable, this does not apply to services that are based on information and communication technology (ICT). Based on such possibilities, there is a growing literature that questions the conventional sequence of "agriculture followed by industry and then services" in the analysis of structural transformation of economies.[1]

The debate on alternative pathways

As mentioned already, models of development with surplus labour postulate growth of modern sectors and the absorption of surplus labour in such sectors. A question that may be raised in this context is whether the term modern sector needs to be coterminous with manufacturing or whether growth and labour absorption can be driven by other sectors. Of course, the historical experience of the currently developed countries and the late developers who have been successful in achieving development indicates that structural change during the early stages of economic growth is led by manufacturing, and the service sector takes over the role of the driver of growth at a subsequent stage of growth. But given the variation in resource endowment and circumstances faced by different countries and the current global economic environment, it may not be realistic to expect all developing countries to be able to follow the same path of economic growth and labour absorption.

Like in many areas of economic and development policies, the rationale for one-size-fits-all approach to structural transformation has also come into question. While the question appeared to be quite relevant in the context of Africa where many countries faced declines in their manufacturing industries during the 1980s and 1990s[2] and the service sector started showing good prospects of growth,[3] it attracted debate in other countries as well (e.g., in India). One strand in this debate[4] takes a pessimistic view of the decline of the manufacturing sector (a phenomenon dubbed as "de-industrialization") and points out that reallocation of labour and other resources away from this to other sectors causes a negative impact on labour productivity growth and hence on the growth of economy as a whole (McMillan and Rodrik, 2011).

But there are others (e.g., Kucera and Roncolato 2014; Roncolato and Kucera, 2014) who point out that the impact of reallocation between sectors (even if it is away from manufacturing) is not always negative, and the overall effect (taking into account the growth in productivity within sectors) could be positive. Be that as it may, it is important to note that while de-industrialization is a reality in many countries, other sectors like services and agriculture (especially diversification within the crop sector and between crop and con-crop activities) can play an important role in bringing about structural transformation in developing economies that could at the same time transfer labour from low productivity to higher productivity activities. But the moot question is whether such alternative pathways hold a real promise for the absorption of surplus labour and for attaining the Lewis turning point within a reasonable period of time.

Structural transformation: some empirical evidence

Developed countries

The outline provided above of structural changes in output and employment appears to be reflected in the historical experience of present-day developed countries. For example, structural change experienced by countries like France, Germany, the UK, and the USA shows a roughly similar pattern: decline in the share of agriculture accompanied by an increase in the share of industries at the initial stages of growth, and a decline in the share of industries at a subsequent stage along with increase in the share of services. The share of agriculture in GDP ranged from a third to half in the UK during the early part of nineteenth century, in France in 1835, and in the USA in 1872. This went down to about a fourth during the subsequent 75–100 years and to around five per cent towards the end of the twentieth century. On the other hand, the share of industry went up to 50 per cent and by the end of the twentieth century declined to 30 per cent. By then, the share of services increased to 70 per cent.[5] One notable feature of that structural change was a similar change in the structure of employment – with the share of different sectors in total employment remaining close to that in output. That implies that economic growth did not result in a major difference in labour productivity in different sectors.

Figures in Table 2.1 show that the pattern of structural change described above continued during the past decade as well. The share of agriculture declined further to between one and two per cent, while that of services increased further to 78–79 per cent. The change in the structure of employment also continued, although some gender-related differences are noticeable. In the manufacturing sector, the share of men is higher than that of women, while the opposite is the case in services. It seems that women are not being attracted to the industrial sector.

Developing countries

Turning to the currently developing countries, development in some of them seems to have followed a pattern similar to that of the developed countries mentioned above. Data for some Asian countries presented in Table 2.2 show such pattern for Republic of Korea, Indonesia, Malaysia, and Thailand. In these countries, the decline in the share of agriculture and increase in that of industries have been quite notable. Quite clearly, manufacturing in these

Table 2.1 Share (%) of Different Sectors in Total GDP and Employment in Selected Developed Countries of the World

Country	Share in GDP (2010)			Share in Employment (2007–10)					
	Agriculture	Industry	Services	Agriculture		Industry		Services	
				Male	Female	Male	Female	Male	Female
Australia	2	20	78	4	2	32	9	64	88
France	2	19	79	4	2	33	10	63	88
Germany	1	28	71	2	1	40	14	58	84
Japan	1	27	72	4	4	33	15	62	80
UK	1	22	78	2	1	29	7	68	91
USA	1	20	79	2	1	25	7	72	92

Source: World Bank: World Development Indicators 2012.

Table 2.2 Change in the Sector Composition of GDP in Selected Developing Countries, 1960–2010

Country	Agriculture (%)		Industry (%)		Services (%)	
	1960	2010	1960	2010	1960	2010
Bangladesh	53	19	11	28	36	53
China	22	10	45	47	33	43
India	43	19	20	26	38	55
Indonesia	51	15	15	47	33	38
Malaysia	34	11	19	44	46	45
Nepal	65	36	11	15	23	48
Pakistan	46	21	16	25	38	53
Philippines	26	12	28	33	47	55
Republic of Korea	38	3	18	39	43	58
Sri Lanka	28	13	21	29	51	58
Thailand	36	12	19	45	45	43

Source: World Bank: World Development Indicators 2004 (CD-ROM), World Development Report 1990, and World Development Indicators 2012.

countries has acted as the engine of growth. But the experience of the countries of South Asia has been different. In Bangladesh and India, for example, the decline in the share of agriculture has not been followed by a similar increase in the share of industry; the increase has been more than proportionate in services. This is particularly the case when one looks at the structure of employment (Table 2.3).

In Republic of Korea, the share of manufacturing in total employment had risen to 23 in 2000 before it started to decline. In Taiwan-China, the peak share of manufacturing in employment was even higher – 32 per cent in 1990. The rise and decline of the share of Malaysia's manufacturing – shown in Figure 2.2 – illustrates the point very clearly. From less than 16 per cent in

Table 2.3 Sector Composition of Employment in South Asia (Percentage of Total Employment)

Country and Period	Agriculture	Industry	Manufacturing	Construction	Services
Bangladesh					
1999–2000	50.7	12.3	9.5	2.8	36.1
2005–06	48.1	14.5	11.0	3.2	37.5
2010	47.6	17.7	12.5	4.8	35.3
2013	45.1	20.8	16.4	3.7	34.1
2016–17	40.6	20.4	14.4	5.6	39.0
India					
1993–94	64.8	14.7	10.5	3.1	20.5
2004–05	58.5	18.1	12.0	5.6	23.4
2011–12	48.9	24.4	12.9	10.6	26.7
Nepal					
1998–99	78.2	10.5	5.8	3.6	11.3
2008–09	73.9	10.8	6.6	3.1	15.3
Pakistan					
2005–06	42.3	20.7	13.8	6.1	37.0
2010–11	44.2	21.3	13.7	7.0	34.4
Sri Lanka					
2004	33.5	24.1	n.a.	n.a.	42.4
2011	33.0	24.0	n.a.	n.a.	42.8

Source: Labour Force Surveys of different countries.

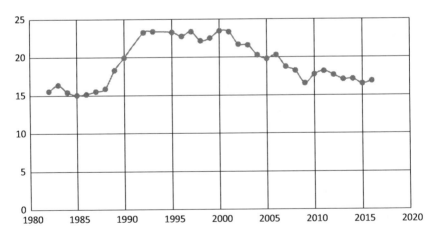

Figure 2.2 Malaysia: Share (%) of Manufacturing in Total Employment, 1982–2016.
Source: Constructed by using data from Department of Statistics, Malaysia Official Portal, Time Series Data. www.dosm.gov.my/v1/index.php?r=column/ctimeseries&menu_id=NHJ laGc2Rlg4ZXlGTjh1SU1kaWY5UT09 (Accessed on 30 January 2018).

1982, the share went up to over 23 per cent during the late 1990s and started to fall after 2001. By 2016, the share had fallen to less than 17 per cent. In contrast, the corresponding figure for India never exceeded 13 per cent. In Bangladesh, it went up to 16 per cent in 2013 and then declined to 13 per cent in 2015–16.

In order to understand the pattern of structural change in South Asian countries (and their contrast with countries of ESEA), it would be useful to look more closely at their growth rates and pattern. In Bangladesh, there has been a steady acceleration in economic growth since the 1990s: from an annual GDP growth of less than five per cent per annum, the country reached six per cent growth in a decade. In 2003–04, growth rate exceeded six per cent and since then has hovered around that mark. Although GDP growth appears to have reached a plateau in recent years, it has remained over six per cent per annum and has crossed seven per cent in 2015–16. Economic growth in India has been more impressive, especially since the mid-1990s. GDP growth rate started accelerating since 1994–95 and ranged between six and nine per cent per annum in most years after that. The annual average GDP growth in India has increased from six per cent during the 1990s to 7.6 per cent during 2000–14 (Annex, Table 2A.1). Sri Lanka also witnessed an acceleration in growth from 5.3 per cent during the 1990s to 6.1 per cent per annum during 2000–14. Nepal and Pakistan's growth record is not so impressive, but Pakistan was able to raise its economic growth during the first half of the 2000s (Amjad and Yusuf, 2014).

Despite such impressive rates of GDP growth, the slow rate of structural transformation in employment observed from Tables 2.2 and 2.3 is something to take note of. In order to understand this, one has to look at the pattern of growth and its drivers. One particular element in that is whether manufacturing has acted as the driver of growth (as discussed above).

In Bangladesh, there has been very little difference between overall GDP growth and growth in manufacturing during 1995–96 and 1999–2000. The ratio increased to about 1.5 during 1999–2000 to 2005–06 but then declined to 1.23 during 2005–10.[6] In India also, industry has not emerged as the driver/engine of economic growth. The elasticity of manufacturing growth with respect to GDP growth declined from 1.14 during 1990–2000 to 1.09 during 2000–10.[7] In Nepal, this elasticity has been declining steadily since mid-1990s and was negative after 2005 (Islam, 2014b). In Pakistan, the figure has fluctuated – declining from 1.34 during the 1980s to 1.04 during the 1990s and then rising to 1.54 during the 2000s.[8] In Sri Lanka, the elasticity varied from 1.6 during the 1980s to 0.7 during 2000–05 (Islam, 2008).

In contrast, in Republic of Korea, the corresponding figure was over 2 during the 1960s, 1.8 during 1970–80 and 1.4 during 1980–90. In Malaysia also, the figure was between 1.5 and 1.8 during the 1970–96 (Islam, 2008).

The conclusion that follows from the figures mentioned above is that in South Asia, manufacturing has not been the driver of economic growth in the same way as it has been in countries like Korea and Malaysia during the early stages of their growth. In order to understand why there has been such divergence of experience between these two groups of countries, it would be necessary to examine the drivers of structural transformation and how they have worked for countries of South Asia. We now turn to this question.

Drivers of Structural Transformation

As mentioned already, a shift in the structure of output and employment needed for producing a high growth of productive employment would require labour-intensive industries to grow at high rates. This pattern of growth would depend on a variety of factors like the pattern of demand in the domestic as well as the external market or the policy environment prevailing in an economy.

Pattern of demand

External demand

External demand plays a major role, especially in open economies. The pattern of comparative advantage and the nature of the trade regime can influence the pattern of industrialization in terms of its sector composition. Conventional trade theory suggests that labour-abundant countries have a comparative advantage in the production and export of labour-intensive goods. Hence, an outward-looking and export-oriented development strategy should result in a high growth of such sectors and a high growth of employment. This process should continue until surplus labour gets exhausted and wage rates start rising, at which point employment elasticity may also start to decline.

Countries of South Asia abandoned the import substitution strategy of industrialization that they had adopted after their independence and shifted to more open and market-oriented economies at various points in time, and in line with such strategies, they adopted measures of trade liberalization.[9] However, the critical question here is whether such a growth strategy automatically results in a change in the structure of production towards more labour-intensive sectors and in high employment growth.

In order to understand whether exports can help developing countries in promoting the growth of their more labour-intensive lines of production, it would be necessary to have estimates of the elasticity of export demand for various categories of products and see whether elasticity is higher for labour-intensive items. Unfortunately, there are not many studies with estimates of export demand elasticity disaggregated at the sector level. One study on India (UNCTAD, 2013)[10] shows that for exports as a whole, income elasticity of demand was higher than unity (1.88) while price elasticity of demand was only 0.54. When disaggregated by items, income elasticity was found to be much higher for items like petroleum products, chemicals, and engineering goods than for items like textile and leather which are much more labour-intensive compared to the former three items. Of the labour-intensive items, gems and jewellery showed very high-income elasticity and close to unity price elasticity of demand.

One study on export demand elasticity for different export items of Pakistan (Hussain, 2010 – covering the period of 1988–2009) showed mixed results. For labour-intensive items like knitwear and other wearing apparel, expenditure elasticity is close to unity, but price elasticity is mixed. For leather, price elasticity is close to unity but expenditure elasticity is low.

Based on limited and rather fragmented studies mentioned above, it is difficult to say anything with confidence about whether external demand is conducive to the growth of labour-intensive goods in the countries of South Asia. Hence, it may be useful to look at alternative – though somewhat indirect – evidence concerning the type of external demand for exports of countries in that region.

According to the standard theory of comparative advantage, developing countries endowed with an abundance of labour are expected to specialize in and export goods that require more labour compared to other scarce factors of production. But data presented in Table 2.4 show that reality may be different from what is predicted by theory. While trade openness has been associated with specialization in and export of labour-intensive manufactures in some countries during certain periods, there are exceptions. In Bangladesh, exports are found at both the labour-intensive and the capital-intensive ends of the spectrum of manufacturing industries. In India and Pakistan, the share of labour-intensive industries declined while that of capital-intensive industries increased. In Sri Lanka, the share of the top five labour-intensive industries declined during the 1980s and then increased during the 1990s to reach the level of 1980 by 2002. Since data in Table 2.4 refer to period up to 2002, it may be useful to look at what happened after that. Some data for Bangladesh, India, and Pakistan are presented in Tables 2.5–2.7.

In India (Table 2.5), the contribution of labour-intensive items like wearing apparel, textile products, and leather and leather products declined substantially between 2000 and 2009. On the other hand, the shares of items like petroleum products, basic metals, electronic machinery, and motor vehicles increased.

In Pakistan (Table 2.6), the experience is more mixed. The shares of some labour-intensive items in the textile group increased, but those of leather and footwear did not increase. The share of jewellery declined so much that it is no longer an important export item. On the other hand, the share of engineering goods increased. One study (Ansari, 2007) undertaken for the Export Promotion Bureau of Pakistan shows that the growth rates of exports of labour-intensive items like garments and leather witnessed notable escalation during 1999–2005 compared to 1993–98 (from 2.66 and −1.74 per cent, respectively during 1993–98 to 11.19 and 10.45 per cent during 1999–2005). But in terms of the structure of exports, the shares of chemicals

Table 2.4 Share of the Five Most Labour-Intensive and Five Most Capital-Intensive Industries in Total Manufacturing Value Added in South Asia

Countries	Share of the Labour-Intensive			Share of the Capital-Intensive		
	1980	1990	2002	1980	1990	2002
Bangladesh	1.78	12.36	22.54[b]	3.09	8.74	32.35[b]
India	9.47	4.01	5.21[d]	21.76	25.01	26.48[d]
Pakistan	15.79	4.14[a]	3.62[e]	21.69	11.61[a]	24.51[e]
Sri Lanka	22.99	4.42	23.25[c]	5.28	10.96	12.57[c]

Source: Calculated from UNIDO, Indstat3, 2005.

a   1991.
b   1997.
c   2000.
d   2001.
e   1996.

Table 2.5 India: Sector Composition of Manufacturing Exports, 1990–2009 (Percentage Share in Total Manufacturing Exports)

Sectors	1990	2000	2009
Coke, petroleum products, and nuclear fuel	3.1	3.7	14.8
Non-metallic mineral products	16.8	19.0	11.4
Chemicals and chemical products	9.5	10.9	11.1
Basic metals	6.2	5.8	10.4
Wearing apparel, dressing, and dying of fur	15.3	15.3	7.5
Textile products	16.2	14.5	6.5
Motor vehicles, trailers, and semi-trailers	2.3	2.4	6.3
Electrical machinery, n.e.c.	1.7	2.3	5.8
Machinery and equipment, n.e.c.	3.8	3.1	4.5
Food products and beverages	9.2	7.5	3.5
Fabricated metal products	2.1	2.7	1.8
Leather and leather-related products	6.1	2.9	1.3
Tobacco and related products	0.9	0.5	0.6
Others	6.7	9.4	14.7
Total	100	100	100

Source: Adapted from UNCTAD (2012), Table 2.3, p. 11.

and pharmaceuticals, petroleum products, and engineering goods registered significant increases (from 0.56, 0.82, and 0.41, respectively, to 1.33, 1.83, and 1.65 per cent, respectively, between the two periods mentioned above) – thus demonstrating the growth in the exports of both labour-intensive and capital-intensive goods. In fact, average growth rates registered by the latter mentioned industries were several times higher than those of the labour-intensive goods mentioned above.

For Bangladesh (Table 2.7), the shares of all labour-intensive items, viz., knitwear, woven garments, leather and leather products, and footwear increased after 2011. How does one explain such experiences?

Table 2.6 Pakistan: Composition of Exports, 2009–10 and 2016–17
(Percentage Share of Various Items in Total Export)

Items	2009–10	2016–17
Food group	15.9	16.7
Textile group, of which	54.9	62.1
(Knitwear)	(9.8)	(12.0)
(Ready-made garments)	(6.5)	(11.1)
Petroleum group	4.5	0.9
Chemical group	3.8	4.0
Engineering goods	1.1	2.9
Jewellery	3.1	Negligible
Leather and leather-related products	4.2	4.3
Footwear	0.5	0.5
Others	4.1	4.3

Source: Calculated from data available in GOP, Ministry of Commerce (2017).

Note: (i) The data are for July–December period of each year. (ii) The figures do not add up to 100 because all items have not been included in the table.

Table 2.7 Bangladesh: Composition of Exports, 2011–12 and 2015–16
(Percentage Share of Different Items in Total Exports)

Items	2011–12	2015–16
Knitwear	39.04	38.99
Woven garments	39.52	43.02
Home textiles	3.73	3.39
Jute goods	2.88	2.18
Leather and leather products	2.73	3.39
Footwear	0.42	0.64
Chemical products	0.42	0.36
Engineering products excluding bicycles	1.11	1.49
Bicycles	0.43	0.29
Petroleum by-products	1.13	0.87

Source: Calculated from data available in Government of Bangladesh, Export Promotion Bureau (2017).

Note: The figures do not add up to 100 because all items have not been included.

It needs to be noted in the context of the question raised above that developing countries may export goods to both developed and developing countries. While the standard prediction based on the theory of comparative advantage may apply to the former, it does not necessarily apply to the latter. Indeed, there is evidence to show that the latter category of exports may include goods, e.g., metal products, machinery, chemicals, transport equipment, etc. (Murakami, 1968) – which may not fit into the conventional description of labour-intensive items. The importance of such goods in total exports may, of course, vary depending on the level of development achieved and the strategy of industrialization pursued by a developing country. It is possible that the weight of such goods in total exports and production may be quite substantial, and their share may not change much (or may increase) even when an open trade regime is introduced. As a result, the emerging pattern of industrialization may not be very employment-intensive. The export structures of India and Pakistan illustrate this possibility. One study (Burange and Chaddha, 2008) found that India enjoys comparative advantage in the exports of labour-intensive items like textiles as well as in scale-intensive items such as chemicals, and iron and steel (the latter belonging to the capital-intensive category).

The upshot of the findings reported above may be summarized as follows. Greater trade openness may help labour-abundant countries to achieve accelerated growth of labour-intensive industries. But a divergence from this standard prediction may occur. Trade liberalization does not necessarily lead to specialization in and exports of labour-intensive goods, and countries may indeed export goods that are at the capital-intensive end of the production spectrum. Such a divergence can act as a constraint on employment growth.

Domestic demand

Domestic demand depends on the level as well as the distribution of income. With an unequal distribution of income and rising inequality, the pattern of demand may shift towards more capital-intensive and imported goods, which, in turn, may have an adverse employment implication. An analysis of the income elasticity of demand for various products would, therefore, be an important element in the identification of constraints on employment growth and potential driver of structural change. However, a literature search indicates that such studies on an up-to-date basis are not readily available. But early studies on the topic[11] do provide some useful insight.[12] One study on India (Gupta, 1997), for example, shows that expenditure elasticity of demand for products of labour-intensive sectors like cotton textiles and footwear are much higher for lower- and middle-income groups than for higher-income groups.

More recent studies on India indicate significant changes in the consumption pattern that have taken place in country. However, the differences in the pattern of consumption between the rich and the poor continue to remain. For example the difference in average expenditure on consumer durables is much more marked than that in the case of food and other basic items (Shukla and Kakar, 2007). And as income inequality widens, the consumption pattern (and hence the pattern of domestic demand) is getting tilted more towards consumer durables which are more capital-intensive by nature.[13]

Estimates of income elasticity of demand for selected consumer goods in Bangladesh (Islam, 2010b) indicate a pattern similar to that observed in India. For example, some items like *gur* (a traditional sweetener) and firewood clearly emerge as inferior goods at high levels of income (top ten per cent of households), implying that an increase in income at that level leads to a decline in the amount spent on these items. And it is quite well known that these items are more labour-intensive compared to similar products (e.g., *gur* compared to sugar, firewood compared to gas and electricity). Second, for some items which use labour-intensive techniques in their production (e.g., *lungi* – a traditional male dress, furniture, shirt and pant, leather shoes, etc.), the income elasticity of demand at high income level (viz., the top ten per cent of households) is lower than for households as a whole. This implies that an increase in income at the topmost level would increase the demand for such items by smaller amounts than if income increases at lower income levels. Third, for items like refrigerator, pressure cookers, etc., (which not only involve the use of capital-intensive technology in their production but are mostly imported in Bangladesh), the income elasticity of demand is much higher for the top ten per cent of the households compared to the overall sample. So, an increase in the demand for such products is unlikely to create much employment within the country (except perhaps in the sales of such items).

The pattern of consumer demand (which, in turn, has its roots in the pattern of income distribution) mentioned above has implications for the growth of sectors that are more employment-intensive. An early study on India (Gupta, 1977), for example, demonstrates that a redistribution of private consumption expenditure in favour of the poorer classes of population would change the output-mix in India in such a way that the average annual growth rate of employment would register an increase of 11 per cent (year of reference was early 1970s). A study on Bangladesh (Islam, 1976) also found positive employment impact of a redistribution of income from upper to lower income groups, although the magnitude was much less notable. One could thus conclude, at least tentatively, that an unequal income distribution and increase in inequality poses a constraint on the growth of sectors that are employment-intensive in nature.

The impact of income distribution on the pattern of consumer demand gets exacerbated when demand gets boosted through credit and subsidy. Indeed, when developing countries move to higher levels of development, it is not uncommon to find consumer demand boosted through such incentives. But it is usually the demand for consumer durables that is supported by such measures, and the employment outcome of the growth of such demand is not necessarily very positive. Credit-driven growth of domestic demand in China and India provides examples of such pattern of growth. In China, the Government's stimulus programme adopted in response to the global economic crisis of 2008–09 included 13 per cent subsidy in rural areas on the purchase of appliances like televisions, refrigerators, washing machines, air conditioners, and computers ("Market Watch" in *Beijing Review,* June 25, 2009). Likewise, in India, credit for the purchase of such items has boosted their demand during the period of high growth (Chandrasekhar and Ghosh, 2008).

Migration – both domestic and international – and remittances sent by workers working outside there area and country have acted as a major factor in boosting domestic demand, especially at low income levels. While domestic migration in states like Bihar in India has benefited low-income groups, international migration has also benefited low-income households. Studies on the use of remittances show that money received is primarily spent on food consumption, education, and housing.[14] All such items of consumption can create linkage effects for labour-intensive goods and services.

The policy environment

When it comes to a discussion of why the pattern of economic growth in countries of South Asia has not led to the kind of structural transformation along conventional lines (especially compared to countries in ESEA), neoliberal explanations usually blame labour market regulations, and the possible impact of economic policies that shape up the incentive structure is overlooked. One could, of course, point out that the labour markets in the countries of ESEA were more flexible than in South Asia, thus creating a more conducive environment for investment in and growth of labour-intensive industries. But if one looks at the experience carefully, one would note that they pursued a set of economic policies, i.e., policies in the realm of trade, tariff, exchange rate, and fiscal policies that encouraged investment in labour-intensive industries. And that has not been the case in the countries of South Asian countries (with of course some exceptions).[15]

In the case of India, for example, one study (Chandrashekhar, 2008) shows that between 1995–96 and 2003–04, money wages in industries rose by about 37 per cent, while the index of the cost of capital (represented by the combined effect of the rate of interest and an index of the price of capital goods) fell by about 18 per cent. Thus there appears to have been a 55 per cent negative shift in the price of capital relative to labour – a major distortion in factor prices that may have favoured capital-intensive sectors and technology. How did that happen? Fiscal and monetary incentives like capital investment subsidy, interest subsidy, export promotion capital goods scheme, credit-linked capital subsidy for technology upgrading of small-scale industries, etc. – all ostensibly aimed at encouraged investment, led to an underpricing of capital.

The kind of factor price distortion mentioned above and its adverse effect on employment can be found in other countries as well. In Nepal, allowing imports of heavy construction equipment at artificially low import duties led to the premature mechanization in the construction sector and decline in the employment generating capacity of the sector. One also needs to note that declines in the carpet and ready-made garment industries in Nepal during the 2000s have been due to a variety of factors that are mostly economic.[16]

In Sri Lanka, the initial round of economic reforms was not followed up by reforms in factor markets as a result of which the relative price of capital and labour does not reflect their true scarcities. So, it is not a surprise that after a period of growth of labour-intensive industries, there has been a stagnation; and after 2005, growth of labour-intensive industries suffered.

In addition to the distortion in the relative factor prices that failed to reflect the relative scarcities of the factors of production, the strategy of development that is being pursued seems to have created conditions for the growth of domestic demand for and production of capital-intensive goods rather than labour-intensive ones. One example of such strategy is the credit-driven demand for consumer durables which by nature are more capital-intensive than labour-intensive consumer goods like clothing, furniture, low-cost housing, etc. whose demand would have grown at faster rates had inequality in income distribution been lower.

There are, of course, examples of success attained through economic policies. High growth of the ready-made garment industry in Bangladesh and of the same industry in Sri Lanka during the initial years after economic liberalization are examples. However, in the case of Bangladesh, policies were too tilted in favour of this single industry, as a result of which the economy has not attained the needed diversification.[17] Sri Lanka's export-oriented development strategy lost steam and gave way to renewed import substitution strategy especially in the 2000s. A number of policies, e.g., special levy on imports, acted as para tariff and provided protection to import competing industries. The overall policy stance of the government in recent years does not appear to be consistent with an outward-looking export-oriented strategy.[18]

Structural transformation: in search of alternative pathways

Alternative pathways: some examples

Alternative pathways to structural transformation may include the service sector[19] as well as diversification of agriculture itself. ICT-based economic activities in India, rural non-farm activities in Bangladesh, diversification of agriculture towards fruits and vegetables in Nepal, and tourism in Nepal and Sri Lanka are examples of such possibilities. First, we look at two examples from the modern service sector, viz., tourism in Nepal[20] and ICT in India[21] and examine their potential as alternative pathways to structural transformation. Later, we shall go beyond specific sectors and look at structural transformation in rural areas with a focus on Bangladesh and the Bihar state of India. Based on these albeit limited experiences, some tentative conclusions about the potential for alternative pathways to structural transformation will be drawn.

Growth and employment in tourism in Nepal[22]

In terms of contribution to GDP and total employment, tourism is a relatively smaller sector than many other sectors of Nepal. Moreover, if the performance of the hotels and restaurant sector is any indicator, growth in the sector has not been smooth. But given the country's established niche in this field, the experience the country has acquired, and the labour-intensive nature of the sector, the sector deserves attention in the context of a strategy for boosting growth and employment.

In 2009, tourism accounted for 2.4 per cent of GDP and nearly two per cent of total employment. The sector contributed 7.5 per cent of the total foreign exchange earnings of the country (compared to 8.88 per cent in 1999/2000). The number of tourist arrivals has increased considerably in recent years from 463,646 in 2000 to 509,956 in January 2010 and to 602,867 in 2011. But spending per person per day by tourists has declined from US$63 in January 2010 to US$47 in January 2011.

Forecasts made by WTTC (2011), using satellite account data show that between 2011 and 2021, the direct contribution of tourism to GDP is likely to grow at an annual rate of 4.8 per cent. Direct employment in the sector is likely to grow at an annual rate of 3.9 per cent. Taking into account the indirect effects, these figures are 5 and 4.1 per cent, respectively.

There is potential for strengthening the linkages between travel and tourism and other sectors of the economy. Currently, there is some linkage of the sector with sectors like wearing apparel, craft products, etc. But the linkage is rather low with agriculture, although one would expect some linkage between hotel and restaurants sector and agricultural products like fruits, vegetables, dairy products, and bakery products. Furthermore, econometric analysis shows that the average length of stay by tourists has a stronger impact on employment generated by the sector than the number of tourist arrivals (Islam, 2014b). Hence, from a policy perspective, it would be important to adopt measures for encouraging tourists to stay longer.

Growth and employment in the ICT sector in India[23]

During the couple of decades from around early 1990s, the ICT sector (defined as the total information technology and IT-enabled services) emerged as the fastest growing sector and a major source of exports in India. The share of this sector in total GDP increased from about three per cent in 2000–01 to 9.5 per cent in 2014–15. With an export of nearly 75 billion US dollars, the share of the sector in total exports was 15 per cent in 2014–15. That this is a highly export-oriented sector is indicated by the share of exports in the sector's output – increased from 49 per cent in 2000–01 to 81 per cent in 2014–15. In 2015, the sector employed a total of 3.5 million people of whom 1.2 million were women. If one remembers that in 2004–05, the sector was employing just about one million people, it is easy to see the phenomenal growth attained, not only in terms of revenue and exports but also in terms of employment.

Although there is a perception that the ICT sector is urban-oriented, a NASSCOM survey[24] found that between a third and a half of the employees are from either non-metro or rural areas. As for education level of the employees, 75 per cent of the indirectly created jobs are filled by those with

HSC or lower level of education. Proportion of women in total employment is also high, although they are over-represented in the low-skill end of the spectrum. The jobs in the sector offer flexibility in terms of working hours and the possibility of working from home. Hence, on the whole, this sector seems to be real growth sector that is capable of generating much-needed jobs for the growing educated workforce.

However, when it comes to the question of an alternative pathway for structural transformation of a vast economy like that of India (with its regional variations), a few sobering remarks may be in order. First, growth rate attained by the sector seems to have slowed down in recent years. One calculation (Hicks, 2015) shows that ten-year annual average growth declined from a massive 40 per cent in 2002 to about 20 per cent in 2014. In fact, growth rate slowed down sharply in 2008–09 and became negative in 2009– 10. Since then, growth has resumed but has not gone back to the levels seen before 2008–09. Likewise, export growth has also declined and fluctuated in recent years – although growth still remained at double-digit level (*RBI Bulletin*, March 2015). Second, even though the number engaged in the sector has increased several-fold, its share in total employment (or labour force) of 472 million (in 2011–12) remains rather small. Third, while the number of job-seekers with paper qualifications meeting the requirements of the sector may be well over its demand, many of them may not meet the standards in terms of technical ability and language skills.

Structural transformation in rural Bihar[25] (India)

Surveys of villages conducted in 1981–83, 1998–2000, and 2009–11 provide valuable data and insight into changes that have taken place in the economy of rural Bihar during the three decades covered by those surveys. While a detailed and insightful analysis of such changes can be found in Rodgers et al. (2013), a glance at some of the major changes that have taken place in the employment and occupational structure may provide one with some ideas on how the structure of rural economies can change even without industrialization. To recount a few points noted by the above-mentioned study:

- In terms of sector composition, while agriculture dominated (with about 80 per cent of employment in the early 1980s), by the end of the first decade of the 2000s, less than half of the main occupations were in the primary sector – the proportion being around a third for men.
- Migration has remained a major source of jobs for male workers of Bihar, but commuting to jobs outside the villages has become more important than before. Migration now is more for non-agricultural work.
- However, occupational diversification through commuting and migration has not benefited all equally. It is the upper echelons of the village class structure (i.e., the landlords and large cultivators) who have benefited more from better jobs with regular and higher pay,

while the agricultural labour households have tended to remain in casual work.

- Migration has led to a change in the gender balance in the rural labour market of Bihar and a rise in the proportion of women in the labour force. In 12 villages that were covered by the surveys mentioned above, female labour force participation rate increased from 56 per cent in 1981–82 to 67 per cent in 2009–10. With men leaving for work outside their villages, women are increasingly working in agriculture. Male labour force participation rate in those 12 villages remained unchanged at 94 per cent.

- As a result of a strengthening of the link between the village labour market and the national market, wage rates have increased substantially. This has made possible increases in incomes of households and improvements in their living conditions.

- While there are sectors/activities where wages are higher than in agriculture, there are those where this is not so. For example, wages of "transport workers" are lower than those of "agriculture equipment operator". The range of wages of construction workers is about the same as for agriculture. The range in brick making is very wide, and the lower end is much lower than in agriculture (Rodgers et al., 2013, Table 3.13, p. 83). These examples indicate that although there has been a diversification in the occupations of workers in Bihar, this does not necessarily entail a move towards activities with higher wages.

Rural transformation through non-farm activities: Bangladesh

Structural transformation of rural areas may be driven by growth of rural non-farm activities in general. But the important question in that respect is the type of economic activities that grow and the productivity and returns associated with them. The key question is the composition of and returns from the non-farm activities that may be growing. Do they reflect real dynamism in the economy or distress adaptation to a situation in which the alternative is no means of livelihood?

Like other developing countries, Bangladesh is also witnessing a process of rural-urban migration. But significant and notable changes are taking place within rural areas as well. Initially, the central role in rural transformation was played by the green revolution that took place during the 1980s and 1990s, but more recent decades have been marked by a diversification in the sources of livelihoods.

According to the *Household Income and Expenditure Survey* (HIES) data, in 1991–92, agriculture accounted for 40 per cent of rural household income. By 2010, this share had fallen to nearly 30 per cent. The share of "business and commerce" increased from 12.4 per cent in 1991–92 to 22.4 per cent in 2000, but then declined to 15 per cent in 2010. The share of wages and salary has also increased. But the most remarkable phenomenon in rural Bangladesh has been the increase in the share of gifts and remittances from 10.6 per cent in 1991–92 to 17.3 per cent in 2010. In fact, income from remittances sent by Bangladeshis working abroad represents a very significant element in the transformation of the rural economy of the country. Such incomes have not only lifted many households out of poverty, but they have also created linkage effects for expansion of many economic activities, especially in the transport and other service sectors.[26]

Alongside diversification of the sources of incomes of rural households, improvement in physical infrastructures (e.g., roads, availability of electricity) has improved connectivity of rural areas with urban areas and rural centres of economic activities. That, in turn, has created necessary conditions for the growth of non-farm activities within rural areas and has also created what may be called rural-urban continuum. The countryside of Bangladesh today offers a landscape that is very different from that of a few decades ago in that in many areas the difference between rural and urban areas gets blurred.[27] It is true that in many instances, it is remittances received from workers working abroad that have transformed the lives and livelihoods of people. But there are also villages where cottage industries, small businesses, or non-traditional agricultural products like vegetables, fruits, flowers, etc. have contributed to some structural transformation in the economy. However, the important question to ask is whether such transformation is sufficient to move the overall economy to a stage where surplus labour is exhausted. Data presented in Tables 2.8–2.10 may throw some light on this important question.

Figures in Table 2.8 provide some indication of what kind (if any) of structural transformation has been taking place in the rural economy of

Table 2.8 Bangladesh: Sector Composition of Employment (Percentage of Employment in the Sector) in Rural Non-Agricultural Activities, 2002–03 to 2013

Sector	Share of the Sector in Total Rural Non-agricultural Activities			
	2002–03	2005–06	2010	2013
Manufacturing	20.94	20.47	22.16	31.68
Construction	7.25	6.67	9.51	7.71
Wholesale and retail trade	28.62	29.93	28.98	23.79
Transportation and storage	14.87	17.71	14.82	12.62
Accommodation and food	2.53	3.06	3.06	2.75
Public administration	3.39	3.00	2.56	2.89
Education	5.54	5.31	4.58	5.35
Health and social work	2.12	1.09	1.50	1.56
Other services	12.70	10.29	12.06	7.97

Source: BBS Labour Force Surveys (various years). For 2013, the published report of the Labour Force Surveys does not provide the required data. So, the numbers and corresponding percentages have been calculated from primary data.

Note: Only the major sectors of employment have been included in this table. So, the percentages don't add up to 100.

Bangladesh as a whole during the 2000s. A few observations may be made on the basis of this data. First, if manufacturing is considered to be important in the process of structural transformation (as has been argued earlier in this chapter), one may note that till 2010, the increase in the proportion of labour force employed there has been very small. In fact, till that time, there was very little change in the structure of employment except for a small increase in the share of construction. However, the situation appears to have changed after 2010, and the share of manufacturing increased sharply. That has been accompanied by a decline in the share of major sectors like construction, trade, and transport. This is quite interesting because if the data are to be taken seriously, one may be led to raise a few questions.

First, is rural Bangladesh finally witnessing a significant change in the structure of its economy towards manufacturing industries? Second, if manufacturing is indeed growing at a high rate, wouldn't that create necessary linkage effects with other sectors like trade and transport and raise their growth as well? We shall look at growth rate of employment in various sectors below. But it may be useful to note that the share of both trade and transport in total employment declined during 2010–13. Likewise, the share of construction also has declined.

Data on numbers employed and their growth in various sectors of the rural economy are presented in Table 2.9. Figures in this table are indicative of some change in the pattern of growth in recent years. First, growth in employment in manufacturing has accelerated gradually, reaching double-digit figure after 2010. Whether this is indicative of a real transformation in the rural economy would depend on what has been happening to output in the sector. Rural–urban breakdown for data on growth in manufacturing output is not available. However, if data on the growth of small and cottage industries (Annex, Table A2.3) are any guide to the growth of manufacturing in rural areas, a couple of observations may be made. First, during the 2005–10 period, growth of output in the sector did exceed eight per cent. If that happened in industries located in rural areas also, one can say that an employment growth of eight per cent per annum was not attained at the cost of decline in labour productivity. However, the situation is different during the 2010–13 period when growth of output in the small and cottage industries sector was well below that of employment reported in Table 2.9. Thus it is quite clear that the acceleration in employment after 2010 did not represent a healthy growth in the sector.

It is also important to note that apart from manufacturing, education and health, growth of employment in other major sectors like construction, trade, transport, etc. was negative – the rate of decline being substantial. Again, data on output growth are not available separately for rural and urban areas. But data on GDP growth by sector (Annex, Table 2A.3) indicate that healthy growth rates (over six per cent per annum) were attained by these sectors in the post-2010 years. If output growth in economic activities in rural areas did not lag too far behind, it is difficult to understand the reason(s) for the

Table 2.9 Bangladesh: Employment in the Rural Non-Agricultural Sector, 2002–03 to 2013

Sectors	Number Employed (Thousand)				Annual Growth Rate (%)		
	2002–03	2005–06	2010	2013	2002–03 to 2005–06	2005–06 to 2010	2010–13
Manufacturing	2,838	3,086	4,193	5,813	2.83	7.96	11.50
Construction	983	1,006	1,800	1,414	0.77	15.66	−7.73
Wholesale and retail trade	3,879	4,513	5,482	4,364	5.18	4.98	−7.32
Transportation and storage	2,015	2,670	2,804	2,316	9.84	1.23	−6.17
Accommodation and food services	343	462	578	504	10.44	5.76	−4.46
Education	751	800	867	982	2.13	2.03	4.24
Health and social work	287	165	283	286	−16.85	14.44	0.35
Other services	1,772	1,551	2,283	1,477			
Total rural non-agriculture	13,554	15,078	18,918	18,348	3.62	5.84	−1.01
Total rural	33,599	36,132	41,663	41,918	2.45	3.63	0.20

Source: BBS Labour Force Surveys (various years).

Note: A few sectors that employ small number of the labour force are excluded from this table. They include mining and quarrying, water, electricity and gas, real estate, ICT, and financial services.

observed negative growth of employment in the major sectors. How manufacturing output and employment could grow without creating any linkage effect on employment in other sectors remains an unanswered question.

An indicator (albeit somewhat indirect) of whether the non-farm sectors, especially in the rural areas, can provide a more attractive alternative compared to agriculture can be provided by a comparison of wages and income from self-employment in such sectors with those in agriculture. Data (Table 2.10) show that in 2005–06, wages in four sectors (viz., fishing, financial service, education, and health and social work) were actually lower than that in agriculture. And that would imply that one was getting into such occupations simply because agriculture could no longer support them (or because they need to supplement their income from their main occupation with engagement in these activities). There are five other sectors where wages were higher than in agriculture, but the difference is less than 30 per cent (which could be taken as a rough indicator of the difference that can be considered sufficient to pull out workers from agriculture). These five sectors are mining, manufacturing, trade, public administration, and community, social, and personal services. These sectors appear to have the potential to act as viable alternatives to agriculture, but their productivity and wages need to improve further before they can act as drivers of growth that is capable of using up surplus labour in a productive manner.

Table 2.10 Bangladesh: Wage Rate (Weekly/Monthly) By Sector/Activities, 2005–06 and 2013

Sector	Wage Rate (2005–06) (Taka Per Week)	Sector Wage Rate as Percentage of Wage in Agriculture	Average Wage/ Salary (2013) (Taka Per Month)	Sector Wage/ Salary as Percentage of Agriculture
Agriculture and forestry	541		9,146[a]	
Fishery	201	37.15	n.a.	
Mining	604	111.65	8,336	92.8
Manufacturing	561	103.70	11,112	121.50
Electricity	1185	219.04	11,698	127.90
Construction	749	138.45	9,800	107.15
Wholesale and retail trade	682	126.06	11,442	125.10
Hotels and restaurants	753	139.19	10,745	117.48
Transport and storage	750	138.63	11,232	122.81
Financial intermediation	463	85.58	14,626	159.92
Real estate, renting, and business	769	142.14	11,919	130.32
Public administration	649	119.96	13,589	148.58
Education	401	74.12	13,998	153.05
Health and social work	176	32.53	12,888	140.91
Other community, social and personal service	669	123.66	15,529	169.79

Source: Calculated from the report of BBS Labour Force Surveys, 2005–06 and 2013.

a   (i) This figure represents agriculture, forestry, and fishing. (ii) n.a. denotes not available separately.

Data of the type presented in Table 2.10 are not available in tabulated form of the BBS Labour Force Surveys of 2010. But data from the 2013 survey could be tabulated to provide a comparative picture (see Table 2.10). And the situation shows improvement in that wage/salary is lower than in agriculture in only one sector (mining). However, in important sectors like manufacturing, construction, transport, trade, and hotels and restaurants, the difference is still less than 30 per cent of agricultural wage.

Income from self-employment[28] in non-farm activities relative to agriculture would be another indicator of whether employment in the former reflects dynamic growth in those sectors. In this respect also, data up to 2005–06 (presented in Islam, 2015) does not enable one to conclude that growth of non-farm activities could be regarded as dynamic. In that year, income in services was lower than in agriculture, while that in manufacturing, trade, and transport was barely better than in agriculture. These figures would appear to indicate that till 2005–06, non-farm activities as a whole or manufacturing, in particular, were not sufficiently attractive in terms of income to pull the surplus labour out of agriculture. Employment in these sectors is more a reflection of the inability of agriculture to support those looking for jobs. The situation may have improved in more recent years.

Concluding observations

There is no doubt that the economies of South Asia have benefited from some alternatives other than manufacturing industries that are providing employment to their growing labour force. While some, e.g., ICT in India and tourism in Nepal provide employment to the educated and skilled (the latter in some cases), others like rural non-farm activities in Bangladesh and outside village employment in Bihar, are a source for a wide variety of jobs. But the question that needs to be addressed is whether such alternatives provide an adequate (from the point of view of mere numbers) and sustainable source of good jobs that are needed to transfer all the surplus labour that are available in the traditional sectors and the new additions to the labour force that are taking place every year.

One set of numbers that are rough and ready and yet could be illustrative may help put the above question in perspective. In India, if growth of labour force is taken to be two per cent per annum, over nine million members may be expected to be added to the workforce of 472 million (as of 2011/12). The number engaged in manufacturing in that year was over 60 million. If growth of manufacturing could be raised to, say, 12 per cent per annum (which is not at all unrealistic), and if elasticity of employment growth is assumed to be 0.5, the sector can generate around 3.6 million jobs per year. On the other hand, the ICT sector currently employs about 3.5 million workers, and the growth of revenue in the sector has been slowing down in recent years. Even if the sector continues to grow at 15 per cent per annum (growth in 2014–15 was 13 per cent), given the current employment generating capability of the sector, it will perhaps not generate more than 50–60 thousand jobs per year. And qualifications required for those jobs will perhaps range from a minimum of HSC to first degree in a technical subject.

If one looks at the service sector as a whole in India, one would see that it accounts for more than a quarter of the currently employed population. But the sector is not an employment-intensive one, as is the case in many countries, and the employment intensity of the major components like trade and transport has been declining. Hence, even with the growth potential that exists in the sector as a whole and in components like the ICT sub-sector, the extent to which they can serve as a real alternative pathway for structural transformation of employment remains a question. Moreover, in lesser developed states like Bihar, migration for jobs outside villages may have provided some alternatives to a rather bleak situation that existed several decades ago. But whether this can be looked at a sustainable solution and viable response for the region's employment challenge is a question that has been raised by researchers with long experience of work on that region (e.g., Rodgers et al., 2013).

In Bangladesh, growth in the crop sector has not only made the country self-sufficient in food grains but has also created linkage effects for growth of non-farm activities in rural areas, and many are diversifying into non-grain crops (especially, vegetables) and activities outside agriculture. However, many such activities are still characterized by low productivity and returns, where people turn to because of a lack of alternative sources of livelihoods. Moreover, several such sectors, e.g., construction, trade, and transport, have experienced negative growth in employment in recent years.

On the other hand, even with the current limited degree of industrialization, the manufacturing sector in Bangladesh creates some 400,000 jobs annually, absorbing over a fifth of the annual addition to the labour force. It is reckoned that with a more diversified growth of labour-intensive manufacturing, the sector could absorb about a third of the additional labour force. Within rural areas, employment in manufacturing has attained acceleration in growth over time.

The limitations of the modern service sector (especially as a source of employment) can also be seen from the example of tourism in Nepal. Currently accounting for just two per cent of total employment, with limited linkages to the rest of the economy, and the fluctuations the sector has been experiencing, it will have to attain much healthier and sustained growth in order to be able to play a more substantial role as a major employer.

Employment in Nepal's manufacturing sector grew at the rate of 3.4 per cent per annum compared to the overall employment growth of 2.2 per cent during 1998–2008. During that period, the sector was generating about 22,000 jobs per year or ten per cent of the annual addition to the labour force. In 1991, the carpet and garment industries together were already employing nearly 90,000 workers, although the number had declined to 42,000 by 2006. If growth in manufacturing industries as a whole could be revived to, say, eight per cent per annum, and employment elasticity is assumed to be 0.6, the sector could generate some 50 thousand jobs which would be nearly 17 per cent of the annual addition to the labour force (which is about 300,000 workers per year).

Of course, a number of factors, e.g., its landlocked nature, difficult terrain, and open border with a large country with a much higher level of industrialization may stand in the way of Nepal's achieving a conventional type of labour-intensive and export-oriented industrialization. This, however, should not imply that no industrialization is possible in the country. The fact that two labour-intensive industries, viz., carpets and garments, achieved significant rates of growth in output and exports during the 1990s and the early part of the 2000s shows that this should be possible. While the sharp decline in the growth of both of these industries may have created a sense of despair about prospects of industrialization in Nepal, their experience may, in fact, be used as the basis for a policy-oriented assessment of the prospects of the sector as a whole.

The conclusion that appears to emerge from the analysis of this chapter can be summed up as follows. Even if one accepts the basic proposition that there can be multiple pathways to structural transformation of an economy, for economies of South Asia, e.g., Bangladesh, India, and Nepal, it is difficult to see how the surplus labour available to them can be fully and productively utilized without industrialization. Of course, there are differences in conditions and possibilities even within South Asia. For example, Nepal may not have the same prospect of industrialization as Bangladesh and India. But the limitations of the service sector as an engine of overall economic growth and as a means of absorbing surplus labour available in the economies seem to be clear.

Annex 2.1

Table 2A.1 Growth of Output in South Asian Countries, 1990–2014 (% per Annum)

Country	GDP		Agriculture		Industry		Manufacturing		Services	
	1990–2000	2000–14	1990–2000	2000–14	1990–2000	2000–14	1990–2000	2000–14	1990–2000	2000–14
Afghanistan	n.a.	8.9	n.a.	3.3	n.a.	8.4	n.a.	3.7	n.a.	n.a.
Bangladesh	4.7	5.9	2.6	4.4	7.3	8.0	7.2	8.3	4.2	5.8
Bhutan	5.2	8.0	1.7	1.9	6.6	9.8	8.9	9.3	7.2	8.8
India	6.0	7.6	3.2	3.3	6.1	7.7	6.9	8.3	7.8	9.2
Maldives	n.a.	7.0	n.a.	−0.2	n.a.	6.6	n.a.	1.4	n.a.	7.0
Nepal	4.9	4.1	2.5	3.3	7.1	2.7	8.9	1.5	6.0	4.7
Pakistan	3.8	4.2	4.4	3.0	4.1	5.3	3.8	6.0	4.4	4.9
Sri Lanka	5.3	6.1	1.9	3.6	6.9	6.9	8.1	5.3	6.0	6.3

Source: World Bank: World Development Indicators 2015. www.wdi.worldbank.org/table/1.1 (accessed on 13 September 2015).

Table 2A.2 Structure of Output of South Asian Countries, 2000 and 2014

Country	Agriculture		Industry		Manufacturing		Services	
	2000	2014	2000	2014	2000	2014	2000	2014
Afghanistan	38	24	24	21	19	12	38	55
Bangladesh	24	16	23	28	15	17	53	56
Bhutan	27	17	36	42	8	8	37	41
India	23	17	26	30	15	17	51	53
Maldives	9	4	15	19	8	5	76	77
Nepal	41	34	22	15	9	6	37	50
Pakistan	26	25	23	21	15	14	51	54
Sri Lanka	20	10	27	34	17	18	53	56

Source: Same as for Table 2A.1.

Table 2A.3 Bangladesh GDP Growth (%), 2005–06 to 2015–16

	2005–06	2006–07	2007–08	2008–09	2009–10	2010–11	2011–12	2012–13	2013–14	2014–15	2015–16
Agriculture	5.44	6.04	3.87	3.09	6.55	3.89	2.41	1.47	3.81	2.45	1.53
Manufacturing	10.81	10.54	7.33	6.69	6.65	10.01	9.96	10.31	8.77	10.31	10.30
Small-scale industry	9.14	9.48	7.15	7.30	8.17	5.67	6.58	8.81	6.33	8.54	7.02
Construction	8.69	6.74	5.99	6.58	7.21	6.95	8.42	8.04	8.08	8.60	8.87
Wholesale and retail trade	6.29	8.37	7.27	5.86	5.85	6.69	6.70	6.18	6.73	6.35	6.61
Hotel and restaurant	5.33	5.53	5.68	5.86	6.01	6.20	6.39	6.49	6.70	6.83	7.00
Transport	8.39	9.442	8.26	8.05	7.55	8.44	9.15	6.27	6.05	5.96	6.51
Education	9.41	8.76	7.14	5.89	5.18	5.63	7.75	6.30	7.26	8.01	13.78
Health	5.10	4.96	5.86	3.04	6.83	6.34	3.81	4.76	5.06	5.18	8.45
GDP	6.67	7.06	6.01	5.05	5.57	6.46	6.52	6.01	6.06	6.55	7.05

Source: Ministry of Finance, Government of Bangladesh, *Economic Review 2016* (in Bengali).

Notes

1 In the context of India, Dasgupta and Singh (2005) explore this possibility.
2 ILO (2011) provides some data.
3 Velde (2008), for example, reported that services have been central to economic growth in the countries of sub-Saharan Africa since 1994 and contributed 47 per cent of real GDP growth during the 2000–05 period, while industry and agriculture contributed 37 and 16 per cent, respectively.
4 See Islam and Islam (2015), Chapter 4 for a summary of this debate.
5 These figures are from Papola (2006).
6 These figures have been calculated from data presented in Islam (2014a).
7 These figures have been calculated by using data from the World Bank: World Development Indicators (various years).
8 These figures have been calculated by the author, using data available in Government of Pakistan: Pakistan Economic Survey 2010–11, Table 1.2.
9 A good account of the evolution of economic policy in South Asian countries is available in Osmani (2009). The SARNET country studies (Amjad and Yusuf, 2014; Chandrasiri, 2014; IHD, 2014; Khanal, 2014; and Rahman, 2014) provide up-to-date accounts of such policies in the respective countries.
10 The period covered by that study was 1970–2008.
11 Islam (2010b) provides an overview and references.
12 In fact, studies carried out during the 1970s under the auspices of the ILO pointed out the importance of income distribution in influencing the mix of products that is produced in a country as the income elasticity of demand for various consumer goods varies between income/expenditure classes.
13 Chandrasekhar and Ghosh (2008) note such a shift in the pattern of consumer demand.
14 See, for example, the study on Bangladesh (BBS, 2013).
15 There is also a renewed debate on the role of industrial policy and technological capability in attaining transformation. See Salazar-Xirinachs et al. (2014) for a set of studies on these issues.
16 See Islam (2014b) for an analysis.
17 For an analysis of this aspect, see Raihan (2015).
18 For further details, see Chandrasiri (2014).
19 Islam and Islam (2015) review empirical evidence from developing countries and point out that the service sector is not necessarily characterized by low productivity and can serve as a driver of growth. Dasgupta and Singh (2005) also make this point, although the study found empirical support for the Kaldor's thesis of manufacturing as the engine of growth. In the context of India, Ghose (2014) provides a detailed analysis of the role of the service sector. But in another chapter, Ghose (2015) argues that India needs manufacturing-led growth in order to generate productive employment.
20 Nepal is a small landlocked country whose economy is predominantly agriculture. Two export-oriented industries, viz., readymade garments and carpet, grew quite rapidly during the late 1990s and early 2000s but declined for a variety of reasons. Tables 2A.1 and 2A.2 provide some basic data on growth and structure of the economy of South Asian countries, including Nepal.
21 India is a large middle-income country whose economy is quite diversified and has attained high growth, especially during the 2000s (see Tables 2A.1 and 2A.2).
22 The following paragraphs are based on Islam (2014b).
23 Figures quoted in this sub-section are from the NASSCOM website, Government of India (GOI), National Statistical Office, Central Statistical Office (2010), *RBI Bulletin* (March 2015), and Hicks (2015).
24 NASSCOM (2015). www.nasscom.in/impact-indias-growth.

25 Bihar is one of the poorer states of India. Its economy is predominantly rural, and the state has traditionally been a source of migrant workers for more developed states of the country.
26 See, for example, Osmani et al. (2010, 2015).
27 For interesting anecdotal accounts of such development, see Hossain and Bayes (2015).
28 The BBS Labour Force Surveys contain a question on monthly income of the self-employed. So, the figures seem to represent the incomes stated by the respondents.

Bibliography

Amjad, Rashid and Anam Yusuf (2014): *More and Better Jobs for Pakistan: Can the Manufacturing Sector Play a Greater Role?* Monograph Series. Graduate School of Development Studies, Lahore School of Economics, Lahore.

Ansari, Javed (2007, July): "Structural Change in Pakistani Exports 1992–2005", *Market Forces*, Vol. 3, No. 2, pp. 1–12. www.pafkiet.edu.pk/marketforces/index.php/marketforces/article/view/153/154.

BBS (various years): *Reports of Labour Force Surveys*. Bangladesh Bureau of Statistics, Dhaka.

——— (2010): *Household Income and Expenditure Survey 2010.* Bangladesh Bureau of Statistics, Dhaka.

——— (2013): *Report on the Use of Remittance (SUR) 2013.* Bangladesh Bureau of Statistics, Dhaka.

Burange, L.G. and Sheetal J. Chaddha (2008, December): "India's Revealed Comparative Advantage in Merchandise Trade", *Artha Vijnana*, Vol. L, No. 4, pp. 332–363.

Chandrasekhar, C.P. (2008): "Re-visiting the Policy Environment for Engendering Employment Intensive Economic Growth". Draft paper, International Labour Office, Geneva.

Chandrasekhar, C.P. and Jayati Ghosh (2008): "Employment and the Pattern of Growth" in Kapila, Raj and Uma Kapila (eds.): *Economic Developments in India.* Academic Foundation, Delhi.

Chandrasiri, Sunil (2014): "Towards Inclusive Growth through More and Better Jobs: Can the Manufacturing Sector Play a Greater Role in Sri Lanka?" Paper prepared for the SARNET project. Institute for Human Development, Delhi.

Clark, C. (1951): *The Conditions of Economic Progress.* Macmillan, London.

Dasgupta, Sukti and Ajit Singh (2005): "Will Services be the New Engine of Indian Economic Growth?" *Development and Change*, Vol. 36, No. 6, pp. 1035–1057.

Fisher, A.G.B. (1939): "Production: Primary, Secondary and Tertiary", *The Economic Record*, Vol. 15, No. 1, pp. 24–38.

Ghose, Ajit K. (2014): "India's Services-Led Growth". Working Paper No. 01/2014. Institute for Economic Development, New Delhi.

——— (2015): "India Needs Rapid Manufacturing-Led Growth". Working Paper No. 01/2015. Institute for Human Development, New Delhi.

Government of Bangladesh, Export Promotion Bureau (2017): *Export Statistics Book 2015–2016.* http://epb.portal.gov.bd/site/files/e51e6097-cdb6-424a-9230-91ace9956929 (Accessed on 6 December 2017).

Government of India (GOI), National Statistical Office, Central Statistical Office (2010): "Value Addition and Employment Generation in the ICT Sector in India". Delhi.

Government of Pakistan, Ministry of Commerce (2017): *Comparative Export of Selected Items.* www.commerce.gov.pk/wpcontent/uploads/2017/01/Comparative_Exp_Selected_Comodities_July-Dec_2016.pdf (Accessed on 6 December 2017).

Gupta, Anand P. (1977): *Fiscal Policy for Employment Generation in India.* Tata-McGraw Hill Publishing Company Limited, New Delhi.

Hicks, Richard (2015): "India IT/Software Statistics: 1980–2015". In *ICT for Development*, 28 April 2015.

Hossain, Mahabub and Abdul Bayes (2015): *Bish Geramer Galpo* (in Bengali: Stories of Twenty Villages). The University Press Limited, Dhaka.

Hussain, Fayyaz (2010): "Pakistan's Export Demand: A Disaggregated Analysis", *SBP Research Bulletin*, Vol. 6, No. 2, pp. 1–13.

International Labour Organization (2011): *Efficient Growth, Employment and Decent Work in Africa: Time for a New Vision.* ILO, Geneva.

Institute for Human Development (2014): *Growth, Labour Markets and Employment: India.* Institute for Human Development, New Delhi.

Islam, Rizwanul (1976): *Factor Intensity and Labour Absorption in Manufacturing Industries: The Case of Bangladesh.* Unpublished Ph.D. dissertation. London School of Economics and Political Science, London.

Islam, Rizwanul (2008): "Has Development and Employment through Labour-Intensive Industrialization Become History?" in Basu, Kaushik and Ravi Kanbur (eds.): *Arguments for a Better World: Essays in Honour of Amartya Sen.* Oxford University Press, Oxford.

——— (2010a): "Pattern of Economic Growth and Its Implication for Employment" in Banerjee, L., A. Dasgupta and R. Islam (eds.): *Development, Equity and Poverty: Essays in Honour of Azizur Rahman Khan.* Macmillan India and UNDP, Delhi and New York.

——— (2010b): *Addressing the Challenge of Jobless Growth in Developing Countries: An Analysis with Cross-Country Data.* Occasional Paper Series No. 01. Bangladesh Institute of Development Studies, Dhaka.

——— (2014a): "The Employment Challenge Faced by Bangladesh: How Far Is the Lewis Turning Point?", *The Indian Journal of Labour Economics*, Vol. 57, No. 2, pp. 201–225.

——— (2014b): *Nepal: Addressing the Employment Challenge through the Sectoral Pattern of Growth.* ILO Country Office, Kathmandu.

——— (2015): "Structural Transformation and Alternative Pathways to the Lewis Turning Point". Paper presented at the International Seminar on Labour and Employment Issues in the Emerging Rural-Urban Continuum: Dimensions, Processes and Policies, 12–14 March 2015, National Institute of Rural Development, Hyderabad.

Islam, Rizwanul and Iyanatul Islam (2015): *Employment and Inclusive Development.* Routledge, London.

Kaldor, N. (1966): *Causes of Slow Growth in the United Kingdom.* Cambridge University Press, Cambridge.

——— (1967): *Strategic Factors in Economic Development.* Cornell University Press, Ithaca.

Khanal, Dilli Raj (2014): "Employment Challenges in Nepal: Trends, Characteristics and Policy Options for Inclusive Growth and Development". Paper prepared for the SARNET project, Institute for Human Development, New Delhi.

Kucera, David and L. Roncolato (2014): "Structure Matters: Sectoral Drivers of Growth and the Labour Productivity-Employment Relationship" in Islam, Iyanatul and David Kucera (eds.): *Beyond Macroeconomic Stability: Structural Transformation and Inclusive Development.* ILO and Palgrave Macmillan, Geneva and London.

Kuznets, S. (1966): *Modern Economic Growth: Rate, Structure and Speed.* Oxford University Press and IBH Publishing House, New Delhi.

———— (1971): *Economic Growth of Nations: Total Output and Production Structure.* Harvard University Press, Cambridge, USA.

Lewis, W.A. (1954): "Economic Development with Unlimited Supplies of Labour", *Manchester School*, Vol. 22, pp. 139–191.

McMillan, Margaret S. and Dani Rodrik (2011): "Globalization, Structural Change and Productivity Growth". Working Paper No. 17143. National Bureau of Economic Research, Cambridge, MA.

Murakami, Atsushi (1968): "Two Aspects of the Export of Manufacturing Goods from Developing Countries", *The Developing Economies*, Vol. 6, No. 3, pp. 261–283.

NASSCOM (2015): www.nasscom.in/impact-indias-growth.

Osmani, S.R., Md. Abdul Latif, Binayak Sen, Rushidan Islam Rahman, Meherun Ahmed, Tareq Ferdous Khan and Rizwanul Islam (2010): *Dynamics of Poverty in Rural Bangladesh: Report of the Benchmark Survey.* Institute of Microfinance, Dhaka.

Osmani, S.R., Meherun Ahmed, Muhammad A. Latif and Binayak Sen (2015): *Poverty and Vulnerability in Rural Bangladesh.* The University Press Limited, Dhaka.

Papola, T.S. (2006): "Emerging Structure of Indian Economy: Implications of Growing Intersectoral Imbalances", *The Indian Economic Journal*, Vol. 54, No. 1, pp. 5–25.

Rahman, Rushidan I. (2014): "Employment for Inclusive Growth and Development in Bangladesh". Paper prepared for the SARNET project, Institute for Human Development, New Delhi.

Raihan, Salim (2015): "Economic Diversification, Structural Change and Employment in Bangladesh". Draft paper prepared for ADB-ILO Employment Diagnostic Study of Bangladesh.

Ranis, Gustav and J. Fei (1961): "A Theory of Economic Development", *American Economic Review*, Vol. 51, pp. 533–565.

Reserve Bank of India (2015): *RBI Bulletin*, March 2015.

Rodgers, Gerry, Amrita Datta, Janine Rodgers, Sunil K. Mishra and Alakh N. Sharma (2013): *The Challenge of Inclusive Development in Rural Bihar.* Institute for Human Development and Manak Publications, New Delhi.

Roncolato, L. and David Kucera (2014): "Structural Drivers of Productivity and Employment Growth: A Decomposition Analysis for 81 Countries", *Cambridge Journal of Economics*, Vol. 38, No. 2, pp. 399–424.

Salazar-Xirinachs, José M., Irmgard Nübler and Richard Kozul-Wright (2014): *Transforming Economies, Making Industrial Policy Work for Growth, Jobs and Development.* International Labour Office, Geneva.

Shukla, Rajesh and Preeti Kakar (2007): "Consumption Level Up as India Shines", *The Economic Times*, 9 February 2007.

UNCTAD (2012): *Twenty Years of India's Liberalization: Experiences and Lessons* (edited by Rashmi Banga and Abhijit Das). UNCTAD, Geneva.

Velde, D.W.T. (2008): "African Growth: Forgotten Issues". IPPG Briefing Paper No. 19. DFID and University of Manchester, Manchester. www.ippg.org.uk/papers/bp19.pdf.

World Bank (2012): *World Development Indicators 2012.* World Bank, Washington, D.C.

WTTC (2011): *Satellite Account of Travel and Tourism Economic Impact: 2011.* World Travel and Tourism Council, London.

3 Conceptualizing the goal of full employment and the SDG framework

Introduction

The post–MDG development agenda, i.e., the Sustainable Development Goals (SDGs), adopted in 2015 – with 2030 as the terminal year for attaining the goals – includes full and productive employment and decent work in one of the goals to be pursued. If this goal is to be pursued seriously by developing countries, it is necessary to start from how the notion of full and productive employment can be conceptualized from a practical point of view. The indicators that can be used to monitor progress in attaining the goal have to be based on the definition and concept adopted.

While the official document listing the SDGs does not go into definitional issues, supplementary documents contain a list of indicators for various goals. The latter includes unemployment rate; labour productivity; proportion of informal employment; average hourly earnings; and the proportion of youth not in employment, education, and training. Several questions arise in this context. First, would the usual definition of full employment be applicable to developing countries? Given the nature of the challenges faced by them in creating productive employment and the importance of structural transformation of their economies (as analyzed in Chapter 2), would it not be necessary to conceptualize full employment differently for them? This question assumes particular significance because the use of the standard definition and measure of unemployment[1] in such countries often is not helpful in monitoring progress towards full employment.[2]

Second, if full employment has to be conceptualized differently, it would also be necessary to find alternative ways of monitoring progress in attaining the goal. In that context, the appropriateness of the indicators suggested in the SDG agenda needs to be examined carefully.

The main purpose of the present chapter would be to address the questions mentioned above. In doing so, possible alternatives will be suggested for monitoring progress towards attaining the goal of full employment in developing countries, and their possible application will be illustrated with particular reference to selected countries of Asia. The chapter is organized as follows. First, the conventional ways of looking at full employment are examined from the point of view of their usefulness in analyzing the problem in developing countries with surplus labour. That is followed by a critique of the indicators of the labour market used to measure progress in attaining the MDGs and of the indicators suggested for the SDGs. Based on the analysis of the first two sections, a set of indicators in an expanded framework are proposed for monitoring the progress of developing countries in moving towards the goal of full employment. These indicators are then used to provide a benchmark of the employment situation in selected countries of South Asia.

Conceptualizing full and productive employment in developing economies

Two broad strands can be found in the discussion on full employment and policies for maintaining it: one is basically welfare oriented in approach and dates back to the early twentieth century while the other is more economic in approach and relatively younger in terms of age. The writings of Sidney Webb (1912) and William Beveridge (1944) can be said to belong to the former strand, although both stood on solid economic arguments. For example, writing in 1912, Sidney Webb advocated for government expenditure as a measure to counteract deficiency in private consumption and external demand for promoting employment and tackling unemployment. He also recommended (i) public employment exchanges for facilitating a better match between job-seekers and employers, and (ii) employment contract with stipulation of fixed hours of work. Although he did not explicitly refer to the notion of full employment, it was clear that his focus was on how the unemployed could be helped by the government in finding jobs on a regular basis. In fact, his brief report also covered the issue of unemployment insurance and training, and how those who are averse to working could be brought into the labour market, albeit in the context of the prevailing situation in the British society.

William Beveridge, in his famous report titled "Full Employment in a Free Society", dealt specifically with the definition of full employment, and defined full employment "as a state of affairs in which there are always more vacant jobs than unemployed men..." (Beveridge, 1944, p. 10). He justified this on the ground that the labour market should be a seller's market rather than a buyer's market so that individuals seeking jobs should not have difficulty finding one. In elaborating his definition of full employment, Beveridge clarified that by full employment he did not mean zero unemployment. In fact, he was aware that there could always be those who are looking for work (a new one or switch from an existing one to another) and would need a bit of time to find a suitable one or could be caught in a seasonal slack. Taking such possibilities into account, he suggested that "we should be able to reduce unemployment to not more than three per cent to cover seasonal slackness and fluctuations of international trade" (Beveridge, 1944, p. 12).

It is clear that for both Webb and Beveridge, reducing unemployment is the starting off point and governments have an important role to play in attaining this goal.[3] The second broad strand in the thinking on full employment is more technocratic in approach and uses the Philips curve[4] for developing the argument. Being of relatively recent in origin, this strand of thinking focusses more on controlling inflation and ensuring price stability. As unemployment is inversely related to inflation, attempt to reduce unemployment below a certain level would result in inflation running at a level which is above the tolerable limit. The level of unemployment at which inflation does not rise is termed the non-accelerating inflation rate of unemployment (NAIRU)[5] and that basically sets the limit for full employment. In such a framework, the rate of unemployment cannot be pushed to zero because inflation starts rising even before that. Thus, even if unemployment rate is above zero, if that is consistent with stable inflation, the state would have to be regarded as one of full employment.

In developed economies where there is normally very little underutilization of labour, the concept and measure of NAIRU may be useful in indicating whether an economy has reached the limit of its productive capacity, and any further expansion may – by raising wages of workers – create inflationary pressures.[6] The situation in developing economies, however, is different. In many of them – especially in situations where there is "surplus labour" – expansion of output can continue by utilizing underutilized labour and other resources without necessarily producing cost-push (or wage-push) inflation of the kind that underlies the notions of Philips curve and NAIRU. Some examples from estimates of NAIRU for developed and developing countries may be useful in illustrating the point.

Estimates made by the OECD for a large number of developed countries indicate that values of NAIRU for 2015 ranged from as low as 3.31 per cent and 3.44 per cent, respectively, for Norway and the Republic of Korea to 9.56 per cent for France and 17.28 per cent for Greece (Table 3.1). For the USA, the estimate was 4.94 per cent. This estimate implies that if unemployment in the USA, for example, drops below 4.94 per cent, inflationary pressures may arise. If one looks at the evolution of monetary policy in that country, one

Table 3.1 OECD Forecasts of NAIRU for Selected Countries

Country	NAIRU (%) for 2015
Norway	3.31
Republic of Korea	3.44
Japan	3.60
Switzerland	4.34
Germany	4.92
USA	4.94
UK	5.57
France	9.56
Greece	17.28

Source: OECD (2017).

would note that the Federal Reserve Board started raising the interest rate from its near-zero level in 2015 when the rate of unemployment was 5.3 per cent. Since then, unemployment rate has fallen further (to 4.1 per cent as of early 2018), and interest rates have also been raised – albeit slowly.

Although official estimates of NAIRU are rare for developing countries, especially for those of South Asia, for illustrative purposes, estimates made by some researchers (Gondal et al., 2014) are presented in Table 3.2. Actual unemployment rates prevailing in these countries are also presented in the same table. A few points may be made on the basis of these data and data on inflation presented in Table 3A.1.

First, in all the countries, actual unemployment rates are systematically lower than NAIRU, which implies that inflation must have been a persistent problem in these countries. The reality, however, is different. While there have been periods of high inflation in all these countries, there is very little evidence of systematic relationship between the unemployment gap and inflation rate. It is only in Pakistan where the increase in unemployment gap was associated with a rise in inflationary pressure. In Bangladesh, inflationary pressure eased during 2005–15, even without a narrowing of the unemployment gap. In India, despite a widening of the gap, inflationary pressure did not register a secular increase. In Nepal, there was some rise in inflationary pressure despite a narrowing of the unemployment gap (Table 3.3).

Table 3.2 Estimated NAIRU and Survey-Based Actual Unemployment Rates in Selected Countries of South Asia

Country	NAIRU	Actual Unemployment Rates	
		Earlier Year	Later Year
Bangladesh	7.849	4.2 (2005–06)	4.5 (2015–16)
India (CWS)	6.064	4.5 (2004–05)	3.7 (2011–12)
Nepal	6.808	1.8 (1998)	2.1 (2008)
Pakistan	6.733	6.1 (2005–06)	5.7 (2010–11)
Sri Lanka	6.035	6.5 (2004)	4.2 (2011)

Source: (i) For NAIRU, Gondal et al. (2014). The period covered by the data is 1971–2012. (ii) The actual unemployment figures have been compiled by the Institute for Human Development, Delhi from country-level labour force survey reports. The figures on India presented in this table refer to the "current weekly status".

Table 3.3 A Summary of Unemployment Gap and Inflation Trends

Country	Unemployment Gap	Trend in Inflation
Bangladesh	Virtually unchanged	Decline
India	Increase	Mixed
Nepal	Decrease	Increase
Pakistan	Increase	Increase
Sri Lanka	Increase	Decline

Sources: Table 3.2 and Annex Table A3.1.

The general point that is being made here is that if estimates of NAIRU (that were referred to above) and actual unemployment rates in the countries of South Asia were used as guide, they would appear to have been in full employment for a long period of time, and there would be no need to worry about their employment problem.[7] If anything, macroeconomic policies would need tightening in order to avoid inflation. That, however, would be a wrong signal, especially given the challenges faced by these countries in absorbing their surplus labour through the growth of productive employment. Use of the unemployment threshold (of three per cent) suggested by Beveridge would be equally inappropriate for such countries.

Full and productive employment and sustainable development goals

Employment goal and the Millennium Development Goals (MDGs)

It is well known that the MDGs (with the terminal date of 2015) were formulated around a target-based format and had a strong development orientation with the goals focussing on income and non-income dimensions of poverty. They came after several decades of disappointing performance in these areas. For many developing countries, this was associated with low or unstable economic growth while there were countries that had this experience despite impressive rates of economic growth. It was, therefore, not surprising that development practitioners and policymakers at both international and national levels focussed on these aspects of development in addition to economic growth. However, when the terminal date of the MDG period drew near and the international community started to look at the attainments and at a possible future development framework, a number of issues came up. Two of them related to economic growth and employment.

The first issue concerned the place of economic growth in a development agenda and whether the MDG framework de-emphasized the growth part of it. One view was that this was indeed the case and there had to be a better balance between the goals economic growth and development. In this context, one may recall that a large part of the second half of the twentieth century was occupied by a single-minded focus on economic growth as the major goal to be pursued with the hope that other developments will follow. This was the case in the development strategies pursued at the country level as well as in policy advice provided by international development agencies. Even when there was an attempt to correct for the shortcomings of that approach through the mechanism of PRSPs, the goal of poverty reduction and other social dimensions of development remained as add-ons rather than being integral parts of an overall growth strategy. The MDG framework at least partly reflected that unease. But when time came to reflect on that framework, economic growth came back into consideration. Of course, this time, issues relating to sustainability of growth, poverty, inequality, and employment were not neglected.

Second, a glaring omission in the MDGs was the lack of a place for employment in the agenda. It may be recalled that the original list of goals and targets did not include productive employment as an item. This was added later, and it took eight years (agreed upon in 2008) to include the new MDG target of achieving "full and productive employment and decent work for all including women and young people" and the associated indicators, viz.

- Growth rate of labour productivity (GDP per person employed).
- Employment-to-population ratio.
- Proportion of employed people living below the poverty line.
- Proportion of own-account and contributing family workers in total employment (vulnerable employment ratio).

The absence of any employment-related target in the original list of MDGs implies that adequate attention was not given to the mechanisms and policies that would be needed to attain the desired development goals listed therein because productive employment is not only a desirable goal by itself, it (along with incomes earned through employment) can also serve as an important instrument for linking economic growth with other goals like reduction of income poverty and hunger, education, and health. Analysis of the critical nexus between economic growth, employment, and poverty reduction undertaken during the years after the adoption of MDGs indicates that while high rate of economic growth is a necessary condition for poverty reduction, it is not sufficient. The pattern of growth in terms of its impact on productive employment plays a key role in translating the benefits of growth into poverty reduction. Moreover, there is no invariant relationship between economic growth and productive employment. Empirical evidence shows that in many countries economic growth has not resulted in the desired rate of growth of productive employment.[8] It is, therefore, important to integrate employment into a development agenda aimed at poverty eradication and the attainment of other social goals in the areas of education and health.

Apart from the late incorporation of productive employment and related indicators into the MDGs in 2008, a few observations may be in order about the indicators themselves and the lack of attention to needed policies for improving upon the outcomes. First, the concept and measurement of employment itself raises problems, especially in developing countries where the absence of social protection for the unemployed compels them to remain engaged in some work (either wage paid or on own-account) merely to eke out a living. When a typical survey question asks a person about his/her status during the reference week, it is highly unlikely to find very many who would say that they were not doing any income-earning work. In this kind of situation, employment-to-population ratio (which is one of the indicators of the employment target) may be more of an indicator of the growth of labour force than of productive employment. Only in some sectors of such economies, e.g., manufacturing and other modern service sectors, the numbers employed and the growth of that number are expected to really reflect demand for them.

Hence, for developing countries, employment-to-population ratio for the economy as a whole may not be a good indicator of productive employment.[9]

The second observation about the employment indicators of MDGs concerns the indicator for vulnerable employment which was measured as the proportion of own-account and family workers. Own-account workers (or self-employed) as a category is very broad and covers a wide range of workers ranging from those engaged in very low productivity residual type of jobs to those who are professionals in specialized occupations and earn decent incomes. Including all of them in the category of vulnerable employment may not reflect the reality. It is, of course, understandable that in the current state of data availability, especially in developing countries, it may not be possible to disaggregate own-account workers into sub-groups by their income and productivity. But this cannot be an argument for not recognizing the shortcoming of the indicator that was being used. Rather, efforts should have been made to bring about improvements at the conceptual level and follow that up by data collection efforts.

A major problem with the employment indicators of the MDGs was that they did not reflect an understanding of the structural transformation that developing countries need to undergo in order to achieve high rates of growth of productive employment. As already mentioned in Chapter 2 of the present volume, the required transformation is from low productivity sectors like agriculture and other traditional sectors to modern manufacturing, transport and communication, and modern services. Of course, such transformation, by itself, may not yield high growth of productive employment. What would be required in addition is high growth of industries that are by nature labour-intensive. If this kind of structural transformation takes place in an economy, it should be reflected in the change in the structure of employment by sectors and sub-sectors. The importance of the pattern of growth expressed through sector and sub-sector composition of growth is indicated by the experience of countries that have been successful in combining high rate of economic growth with high rate of employment, e.g., Republic of Korea and Malaysia in the early stages of their economic growth, Indonesia, Thailand, etc. The important aspects of the pattern of growth are (i) high growth of manufacturing industries in relation to overall GDP growth and (ii) high rate of growth of labour-intensive industries and other labour-intensive sectors. In selecting indicators of employment performance, this feature of developing countries should be taken into account. The employment indicators incorporated into the MDGs in 2008 did not reflect the importance of the pattern of growth outlined above. An important question in this regard is whether the SDG framework made any improvement on that score.[10]

The goal of full and productive employment in the Sustainable Development Goals

In 2015, leaders of 193 countries of the world unanimously adopted the post-2015 international development agenda for the period 2015–30. Termed Sustainable Development Goals (SDGs), they are meant to provide the framework for global development after the terminal year (2015) of the MDGs. With 17 goals and 169 targets[11], SDGs represent a bold new agenda to end poverty, fight inequality, tackle the adverse effects of climate change, and ensure a sustainable future for all. Goal 8 of the SDGs includes, in addition to sustained and inclusive economic growth, full and productive employment, and decent work for all.[12] Like each of the goals, Goal 8 has also been elaborated through a number of "targets" and "indicators". Table 3.4 presents the targets and indicators that are relevant for the goal of full and productive employment.

It can be seen from Table 3.4 that the goal of full and productive employment is articulated in target 8.5. A look at this target would indicate the comprehensive nature of the goal of full employment and decent work. Separate mention is made of (i) productivity, (ii) men and women, (iii) youth, (iv) persons with disabilities, (v) equal pay for work of equal value, and (vi) decent work. The last, if one follows ILO's conceptualization, would include

Table 3.4 Sustainable Development Goal 8: Targets and Indicators Relating to Full and Productive Employment

Targets	Indicators
8.2. Achieve higher levels of productivity through diversification, technological upgrading and innovation, including through a focus on high value–added and labour–intensive sectors	8.2.1. Annual growth rate of GDP per employed person
8.3. Promote development-oriented policies that support productive activities, decent job creation, entrepreneurship, creativity and innovation, and encourage the formalization and growth of micro-, small-, and medium-sized enterprises, including through access to financial services	8.3.1. Proportion of informal employment in non-agricultural employment, by sex
8.5. By 2030, achieve full and productive employment and decent work for all women and men, including for young people and persons with disabilities, and equal pay for work of equal value	8.5.1. Average hourly earnings of female and male employees, by occupation, age, and persons with disabilities 8.5.2. Unemployment rate by sex, age, and persons with disabilities
8.6. By 2020, substantially reduce the proportion of youth not in employment, education, or training	8.6.1. Proportion of youth (aged 15–24 years) not in education, employment, or training
8.B. By 2020, develop and operationalize a global strategy for youth employment and implement the Global Jobs Pact of the International Organization	8.B.1. Total government spending in social protection and employment programmes as a proportion of the national budgets and GDP

Source: United Nations: Sustainable Development Knowledge Platform: Sustainable Development Goal 8. https://sustainabledevelopment.un.org/sdg8 (Accessed on 3 May 2018).

in addition to productive employment, social protection, rights at work, and social dialogue between workers, employers, and governments.

Two indicators – one focussing on unemployment rate (Indicator 8.5.2) and another on "average hourly earnings" (Indicator 8.5.1) are mentioned alongside the target of full employment – presumably for purposes of monitoring performance in achieving the target.

If one casts a wider glance and looks at other targets and indicators relating to employment, one would note a few points.

- For attaining the target of improving productivity, mention is made of economic diversification, technology, and labour-intensive sectors. But one single indicator, viz., GDP per person, has been identified for monitoring this target.
- For promoting the growth of decent jobs, suggestion is made for promoting the growth of micro-, small-, and medium-sized enterprises and formalization of jobs in those sectors. The indicator relating to this target is the proportion of informal employment in non-agricultural employment.
- The target of reducing the number of young people not in employment, education, and training is associated with a direct indicator on their number/proportion.
- Government spending on social protection and employment programmes as a proportion of national budgets and GDP is mentioned as an indicator, but that is related to youth employment.

What do all the above amount to from the point of view of assessing the performance of developing countries with respect to the goal of full and productive employment? As already argued earlier in the present chapter, measures of open unemployment are of very little use for this purpose. Of course, there is mention of the need for "diversification" and growth of "labour-intensive sectors" as pathways to attaining higher productivity. The importance of micro- and small enterprises has also been recognized among the targets. But there is nothing in terms of indicators with which the performance of an economy in attaining the required degree of structural transformation in employment can be assessed.

It may, of course, be argued that the proportion of informal employment in total non-agricultural employment might provide some indication of whether an economy is moving towards better quality jobs. Indeed, the hypothesis of an inverse relationship between informal employment and per capita income may get support from cross-country data – the proportion of informal employment is lower at higher levels of income. But the recent experience of some developing countries, especially in South Asia, indicates that at the country level and over time, the process of decline in informal employment with economic growth may not be working as anticipated (see below). Persistence of such employment even in economies with good record on economic growth is an issue of concern, and it is important not only to monitor the situation in that respect but also to gear public policy for addressing the challenge. And we shall return to this issue soon in the present chapter. But the point to note is that the proportion of informal employment, by itself, cannot adequately capture what happens in an economy in terms of structural transformation of output and employment, and the transfer of workers from jobs characterized by low levels of productivity to those with higher productivity.

Indicators of progress in creating productive employment: an expanded framework[13]

The observations made above about the limitations of employment indicators employed in the MDGs and SDGs should provide pointers to how the issue of productive employment could be addressed in the context of developing countries. In order to identify indicators that would be useful in signalling growth of productive employment, it would be necessary to go beyond the standard definition of the term employment and the measure that results from such a definition. Taking into account the characteristics of labour markets in developing countries and the importance of the pattern of growth and need for structural change in the sector composition of employment (as discussed in Chapter 2), various possibilities could be considered[14]:

- Employed persons who are not underemployed (preferably by a productivity or income measure)
- Persons in regular wage employment as proportion of total employment
- Persons in regular wage employment in non-agricultural sectors as proportion of total employment in those sectors
- The rate of growth and proportion of total employment in manufacturing, construction, and modern services
- The rate of decline in unpaid family work
- Proportion of total employment in the informal segment of the economy and the rate at which it declines
- The proportion of the workforce who are below the poverty line
- Labour productivity and real wages

A few words may be in order about the rationale for the indicators suggested above. Take underemployment first. It has already been mentioned that in most developing countries, the rate of open unemployment is found to be rather low, and it is not a very useful indicator of the labour market situation. In many countries, underemployment – by income or time criteria – is a common phenomenon, especially in agriculture and other traditional sectors. Although it is not easy to measure the degree of underemployment, various alternatives including time and income measure are available. Clearly, if one is trying to identify those engaged in productive employment, a starting point may be to exclude the underemployed from the total numbers employed and use that as an indicator. This, of course, is not a satisfactory solution because those who are underemployed may not be engaged in entirely unproductive work. The point here is one of relative levels of productivity, and the suggestion is that those who are not underemployed by any of the currently used measures may be regarded as engaged in more productive employment.

The indicators suggested in the bullet points second through fifth above emanate from the framework of economic growth and structural transformation that has been discussed in Chapter 2. To recall briefly, in order to be successful in creating productive employment, economic growth has to engender a process through which labour force moves from low productivity traditional sectors like agriculture to those where productivity is higher, e.g., manufacturing, trade, services, etc. In terms of status in employment, the change has to be from unpaid family work to either own-account work or wage employment and from casual employment to regular wage-/salary-based work. Furthermore, the analysis in Chapter 2 shows that manufacturing has to act as the engine of growth, although the feasibility of that happening in all countries may be questioned and the possibility of alternatives like services could be examined. Hence the rate of growth of employment in manufacturing (as well as modern services) and its share in total employment could be useful indicators of progress towards expanding the base of productive employment.

Given the recent experience of low growth of employment as a whole and of wage/salaried jobs in particular, creating one's own job is being increasingly emphasized by development practitioners and policymakers. But that should not reduce the importance of wage employment as an indicator of progress towards productive employment. The extent of wage/salaried employment created by the modern sectors of the economy should be a major indicator of the employment intensity of growth.

While structural change in an economy and in the composition of employment is important from the point of view of productive employment, large proportions of the total labour force in developing countries remain employed in agriculture. Hence, in addition to transferring workers from agriculture to modern sectors, development strategies must aim at raising productivity within agriculture so that real wages and earnings of those who remain there may improve.

Labour markets of many developing countries are characterized by high proportions engaged in the so-called informal segment of the economy which consists of those who are outside the formal segment as well as those who are linked to the formal segment in various ways and yet are informally employed (in the sense of not being covered by the regulations and practices of the formal sector that engages them). Progress in development has to be associated with a reduction in this segment of employment. This, of course, is not to suggest that all those who are employed in this segment suffer from low productivity. On the contrary, the informal sector in developing countries can be quite heterogeneous in terms of levels of operation as well as the levels of productivity and incomes of workers engaged in them. As for an indicator relating to informal employment, the attempt should be to identify the component where labour productivity and returns are low and monitor changes therein – the target being to reduce the share of this component.

An important issue concerning the labour market indicators is whether it is possible to specify targets for them. Although the answer is not straightforward, some indicative figures can be suggested on the basis of the experience of developing countries who have attained greater success with respect to both economic growth and employment. Take, for example, the proportion of employees in total employment. Table 3.5 presents data on this for selected countries of East and South East Asia (ESEA). Out of the four countries for which data are presented, Republic of Korea already attained the status of developed country at the beginning of the present millennium while the others are at various stages of development. A few observations may be made about the structure of employment in these countries and changes therein as their economies grew.

During the early stages of their economic growth, Korea and Malaysia attained rapid growth of labour-intensive industrialization. That pattern of growth enabled them to create employment based on wages and salary at high rates, which, in turn, led to a rapid change in the structure of employment towards regular employees. A similar pattern of growth was attained by Indonesia and Thailand – albeit somewhat later and at different rates. And the share of employees increased in those countries as well. It may be useful to look at the figures of Table 3.5 with this background in mind. In 1998, the share of employees in total employment was 62 and 73 per cent in Korea and Malaysia, respectively. The corresponding figure for Thailand was 36 per cent while that for Indonesia (in 2001) was 33 per cent. By 2014/2015, the figures for Korea and Malaysia stood at 73 per cent. In 2017, the figures for Indonesia and Thailand had gone up to 49 and 47 per cent, respectively. These figures, especially those of Korea and Malaysia, may provide at least some rough idea as to where countries of South Asia should aim at seeing themselves in this regard in the terminal year of SDGs.

Table 3.5 Share of Employees in Total Employment in Selected Countries of Asia

Country	Share (%) of Employees in Total Employment	
	1990s	*Recent Year*
Indonesia	33.27 (2001)	48.9 (2017)
Republic of Korea	61.67 (1998)	73.22 (2014)
Malaysia	73.35 (1998)	73.90 (2015)
Thailand	36.50 (1998)	47.1 (2017)

Source: Calculated from data available from the ILO statistical website www.ilo. org/ilostat/faces/help_home/data_by_country?_adf.ctrl-state=lfizq94u7_ 312&_afrLoop=644504662805072#!

Table 3.6 The Share (%) of Informal Employment in Total Non-Agricultural Employment

Country	The Share of Informal Employment (%) and Year
Indonesia	72.6 (2009)
Republic of Korea	25.8 (2005)
Malaysia	11.4 (2015)
Thailand	42.3 (2010)

Sources: For Korea, OECD (2008); for Malaysia, Government of Malaysia, Department of Statistics (2015). For Korea, the source is the Korea Labour and Income Panel Study. For Malaysia, it is Informal Sector Workforce Survey. The figures for Indonesia and Thailand are from ILO (2012).

Observations similar to the above may be made on using share of informal employment as an indicator of progress towards full employment. Data on the share of informal employment in total non-agricultural employment in the four countries mentioned above are presented in Table 3.6. The figures range from 11.4 per cent in Malaysia to 72.6 per cent in Indonesia. Malaysia is somewhat different from the other countries in this respect because that is a country with relatively small population, especially in relation to the resources available. Rural–urban migration and growth of informal sector economic activities has not been a significant phenomenon in that country, and that's why the share of informal employment is so low in that country. As for Korea, the figure of 25.8 per cent can be explained by the rapid growth attained by the country over a long period of time and the absorption of surplus labour in the modern sector. Indonesia and Thailand also attained some success in this regard – though the extent varies. Although it is difficult to suggest what should be the target for reduction in the share of informal employment, the examples should provide some idea about the desirable direction of change and its speed. For countries of South Asia, a target of about 60 per cent by 2030 may not be too unrealistic.

How are the countries of South Asia doing?

Use of the "expanded framework" for assessing progress in creating productive employment at the country level would make considerable demand on data. While labour force surveys can be a source for several of the items, there are items (wages, labour productivity, etc.) on which data from other sources would be needed. In most countries, such surveys are carried out only at intervals, and data tend to get outdated by the time the results are available in published form. Furthermore, the use of standard internationally recommended definitions and measures also creates limitations on their usefulness. Sometimes, changes made in definitions/measures and categories used and tables prepared also create difficulty in analyzing trends. Considering these difficulties and limitations, a few items from the augmented framework mentioned above are used here to assess where the countries of South Asia stand in terms of full and productive employment.[15]

Underemployment

As already mentioned earlier, in developing countries with surplus labour, underemployment can be a useful alternative indicator of the employment situation, especially if the objective is to assess progress towards attaining the goal of full employment. However, the concept of underemployment is also not without complexity, and hence measures also vary. Two alternatives that are often suggested are visible and invisible underemployment. Visible underemployment refers to the underutilization of the available labour time of an individual and willingness of the individual to work longer. This is also referred to as the time measure of underemployment.[16] Invisible underemployment is an analytical concept referring to the productivity and income-generating capacity of work in which one is engaged. There is no universally accepted measure of such underemployment. It could be measured in terms of productivity associated with or income generated by employment.

Labour force surveys in developing countries, especially those in South Asia, usually provide a measure of visible underemployment in terms of time criterion and categorize those working less than 35 (or 40) hours a week as underemployed. Table 3.7 presents some data. Sometimes, an additional criterion, viz., whether looking for/sought or were available for additional work is also used. When this criterion is applied in addition to that of working less than 35 hours per week, the observed rate of underemployment is usually found to be rather low. For example, in Bangladesh, the labour force survey of 2013 applied both the criteria, and underemployment rate was found to be four per cent. But the rate turned out to be 17.8 per cent when calculation was made by using only the time criterion. Likewise, in Pakistan and Sri Lanka, where both the criteria were applied, the rate of underemployment was found to be very low.

If the figures of Table 3.7 were to be taken seriously, it would appear that like unemployment, underemployment is also not a problem in the countries of South Asia. But it should be understood that these low figures are due simply to the criteria used in measuring the phenomenon. First, even those who are working less than a certain number of hours may genuinely feel that they are working quite hard and are entitled to some rest time. Second, a question about willingness to work additional hours without any reference to the rate of wage/salary for such work can be regarded as vague if not incomplete. And a negative answer to such a question should have no implication for potential supply of labour. If the respondents were told about the availability of more remunerative work, the response could have been different. If underemployment were to be used as an indicator of the employment situation, it should be measured in such a way that it would reflect productivity and incomes associated with the employment.

Table 3.7 Time-Related Underemployment in Countries of South Asia (Percentage of Employed Persons)

Country and Year	Underemployed as % of Employed Persons	
	Definition 1	*Definition 2*
Bangladesh		
2010	20.3	n.a.
2013	17.8	4.0
2016–17	n.a.	2.4
India		
2011/12	11.7	6.7
Nepal		
1998	4.2	n.a.
2008	6.8	n.a.
Pakistan		
2010–11	15.1	1.3
2012–13	n.a.	1.6
2014–15	n.a.	1.1
Sri Lanka		
2012	n.a.	2.9
2016	n.a.	2.4

Sources: Labour force surveys of different countries.

Note: (i) Definition 1: Those who have worked <35 hours during the reference week as percentage of total employed persons. (ii) Definition 2: Those who worked <35 hours during the reference week and were available for additional work. (iii) In Bangladesh, from 2013 onwards, the threshold has been changed from 35 hours per week to 40 hours per week.

The share of regular wage employment in total employment

Although data on wage employment are collected through the labour force surveys in most countries of South Asia, the data that are available are not without problems. First, all wage employment should not be taken as an indicator of productive employment because some of them could be in the informal economy and may be characterized by low productivity. Second, sometimes casual employment may also be included in the category dubbed as "employees". In such cases, the proportion of employees in total employment may not be a good indicator of productive employment. It would be important to keep these caveats in mind while looking at the data presented in Table 3.8.

One general observation that may be made is that the share of employees in total employment in the countries of South Asia are much lower than the level attained by Republic of Korea and Malaysia in the late 1990s. Of course,

Table 3.8 Share of Employees in Total Employment

Country	Share (%) of Employees in Total Employment	
	Earlier Year	Recent Year
Bangladesh	12.6 (1999–2000)	39.1 (2016–17)
India	47.2 (1999–2000)	47.8 (2011–12)
Nepal	43.5 (1998/99)	45.8 (2008)
Pakistan	39.9 (2001–02)	38.7 (2014–15)
Sri Lanka	59.8 (1995)	57.8 (2016)

Source: Labour force surveys of different countries.

Note: In the case of Bangladesh, the definition of "employees" in the earlier year was different from that used in the recent year. In the latter, "day labourers" have been included in the category titled "employees" along with regular wage paid employees, whereas in the earlier year, "day labourers" were shown as a separate category.

the levels in Sri Lanka and India compare favourably with those in Indonesia and Thailand. Second, the data for South Asian countries do not indicate any improvement in this regard except for Bangladesh where at least part of the sharp increase is almost certainly due to the inclusion of "day labourers" in the category of employees.

Employment in manufacturing

As already mentioned above (and also in Chapter 2), industrialization has to be the cornerstone of development effort. Since productivity of labour in that sector is expected to be higher than in the traditional sectors, growth of employment in manufacturing should be one of the key indicators of progress towards creation of productive employment in an economy. The development experience of the countries of ESEA which have been successful provides strength to this argument. For example, manufacturing in Korea was able to attain an annual growth of over 17 per cent during the 1960s and 1970s, and nearly 13 per cent during the 1980s. During the 1970s, elasticity of employment with respect to output in the sector was 0.69, which implies that during that period annual employment growth was over 11 per cent. During the subsequent decade, elasticity of employment had declined to below 0.5; but with output growth of 13 per cent, annual employment growth was still over six per cent. In Malaysia, annual growth of output in manufacturing was 11.7, 9.3, and 13.2 per cent during the 1970s, 1980s, and 1990–96, respectively. With employment elasticity of 0.67 and 0.71 during the 1980s and 1990s, respectively, employment growth in the sector was over six per cent and nine per cent during those decades.

The experience of Korea and Malaysia mentioned above indicates that an employment growth of over six per cent in manufacturing should not be an unrealistic target. Of course, one has to take into account the difficulties of replicating the experience of some countries in others, and there are a variety of reasons for growth of manufacturing employment to be lower in South Asian countries (as already discussed in Chapter 2). But the experience of countries that have been successful in absorbing surplus labour through high growth of productive employment indicates what is possible.

Data on employment growth in manufacturing industries in some of the countries of South Asia presented in Table 3.9 show that Bangladesh was the only country in the region where an annual growth of over six per cent was attained – and that also for a few years. It has declined since then, and data for very recent years (e.g., 2016 and 2017) show that employment growth in the sector has slowed down further. In other countries, employment growth in the sector has been lower and has fluctuated. In Sri Lanka, for example, there was a period of negative growth. In India, growth has declined from over three per cent to just 1.5 per cent.[17]

Employment in the informal economy

Data presented in Table 3.10 show that the incidence of informal employment is very high in the countries of South Asia, except in Sri Lanka. Moreover, the progress in reducing it has been very slow – except, perhaps, in Pakistan. So, the conventional hypothesis that the incidence of informal

Table 3.9 Growth of Employment in Manufacturing

Country	Annual Growth of Employment in Manufacturing (%)
Bangladesh	
2005–06 to 2010	6.34
2010 to 2015–16	5.12
India	
1993–94 to 2004–05	3.2
2004–05 to 2011–12	1.5
Nepal	
1998 to 2008	3.41
Pakistan	
1999–2000 to 2005–06	4.41
2005–06 to 2014–15	3.46
Sri Lanka	
2006 to 2010	−1.75
2010 to 2012	3.35
2013 to 2016	1.31

Sources: Calculated from data available from labour force surveys of different years.

Table 3.10 Employment in the Informal Economy

Country	Share (%) of The Informal Sector in Total Non-Agricultural Employment	
	Earlier Year	Recent Year
Bangladesh	78 (2005–06)	85 (2016–17)
India	91 (1999–2000)	83.8 (2011–12)
Nepal	n.a.	92.1 (2008)
Pakistan	85.6 (2010–11)	72.6 (2014–15)
Sri Lanka	62.7 (2011–12)	60.2 (2016)

Sources: Labour force surveys of different years.

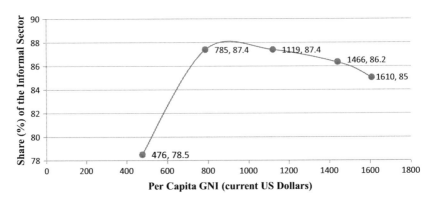

Figure 3.1 Bangladesh Share of the Informal Sector in Non-Agricultural Employment and per Capita Income.

Sources: Data on informal sector employment are from labour force surveys while the per
capita GNI figures are from the Statistical Pocketbook of Bangladesh of various years.

employment would decline with economic growth does not seem to be
borne out by the actual experiences, especially of Bangladesh and India. The
proportion of informal sector employment has remained high in those two
countries despite the rapid economic growth attained by them during the
2000s. Figure 3.1 shows that in Bangladesh, a doubling of per capita GNI
has been associated with only a small reduction in the share of the informal
sector employment.

Labour productivity

GDP per employed person has been used as a proxy for overall labour productivity and has been calculated by using the World Bank's World Development
Indicators data. A few observations may be made on the basis of the results
presented in Table 3.11. First, Bangladesh, India, and Sri Lanka appear to
have done well in terms of both the actual level and gradual acceleration in labour productivity. While Bangladesh has attained a secular increase, growth
of labour productivity in India and Sri Lanka declined after 2012. Second,

Table 3.11 Growth of GDP per Employed Person, 1992–2016 (Annual, %)

Country	1992–2002	2002–12	2012–16
Bangladesh	1.65	3.94	5.22
India	3.69	6.50	5.14
Nepal	1.79	2.32	0.91
Pakistan	0.65	0.59	1.43
Sri Lanka	2.65	5.57	4.23

Source: Calculated by using World Development Indicators data on GDP per employed person available online at https://data.worldbank.org/indicator/SL.GDP. PCAP.EM.KD?view=chart&year_high_desc=false (Accessed 7 May 2018).
Notes: (i) The estimates of GDP per person in the source mentioned above use ILO "modelled estimates". (ii) For estimating growth rates between two years, three-year averages have been used as beginning and end of period figures. For example, for the 1992 figure, the average of 1991–1993 has been used.

growth of labour productivity in Nepal and Pakistan was not only lower than in other countries, but it has also been unstable in these two countries.

A summing up

Conceptualization of full employment as done under the welfare-oriented approaches of Sydney Webb or William Beveridge or through the technocratic approach encapsulated by the framework of NAIRU is not very useful for developing economies characterized by the existence of surplus labour. In such situations, the application of the standard measure yields rather low rates of unemployment and does not help much in understanding the real employment situation. What is critical in developing economies is structural transformation of the economy enabling people to move from low-productivity employment to those with higher productivity and earnings.

Although the targets and indicators adopted under the SDG of full and productive employment and decent work do have elements that reflect some of the challenge mentioned above, the major focus remains on unemployment rate. The list of indicators (except, to some extent, the proportion of informal employment) does not include anything through which the process of structural transformation – especially of employment, and success attained in that regard can be assessed and monitored. Elements that would be important in that context include the proportion of regular wage- and salary-based employment, especially in the formal sector, and related to that, growth of employment in the manufacturing sector and other modern sectors where labour productivity and earnings are expected to be higher than in traditional sectors where a large part of workers are currently employed. Taking this into account, an "expanded framework" with a number of indicators has been proposed in this chapter for purposes of monitoring progress in moving towards full and productive employment in developing economies.

One needs to understand, however, that for developing economies, the notion of full and productive employment is not amenable to a neat definition, and that it would be difficult to translate this goal into clearly articulated and quantifiable targets and indicators. Moreover, all the indicators may not be relevant in the same manner for all countries irrespective of the characteristics of their economies. What would be important is for countries to formulate, within the common broad framework, their own set of indicators and use them to assess their performance and progress.

Some of the indicators of the expanded framework mentioned above have been used to examine how the countries of South Asia are faring in terms of creating productive employment. In doing so, a comparative approach is taken and the performance is compared with that of some countries of ESEA, especially Republic of Korea and Malaysia. On the whole, both in terms of the growth of employment in manufacturing and the proportion of regular wage- and salary-based employment, the performance appears to be rather mixed, and the countries of South Asia appear to have a long way to travel. Not surprisingly, proportion of employment in the informal economy remains at very high levels and has not shown much relationship to the rate of economic growth. The good news, however, is the growth in productivity attained by some countries, especially by Bangladesh and India, and to some extent, by Sri Lanka. This was despite low growth of manufacturing employment (e.g., in India) and high proportion of informal employment. But increase in labour productivity has not always been associated with increase in real wages of workers – a subject to which we shall turn in the next chapter.

Annex 3.1

Table 3A.1 Inflation Rates in Selected Countries of South Asia, 2000–16

Year	Bangladesh	Year	India	Nepal	Pakistan	Sri Lanka
2000–01	1.58	2000	7.2	3.5	3.6	1.5
2001–02	2.36	2001	3.6	2.4	4.4	12.1
2002–03	4.37	2002	3.4	2.9	3.5	10.2
2003–04	5.83	2003	5.4	4.8	3.1	2.6
2004–05	6.48	2004	6.4	4	4.6	7.9
2005–06	7.17	2005	4.4	4.5	9.3	10.6
2006–07	7.22	2006	5.2	8	7.9	10
2007–08	9.93	2007	5	6.4	7.8	15.8
2008–09	6.66	2008	8.7	7.7	12	22.6
2009–10	7.31	2009	2.1	13.2	20.8	3.4
2010–11	8.51	2010	9.2	10.5	11.7	5.9
2011–12	8.69	2011	8.9	9.6	13.7	6.7
2012–13	6.78	2012	9.9	8.2	11	7.5
2013–14	7.35	2013	9.4	9.9	7.3	6.9
2014–15	6.45	2014	6	9.1	8.6	3.3
2015–16	6.05	2015	4.9	7.2	4.5	3.8
		2016	4.7	9.9	2.9	4

Sources: (i) Bangladesh: Bangladesh Bureau of Statistics: *Statistical Pocketbook* (various years), BBS, Dhaka. (ii) Other countries: Asian Development Bank: *Asian Development Outlook* (various years), ADB, Manila.

Table 3A.2 GDP per Employed Person (in Constant 2011 PP Dollar)

Year	Bangladesh	India	Nepal	Pakistan	Sri Lanka
1991	4,062	4,785	2,635	11,528	10,659
1992	4,159	4,924	2,662	12,013	11,353
1993	4,226	5,034	2,676	11,903	11,845
2001	4,802	6,903	3,186	12,540	14,070
2002	4,859	6,975	3,135	12,569	14,625
2003	4,997	7,306	3,202	12,714	15,265
2011	6,852	12,653	3,915	13,159	23,605
2012	7,189	13,268	4,000	13,330	25,950
2013	7,528	13,829	4,062	13,628	26,024
2015	8,215	15,490	4,185	14,093	28,903
2016	8,649	16,305	4,098	14,295	29,903
2017	9,572	16,774	4,134	14,066	30,409

Source: World Bank: World Development Indicators, GDP per employed person.

Notes

1 According to the standard definition of unemployment recommended by the International Labour Organization and adopted almost universally, those who have not worked even one hour during the reference period of one week, were available for work and have been looking for work are regarded as unemployed.
2 Unemployment rate measured by using the standard definition does not reflect the real situation in the labour market for a variety of reasons. First, because of the absence of social protection like unemployment insurance in many countries, a poor worker has very little alternative other than eking out a living through some form of work, whatever the means and form are. Second, in many developing economies, the traditional sectors like agriculture, non-farm activities in rural areas and myriad activities in the urban informal economy constitute the major sources of employment where the notion of job search is often subject to interpretation. And hence, the question whether someone was looking for work during a given period is likely to be interpreted and responded in different ways – often not producing the real situation of the respondent.
3 Although their analysis and recommendations were made in the context of a developed country, a good deal of what they said about the role of governments remains relevant for developing countries today. Kalecki's (1943) contribution on employment policies may also be noted in this context.
4 Named after A. W. Phillips who, in an article in 1958 (Phillips, 1958), pointed out that the relationship between unemployment rate and change in money wage rate in the UK was negative. According to his finding, at high rates of unemployment, a sizeable reduction in unemployment could be achieved through a small rise in money wage rate while at low rates of unemployment, a further reduction would cause a sharper rise in money wage rate.
5 The concept of NAIRU has emerged out of a debate between the monetarist and Keynesian approaches to explaining macroeconomic phenomena like unemployment and inflation. While the former expressed doubt about the downward sloping Phillips curve as originally hypothesized, the latter kept faith in it and asserted the existence of a non-inflationary rate of unemployment (NIRU). Milton Friedman and Edmund Phelps argued (summarized by Friedman, 1976) that unemployment can go below natural rate only temporarily, and in the long run, there will be no inflation-unemployment trade-off (as suggested by the Phillips

curve). In other words, the long-run Phillips curve is vertical. The Keynesian position was articulated by Modigliani and Papademos (1975) in which they developed the concept of NIRU. The concept of NAIRU emerged out of that, and according to Marco A. Espinosa-Vega and Steven Russel (1997), it was James Tobin who first used the expression NAIRU. Espinosa-Vega and Russel (1997) provides a good exposition of the theory and history of NAIRU.

6 For a survey-based analysis of the notion of full employment in the context of developed countries, see Goldberg et al. (2005).

7 For example, the Reserve Bank of India (which is the country's central bank) argues that if inflation rises beyond a certain level, economic growth may be adversely affected and unemployment rate may go up rather than down. In other words, the Phillips curve may be "backward bending" from some point. They are using an estimate of the threshold inflation for India which is in the range of four to six per cent. This estimate is being used to anchor monetary policy, and it is being argued that even if this might involve "some marginal sacrifice of growth in the short-run", by containing inflation, the central bank could best contribute to sustainable employment and growth (Reserve Bank of India, 2011).

8 These were found in a number of country level and cross-country studies, e.g., Islam (2006a, b) and Khan (2007).

9 The observation made above may be relevant for developed countries as well because in many of them, large proportions of the employed are engaged in part time and other atypical forms of employment; and counting all of them as employed may not be appropriate from the point of view of measuring progress towards full productive employment.

10 For a critique of the MDGs and SDGs from human rights perspective, see Frey and MacNaughton (2016).

11 UN General Assembly: *Transforming Our World: The 2030 Agenda for Sustainable Development.* www.un.org/ga/search/view_doc.asp?symbol=A/70/L.1&Lang=E (Accessed on 4 May 2018).

12 Goal 8 is worded as: Promote Sustained, Inclusive and Sustainable Economic Growth, Full and Productive Employment and Decent Work for All.

13 Countries may voluntarily adopt an expanded framework to monitor progress in attaining the SDGs. One example is India where the government has already drafted a set of indicators for their monitoring purposes. For goal 8 also, there is such a list of indicators. See Government of India, Ministry of Statistics and Programme Implementation (2017).

14 The list presented here draws from Islam (2013). See also Majid (2014) for suggestions on indicators for measuring and monitoring employment and unemployment in developing countries. His list also includes proportions of regular employment and of the working poor.

15 It may be mentioned here that a number of countries have already started preparing reports on progress made in attaining the SDGs. If the reports by the governments of Bangladesh, India, and Pakistan – GOB (2018), GOP (2018), and United Nations and NITI Aayog (2018) – are any indicator, it is clear that the officially suggested set of indicators are being applied. But such mechanical application of indicators and reporting of situation and progress may not be very helpful in attaining real progress.

16 The ILO (2013) is suggesting another measure of labour underutilization that considers, in addition to time underutilization, "potential labour force" which is a concept defined to include three mutually exclusive groups: (i) unavailable job seekers – persons without employment who are seeking employment but not available, (ii) available potential job seekers – persons without employment and not seeking employment but are available, and (iii) willing potential job seekers – persons without employment who are neither seeking employment nor available for employment but want employment. In addition, there may be "discouraged

job-seekers" who are unemployed and willing to work and yet are not actively seeking jobs because of the perception of the lack of jobs.

17 The data used here are from labour force surveys. There are studies that use data from surveys of industries, e.g., Ghose (2014) on India and Amjad and Yusuf (2014) on Pakistan. But such surveys usually are not comprehensive in their coverage of industries, and thus, may not provide a real picture of the growth of employment in the sector as a whole.

Bibliography

Amjad, Rashid and Anam Yusuf (2014): *More and Better Jobs for Pakistan: Can the Manufacturing Sector Play a Greater Role?* Graduate Institute of Development Studies, Lahore School of Economics, Lahore.

Bangladesh Bureau of Statistics (various years): *Labour Force Survey*, various years. Bangladesh Bureau of Statistics, Dhaka.

Beveridge, William (1944): *Full Employment in a Free Society*. George Allen and Unwin Ltd., London.

Frey, Diane F. and Gillian MacNaughton (2016, April–June): "A Human Rights Lens on Full Employment and Decent Work in the 2030 Sustainable Development Agenda", *Journal of Workplace Rights*, pp. 1–13.

Friedman, Milton (1976): "Wage Determination and Unemployment". Chapter 12 in *Price Theory*. Aldine Publishing Company, Chicago.

Ghose, Ajit (2014): "India Needs Manufacturing-Led Growth". Working Paper WP 01/2015. Institute for Human Development, Delhi.

Goldberg, Gertrude Schaffner, Helen Lachs Ginsburg and Philip Harvey (2005): "What Do We Mean By Full Employment? A Survey". Paper prepared for the 11th Annual Workshop of European Economists for an Alternative Economic Policy in Europe, Brussels, 23–25 September 2005.

Gondal, Shabbir Ahmed, Zahir Hussain and Rana Ejaz Ali Khan (2014): "Measurement and Policy Implications of NAIRU in SAARC Countries", *Pakistan Journal of Commerce and Social Sciences*, Vol. 8, No. 3, pp. 867–886.

Government of Bangladesh (2018): *Sustainable Development Goals Bangladesh First Progress Report 2018*. General Economic Division, Planning Commission, Dhaka.

Government of India, Ministry of Statistics and Programme Implementation (2017): Office Memorandum on Draft National Indicator Framework for Sustainable Development Goals, 8 March 2017. http://mospi.nic.in/sites/default/files/announcements/SDG_DraftNational_Indicators8mar17.pdf (Accessed on 10 May 2018).

Government of Malaysia, Department of Statistics (2015): *Informal Sector Workforce Survey Report Malaysia 2015*. https://dosm.gov.my/v1/index.php?r=column/ctheme&menu_id=U3VPMldoYUxzVzFaYmNkWXZteGduZz09&bul_id=UUFsUEJn NGFhcDE1TndNUlg4OEZCQT09# (Accessed on 11 May 2015).

Government of Pakistan, Finance Division (2006): *Pakistan Economic Survey 2005–06*. Islamabad.

Government of Pakistan, Planning Commission (2018): *Sustainable Development Goals (SDGs) National Framework*. Planning Commission, Islamabad.

Government of Pakistan, Statistics Division, Pakistan Bureau of Statistics (various years): Labour Force Survey, various years including 2001–02, 2006–07 and 2014–15.

Government of Sri Lanka, Department of Statistics, Ministry of National Policies and Economic Affairs (2013 and 2017): *Sri Lanka Labour Force Survey*, Annual Report, 2012, 2016.

Institute for Human Development (2015): *Growth, Labour Markets and Employment: India*, Delhi.

International Labour Office (2012): *Statistical Update on Employment in the Informal Economy*, Unpublsihed Draft. ILO, Geneva, 2012. file:///C:/Users/Islam/Downloads/Statistical%20update%20on%20employment%20in%20the%20informal%20economy.pdf (Accessed on 11 May 2018).

——— (2013): "Statistics of Work, Employment and Labour Underutilization", Report II of the 19th International Conference of Labour Statisticians. 2–11 October 2013, ILO, Geneva.

Islam, Rizwanul (2006a): "The Nexus of Economic Growth, Employment and Poverty Reduction: An Empirical Analysis" in Islam (2006b).

——— (2006b): *Fighting Poverty: The Development-Employment Link*. Lynn Rienner, Boulder and London.

——— (2013): *Integrating Productive Employment into the Post 2015 Development Agenda.* Southern Voice Occasional Paper 3, Centre for Policy Dialogue, Dhaka.

Kalecki, Michael (1943): "Political Aspects of Full Employment", *Political Quarterly*, Vol. 14, No. 4, pp. 322–331.

Khan, A.R. (2007): *Asian Experience of Growth, Employment and Poverty: An Overview with Special Reference to the Findings of Some Recent Case Studies*. ILO, Geneva and UNDP, Colombo.

Marco A. Espinosa-Vega and Steven Russel (1997): "History and Theory of the NAIRU: A Critical Review". *Federal Reserve Bank of Atlanta Economic Review*, Second Quarter 1997, pp. 4–25.

Majid, Nomaan (2014, July–September): "Measuring Employment in Developing Countries", *World Economics*, Vol. 15, No. 3, pp. 1–31.

Modigliani, Franco and Lucas Papademos (1975): "Targets for Monetary Policy in the Coming Year". *Brookings Papers on Economic Activity*, Vol. 6, No. 1, pp. 141–163.

OECD (2008): *Employment Outlook 2008*. https://read.oecd-ilibrary.org/employment/oecd-employment-outlook-2008_empl_outlook-2008-en#page88 (Accessed on 10 May 2018).

OECD (2017): *Economic Outlook* No. 102, November 2017. www.stats.oecd.org/Index.aspx?QueryId=61365# (Accessed on 1 May 2018).

Phillips, A.W. (1958, November): "The Relationship between Unemployment and the Rate of Change of Money Wage Rates in the United Kingdom, 1861–1957", *Economica*, Vol. 25, pp. 283–299.

Reserve Bank of India (2011): Annual Report, Part II Economic Review, August 25, 2011. http://rbi.org.in/scripts/AnnualReportPublications.aspx?Id=999 (Accessed on 1 May 2018).

United Nations and NITI Aayog (2018): *SDG India Index Baseline Report 2018*. New Delhi.

Webb, Sidney (1912): *How the Government Can Prevent Unemployment*. The National Committee for the Prevention of Destitution, London.

World Bank: *World Development Indicators, GDP per Employed Person*. https://data.worldbank.org/indicator/SL.GDP.PCAP.EM.KD?view=chart&year_high_desc=false (Accessed on 7 May 2018).

Zaman, Khalid, Muhammad Mushtaq Khan, Mehboob Ahmed and Waseem Ikram (2011, February): "Inflation, Unemployment, and the NAIRU in Pakistan (1975–2009)", *International Journal of Economics and Finance*, Vol. 3, No. 1, pp. 245–254.

4 Labour market outcomes and inclusive development[1]

Introduction

During the second half of the twentieth century and the first decade of the current millennium, development paradigm has undergone several shifts in focus. The journey that started with a trickle down approach and passed through redistribution with growth, structural adjustment, and pro-poor growth is now docked at inclusive growth. Although the term inclusion may be conceptualized in different ways, it is important to focus on both the process and outcome. While the process of inclusion can be captured through measures relating to employment, the outcomes can be assessed in terms of income relative to some benchmark of poverty, inequality, or other dimensions of human development like education and health. Another important element of inclusion is the degree of social protection provided by a society. Characterized this way, labour market outcomes like employment, wages, returns to self-employment, and social protection are of direct relevance for inclusive growth. A number of questions may be raised in this context.

- Is economic growth leading to the growth of productive employment that is needed for absorbing the new members of the labour force and for transferring workers from sectors characterized by low productivity to those with higher productivity?
- Is sector composition of employment changing in a way that contributes to poverty reduction (through higher incomes of workers)?
- Is access to social protection expanding along with economic growth?
- Is economic growth associated with growth of labour productivity and rise in real wages?
- Are real wages rising to contribute to reduction in poverty and inequality?
- What is happening to the share of wages in national income and in value added?

As already mentioned in Chapters 2 and 3, the experience of countries that have been successful in their development effort, e.g., Republic of Korea, Malaysia, and Taiwan (China) shows that economic growth was associated with high rate of labour absorption in modern sectors, and a corresponding reduction in the share of jobs in the informal economy and a rise in the access to social protection. But employment growth was not achieved at the cost of labour productivity. In fact, labour productivity increased and real wages also rose.

The present chapter attempts to address some of the above questions with particular focus on the experience of the countries of South Asia. Using the concept of employment elasticity with respect to output growth, it shows that the labour absorptive capacity of the countries of the region has been low and has declined. The process of transformation of the structure of employment has been slow, and as a result, the informal economy has remained the predominant source of jobs for the growing labour force. That, in turn, has meant limited access to social protection because there is a negative relationship between the proportion of employment and the informal economy and access to social protection. As for real wages, the experience is mixed at best. They registered increases in some sectors and in some years – thus showing potential for making contribution to poverty reduction. But in some instances, growth in real wages was not sustained and has not been enough to make any impact on inequality.

The chapter is organized as follows. The second section looks at the nexus between economic growth and employment and examines the outcome of economic growth in terms of employment. The third section goes back to the issue of informal employment and relates it to the challenge of social protection. Then we look at what has happened to wages of workers, with particular focus on gender difference. Some concluding observations are made in the last section.

The nexus between economic growth and employment

High rate of economic growth is an objective that countries at all levels of development aim to attain. However, this cannot be a goal by itself, especially for developing countries of South Asia where, despite notable progress, the incidence of poverty remains high. High rate of economic growth is, of course, a necessary condition for poverty reduction, but a number of studies have demonstrated that this is not sufficient; the pattern and sources of growth and the manner in which its benefits are distributed are critical from the point of view of achieving the goal of poverty reduction (Islam, 2006a, Khan, 2006). There are country experiences demonstrating that the relationship between economic growth and poverty reduction is not invariant, and that variables relating to employment and labour market are critical in determining the poverty reducing outcome of growth.[2] Empirical exercise based on cross–country data (Islam, 2006a) demonstrates that the employment intensity of economic growth has a significant influence on the rate of poverty reduction.

There are different ways of looking at the relationship between economic growth and employment. One that is commonly employed is to estimate the elasticity of employment growth with respect to output growth and see its level and trend. But employment elasticity reflects the inverse of labour productivity: while an elasticity higher than unity implies decline in productivity, an elasticity lower than unity means that employment expansion is taking place alongside increase in productivity. A rise in productivity would lead to a reduction in employment elasticity. However, this measure of employment intensity of growth is not without its limitations.

One limitation that is obvious is that for many developing countries, overall employment growth cannot be taken as a reflection of labour demand alone because for a variety of reasons, employment growth may not correctly reflect demand for labour. However, for organized sectors like manufacturing, employment would perhaps reflect demand side more closely than overall employment, and hence, it may be more meaningful to look at the relationship between employment and output growth of such sectors.

Another limitation of employment elasticity as a measure of employment intensity of growth is that the estimated value could be high with a combination of low output growth and high employment growth. This cannot be a desirable outcome especially if productive employment is the goal and is looked at as a mechanism for poverty reduction. It would, therefore, be important to look at the underlying figures of output and employment growth in order to have a clear understanding of the real nature of economic growth that is taking place.[3]

Studies on employment intensity of economic growth in developing countries date back to the early 2000s when a number of country studies as well as a cross-country study were published (Islam, 2006b). Another study (Khan, 2007) covered countries of South Asia as well as of East and South East Asia (ESEA), thus providing a comparative perspective of the experiences of the sub-regions.[4] Subsequently, a study focussing on manufacturing industries in a larger set of developing countries were undertaken in order to examine what has happened to the employment intensity of growth within that sector (Islam, 2010b; Islam and Islam, 2015, Chapter 2). Studies carried out under a project of the Institute for Human Development[5], Delhi, covered five countries of South Asia, viz., Bangladesh, India, Nepal, Pakistan, and Sri Lanka, and provide updates and extensions to the earlier studies. The abovementioned studies provide useful and interesting data for analyzing the nexus between economic growth, employment, and poverty reduction. To begin with, a few major findings from the earlier set of studies may be highlighted.

First, there is no invariant relationship either between economic growth and employment or between economic growth and poverty reduction. While high rate of economic growth is a necessary condition for generating productive employment and for achieving poverty reduction on a sustained basis, it is not a sufficient condition. Much depends on the pattern and sources of growth and to what extent the poor benefit from it. Second, one variable that has a significant impact on the rate of poverty reduction in relation to economic growth is employment intensity of economic growth. In other words, what happens to employment and labour markets is important for translating the benefits of economic growth into poverty reduction. Third, what happens to the structure of the economy as a result of economic growth is also important from the point of view of poverty reduction. Transfer of workers from sectors characterized by low labour productivity (e.g., agriculture and other traditional economic activities) to those with higher productivity (e.g., manufacturing and modern services) helps increase incomes of the poor. Fourth, education and skills make a contribution to poverty reduction from the supply side of the equation by enabling the members of the labour to benefit from productive employment that may be created through growth of output (Islam, 2006a).

A comparison between the 1980s and the 1990s shows that employment intensity of economic growth (measured through the elasticity of employment growth with respect to output growth) as a whole and for major sectors, by and large, declined during the latter period (Khan, 2007; Islam, 2010b, 2014a). Data for the 2000s indicate that this trend continued after the 1990s (Islam, 2010b). This is an important finding indicating that the employment generating ability of economic growth has been declining over time. A comparison between countries of South Asia and ESEA shows that the latter group of countries, during their early stages of economic development, were characterized by higher degrees of employment intensity of growth. In fact, growth in some of them, especially Malaysia, has remained more employment–intensive compared to some countries of South Asia. This is contrary to what one would expect if levels of development and relative factor endowments were to be taken into account.

Studies carried out under the SARNET project (mentioned above) covering Bangladesh, India, Nepal, Pakistan, and Sri Lanka provide useful extensions to the data and analysis presented in the studies mentioned above. First, it has been possible to compile estimates of elasticity of employment for the economies as a whole and the broad sectors for different sub-periods extending up to the first decade of the new millennium.[6] Second, it is also possible to examine what has been happening to labour productivity (which, of course, is the mirror image of employment elasticity) and whether there has been a trade-off between growth of employment and improvement in labour productivity. The relevant data are presented in Tables 4.1 and 4.2.

Data presented in Table 4.1 indicate, by and large, a continuation of the trend observed in earlier studies (mentioned above) – i.e., of a decline in the employment intensity of economic growth. The decline (during the 2000s) in employment intensity for the economy as a whole and for the manufacturing sector is quite striking for India, Nepal, and Sri Lanka. This has happened in India despite high economic growth attained during that period[7]. Likewise, growth in Sri Lanka has also been respectable during that period, and yet, employment intensity of growth has declined sharply. In Nepal, this has happened during a period of declining economic growth. So, while one can ascribe the decline in India and Sri Lanka to the pattern of economic growth, for Nepal, the problem is both low output and employment growth.

Table 4.1 Elasticity of Employment with Respect to Output, Selected Countries of South Asia

Country and Periods	GDP	Agriculture	Manufacturing	Construction	Services
Bangladesh (Rahman, 2014; Islam, 2015b)					
1995–96 to 1999–2000	0.54	0.73	0.26	0.27	0.21
1999–2000 to 2005–06	0.59	0.82	0.78	0.63	0.69
2005–06 to 2010	0.55	0.71	0.87	2.42	0.27
2010–13	0.39	0.20	1.28	−0.77	0.21
2013 to 2015–16	0.18	−0.52	−0.47	2.81	0.81
2010 to 2015–16	0.27	−0.06	0.47	0.54	0.45
India (IHD, 2014)					
1983–84 to 1993–94	0.42	0.49	0.41	1.16	0.39–0.67[a]
1993–94 to 2004–05	0.29	0.26	0.47	0.94	0.06–0.99[a]
2004–05 to 2011–12	0.04	−0.42	0.13	1.15	0.12–0.59[a]
Nepal (Khanal, 2014)					
1991–2001	0.64	0.32	2.15	3.76	1.55–2.60[a]
2001–11	0.18	0.25	−4.85	0.47	−1.43 to 0.74[a]
Pakistan (Amjad and Yusuf, 2014)[b]					
1981–90	0.30	0.45	0.26[c]	n.a.	0.42
1991–2000	0.55	0.36	0.24[c]	n.a.	0.82
2001–10	0.79	1.19	0.82[c]	n.a.	0.80
Pakistan (Arif and Farooq, 2011)[b]					
1992–98	0.81	n.a.	n.a.	n.a.	n.a.
1998–2001	0.50	n.a.	n.a.	n.a.	n.a.
2001–05	0.43	n.a.	n.a.	n.a.	n.a.
Sri Lanka (Chandrasiri, 2014)					
1981–94	0.44	0.38	1.28	n.a.	0.25
1994–2005	0.52	0.18	1.31	n.a.	0.57
2005–12	0.085	0.67	0.06	n.a.	0.03

a In these cases, data are available for sub-sectors of the service sector, e.g., trade, transport, finance and real estate, and community, social, and personal services. The figures mentioned here are the lowest and the highest of those figures.
b The figures for Pakistan have been estimated by the present author from data on output and employment growth that are available in the sources cited.
c These figures are for industry as a whole not for manufacturing.
n.a. denotes not available.

Bangladesh presents a mixed picture. Employment elasticity for the economy as a whole registered a small increase during the first half of the 2000s compared to the second half of the 1990s. That was the result of increases in employment elasticity of all sectors – agriculture, manufacturing, construction, and services. However, there was a reversal in this trend during the second half of 2000s when overall employment elasticity declined somewhat. At the sector level, employment elasticity increased in manufacturing and construction but declined in agriculture and services (the latter quite sharply). During 2010–13, overall employment elasticity declined further, and that happened despite manufacturing becoming more employment-intensive. Employment elasticity declined sharply in agriculture and construction, and the declining trend in services continued. Several things seem to be happening. On the one hand, the manufacturing sector which is dominated by the labour-intensive ready-made garment industry continued to be employment-intensive to the extent that employment growth exceeded that of output growth. On the other hand, the ability of agriculture to absorb additional labour declined sharply. And after a high rate of growth of employment in the construction sector during 2005–10, there was a reversal in the subsequent years. The net result was that overall employment elasticity registered a decline.

Several points may be worth noting in the case of Bangladesh. First, for a variety of reasons, agriculture can no longer be counted on as a source of much additional employment. Second, growth in the construction sector appears to have slowed down after several years of high growth and job creation. Likewise, the service sector does not seem to be very labour-intensive any more. Third, the weight of the manufacturing sector in total GDP is still rather low, and hence even a high degree of employment intensity in the sector is unable to offset the low labour absorption in other sectors. In fact, higher than one employment elasticity in the sector is indicative of declining labour productivity which is not desirable from the point of view of competitiveness and future growth of the sector. It thus seems that maintaining a desirable degree of employment intensity of growth would depend on a variety of factors, including attaining higher growth, especially of manufacturing and construction, and higher growth of those segments of the service sector that combine growth potential with the ability to create productive employment.

Pakistan's experience appears to be less straightforward compared to the trend in the other countries described above. Data provided by Amjad and Yusuf (2014) indicate a rise in employment elasticity during 2001–10 compared to the 1990s and 1980s – overall as well as for manufacturing. On the other hand, Arif and Farooq (2011), who provide data up to 2005, show that overall employment elasticity during 2001–05 was lower than during 1998–2001 and 1992–98. A closer look at the data for the 2000s shows that while the first half of the decade was a period of rising growth, the second half saw the opposite.[8] Unlike in developed countries, in developing countries with large informal sector, a decline in economic growth does not automatically lead to a decline in employment (except in the formal segments of the economy). This may have happened in the case of Pakistan during the 2005–10 period. And that may have resulted in a high employment elasticity for the decade as a whole. This, however, is merely a conjecture, and with the conflicting sets of data, it is not possible to be more confident.

Table 4.2 Growth of Labour Productivity in Selected Countries of South Asia
(% per Annum)

Country and period	GDP	Agriculture	Industry	Services
Bangladesh				
1995–96 to 2006	0.16	−1.80	1.25	0.23
2006 to 2010	2.65	2.03	−1.08	5.13
India				
1993–94 to 2004–05	4.11	1.64	1.55	4.82
2004–05 to 2011–12	7.09	4.67	4.96	6.82
Nepal				
1991 to 1998–99	0.66	−2.33	−10.76	9.10
1998–99 to 2008	1.22	1.31	−0.19	−1.59
Pakistan				
1996 to 2005–06	0.72	0	0.59	0.31
2005–06 to 2010–11	0.28	−1.79	−0.06	2.07
Sri Lanka				
1997–2006	2.00	−3.63	1.18	3.59
2006–11	3.52	1.01	2.66	2.71

Sources: Employment data from national labour force surveys and output data from the national accounts statistics of the respective countries have been used to calculate output per worker at constant prices.

As expected, data on labour productivity (Table 4.2) are consistent with the estimates of employment elasticity. When the latter increases, labour productivity declines and vice versa. Particularly notable are:

- Bangladesh, 2005–06 to 2010 compared to 1995–96 to 2005–06: decline in the growth of labour productivity in industry, while labour productivity growth as a whole increased.
- India, 2004–05 to 2011–12 compared to 1993–94 to 2004–05: increase in the growth of labour productivity as a whole as well as in all sectors.
- Nepal, 2000s compared to the 1990s: increase in the growth of overall labour productivity as well as for agriculture and industry.
- Pakistan, 2005–06 to 2010–11 compared to 1996 to 2005–06: decline in labour productivity growth – overall as well as for agriculture and industry.
- Sri Lanka, 2006–11 compared 1997–2006: increase in the growth of labour productivity – overall as well as in agriculture and industry.

The conclusion that one may reach is that with exceptions like Pakistan, economic growth during the 2000s has been associated with increases in the growth of labour productivity and declines in employment elasticity – overall as well as in major sectors. These countries thus faced a trade-off between growth of employment and labour productivity.

The challenge of social protection

Economic growth and social protection

Till about the end of the twentieth century, social protection was not very high on the agenda either in developed or in developing countries. There was even a tendency to invoke the debate between the "growth first model" versus the "European social model" and the perceived superiority of the former as a justification for relegating the importance of social protection. Indeed, in the developed world, countries that achieved high economic and employment growth appear to be the ones characterized by lower unemployment rates as well as lower levels of unemployment benefits. Amongst the OECD countries, for example, the USA is known to have been able to achieve higher economic growth (in terms of GDP growth) than, for example, the countries in western Europe – at least during the two decades before the global economic crisis of 2008–09.[9] And the duration of unemployment benefit as well as expenditure on unemployment compensation has been consistently lower in the USA compared to the latter.[10]

Countries in the developing world generally did not have any unemployment benefits, and social protection in them – covering mainly the formal sector workers – basically was in the form of severance benefits (of varying duration), pensions and provident fund, and programmes of social assistance. For workers outside the formal sector, there was virtually no social protection except for some programmes of social assistance and labour market programmes targeted at specific groups. Even in countries that had achieved high rates of economic growth on a sustained basis for some time, e.g., those in ESEA, there was not much thinking about unemployment benefit until they were hit by a severe economic crisis in 1997–98. High rates of output growth that were generally associated with high rates of employment growth in higher productivity activities like manufacturing, construction and services, and some increases in real wages appeared to have made it possible for policymakers in those countries to postpone thinking about social protection for workers.

The experiences mentioned above perhaps gave rise to the question whether high rates of economic and employment growth could obviate the need for social protection or at least make its case somewhat weaker. Even apart from the normative issue of the desirability of social protection, two points need to be considered in this context. The first relates to economic growth itself: what has been the experience with respect to growth – both in terms of rates and stability. The second point relates to the outcome of economic growth in terms of employment growth. Let us look at both points briefly.

As for economic growth, market-based economies of the present-day world face uncertainties of different kinds, the result of which is frequent fluctuations in growth and occasional recessions. Developing countries don't remain immune from such instability in growth and recessions. The impact of economic downturns and recessions on employment and labour market is usually negative, and recovery in labour markets often takes longer than economic recovery. In such situations, it is the general people, especially those dependent on their own labour, who are the ultimate sufferers. Measures are needed to provide them with protection and ability to cope with such an environment.

As for the employment outcome of economic growth, it has already been shown above that the employment intensity of economic growth in South Asia has been low and declining in recent years. Growth of employment in the formal sector has been rather low, and much of the employment growth takes place in the informal segments of the economy. In this kind of a situation, the prospects of high rates of employment-intensive growth of the kind achieved by the East and South East Asian countries during the past few decades do not appear to be bright.[11] Unless there is a willingness on the part of policymakers to re-think and re-orient development strategies, economic growth may not become significantly more employment-intensive than at present. Hence, it would be important to develop a strategy for social protection alongside the growth strategy.

The challenge posed by a large informal sector

In the context of developing countries, an important aspect of the structure of labour markets is the duality that characterizes them – a small formal sector co-existing with a large informal sector. This has important implications for the coverage and type of social protection. For example, higher employment growth in the formal sector can facilitate a greater coverage of workers through various social insurance schemes. If, on the contrary, a high proportion of the labour force is engaged in the informal economy, alternative mechanisms for providing social protection are required. The high proportion of the employed labour force in self-employment and in informal employment does pose an additional challenge for developing countries in this respect. For those who are self-employed, it is not so easy to arrange for insurance against ill health and inability to work due to unforeseen contingencies and make provision for incomes during old age.[12] The same applies to those who are in informal employment because it is difficult to use formal mechanisms of social protection, especially those based on insurance, in such cases. Conventional mechanisms of social protection, e.g., unemployment allowance, pensions, etc., may not be applicable to the vast number of people in these categories. But rather than overlooking and ignoring the need for social protection for them, it is essential to identify alternative measures, and if necessary, innovative mechanisms for providing social protection.

The challenge posed for social protection by the high proportion of employment in the informal economy is illustrated by Figure 4.1 where social

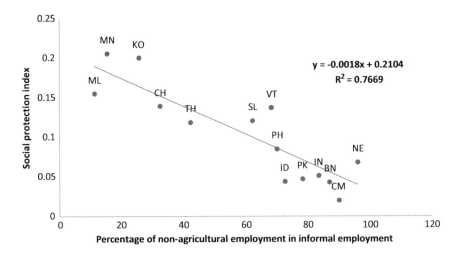

Figure 4.1 Social Protection Index and Informal Employment.

Note: BN=Bangladesh, BH=Bhutan, CM=Cambodia, CH=China, IN=India, ID=Indonesia, KO=Korea, ML=Malaysia, NE=Nepal, PK=Pakistan, PH=Philippines, SL=Sri Lanka, TH=Thailand, VT=Vietnam

Source: Constructed by the author using figures for Social Protection Index from ADB (2013) and figures for informal employment from ILO (2012) and national sources.

protection index[13] for selected countries of Asia has been plotted against data on the share of informal employment in total non-agricultural employment. This plotting shows a negative correlation between the two variables – indicating that improvements in the coverage of social protection come with increase in the share of formal sector employment.

The conventional wisdom in development discourse is that high and sustained economic growth should result in more formal sector employment. And given the negative relationship between informal employment and social protection, higher levels of income should lead to an improvement in social protection. Indeed, data from selected Asian developing countries on GDP per capita and social protection do point towards this possibility (Figure 4.2). However, it needs to be noted that although the relationship between these two variables is positive, it is not linear. The rate of improvement in social protection index declines at higher levels of income – indicating that the relationship between economic growth and social protection should not be taken for granted. Public policy has an important role to play in that regard.

The low level of social protection in the countries of South Asia can be seen from a few other indicators. One general indicator of this is what is spent by governments for providing social protection to its citizens. Data on public social expenditure as percentage of GDP (Table 4.3) show that in general, countries of South Asia lag behind those of ESEA. The exceptions are Sri Lanka where the spending is much higher than in other South Asian countries, and Indonesia where the spending is much lower than other countries

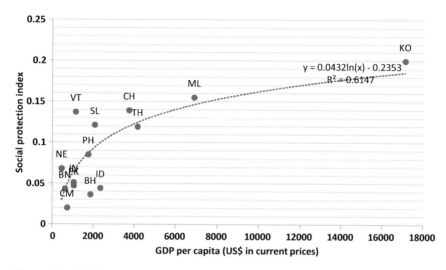

Figure 4.2 Social Protection Index and GDP per Capita at Current Prices, 2009.
Note: BN=Bangladesh, BH=Bhutan, CM=Cambodia, CH=China, IN=India, ID=Indonesia, KO=Korea, ML=Malaysia, NE=Nepal, PK=Pakistan, PH=Philippines, SL=Sri Lanka, TH=Thailand, VT=Vietnam
Source: Constructed by the author using data from ADB (2013).

Table 4.3 Public Social Protection Expenditure as Percentage of GDP

Country	Public Expenditure on Social Protection as Percentage of GDP (Year)
Bangladesh	1.7 (2014)
India	2.7 (20114)
Nepal	3.0 (2015)
Pakistan	0.2 (2014)
Sri Lanka	6.5 (2015)
China	6.3 (2015)
Republic of Korea	10.1 (2015)
Indonesia	1.1 (2015)
Malaysia	3.2 (2015)
Thailand	3.7 (2015)
Vietnam	6.3 (2015)

Source: ILO (2017), Table B.16.

of the same region. The countries that stand out in the region as a whole are China, Korea, Sri Lanka, and Vietnam.

The SDG indicator 1.3.1 – percentage of population covered by at least one social protection benefit – can also be used to see where various countries stand in this regard. Table 4.4 presents data for some countries. Again, China, Korea, and Vietnam stand out with their higher figures compared to the countries of South Asia.

Table 4.4 Percentage of Population Covered by at Least One Social Protection Benefit (2015 or Latest Available Year)

Country	Percentage of People Covered
Bangladesh	28.4
India	19.0
Sri Lanka	30.4
China	63.0
Republic of Korea	65.7
Vietnam	37.9

Source: ILO (2017), Table B.3.

Note: Data for Malaysia, Nepal, and Pakistan are not available.

Table 4.5 Percentage of the Unemployed Receiving Unemployment Benefits under Contributory and Non-Contributory Schemes

Country	Percentage of the Unemployed Who Receive Benefits
India	3.0 (2008)
China	18.8 (2015)
Republic of Korea	40.0 (2014)
Thailand	43.2 (2015)
Vietnam	45.0 (2015)

Source: ILO (2017), Table B.6.

Another indicator on which some data are available is the proportion of unemployed who receive unemployment benefit under contributory and non-contributory schemes (Table 4.5).

Unfortunately, data on this indicator are available for only one South Asian country, viz., India. As with the other indicators mentioned above, India lags way behind countries of ESEA in this case as well.

In situations where social protection system is weak or inadequate, the poor usually depend on traditional support systems based on family and community. For example, during the Asian economic crisis of 1997–98, many workers who lost jobs in Indonesia and Thailand had to return to their rural households and rely on support from their families. At that time, there was a good deal of talk about so-called "Asian values". But what happened in reality was sharing of family's incomes and the creation of a new class of poor. On the other hand, in Republic of Korea, the social protection system was strengthened at that time by increasing the number of people covered by unemployment insurance. In addition, an attempt was made to prevent increase in the rate of unemployment by introducing a public works programme. In Thailand as well, debates and discussion on the possibility of introducing unemployment insurance started at that time.

While conventional thinking is that social protection may not be economically feasible in developing countries, empirical exercises show that it should be possible to introduce at least some basic social protection measures, e.g., old age allowance and unemployment benefits, etc. in such countries. One exercise (Lee, 1998) showed that in Indonesia and Thailand, the expenditure that will be needed to replace half of the regular incomes for the unemployment for a period of six months can be feasibly shared between the government, employers, and workers.

A good example of what can be done to provide social protection for those engaged in the unorganized sector is demonstrated by the adoption, in India in 2008, of the Unorganized Workers' Social Security Bill. Under this Act, provision was made to bring 340 million people (out of a total labour force of 458 million) under the cover of pension, basic health, life, and disability insurance as well as group accident insurance within a period of five years. This shows that it is not unpractical or a luxury to think of providing social protection to those who are engaged in the informal economy. What is important is political will and the adoption of innovative approaches.[14]

Real wages and inclusive development

Wage is a key labour market outcome and has important implications for inclusive development. Increases in real wages and earnings can play an important role not only in reducing poverty but also in reducing inequality in the distribution of income. It needs to be noted, however, that a rise in real wages may not necessarily help poverty reduction, especially if it is associated with a decline in the quantity of employment (e.g., the number of days for which employment is available in a year for an agricultural labourer). The latter may actually neutralize the positive effect of the rise in real wages and prevent total earnings from increasing.

Likewise, a rise in real wages may not help improve income distribution if labour productivity increases at a faster rate than real wages. The gains from productivity increase may be unevenly shared by the factors of production, and the share of labour in value added may even decline. That, in turn, may have an adverse effect on personal income distribution.

If one looks at data on trends in real wages in the countries of South Asia (Table 4.6), a somewhat mixed picture emerges. First, let us look at wages of agricultural labourers – a category on which studies and data are more easily available. Although several countries, especially India and Bangladesh, witnessed an acceleration in economic growth since the mid-1990s, real wages of such workers started to rise significantly only after the mid-2000s (Table 4.6).[15] In Nepal and Sri Lanka also, real wages of agricultural workers registered healthy growth during the second half of the 2000s. Pakistan appears to be an exception to this trend where real wages in agriculture declined between 2007 and 2012.

An important question is whether the rise in real wages is sustained over a period of time or represents short-term changes. An example is provided by the trends in wages in Bangladesh agriculture. Data on real wages in agriculture for recent years are not available from official sources. What is available are data on changes in nominal wages and in consumer prices, which have

Table 4.6 Real Wages of Agricultural Workers in Selected Countries of South Asia

Country and Category	Real Daily Wages (US$, Constant 2010)			Percentage Change		
Bangladesh	*2000*	*2005*	*2010*	*2000–05*	*2005–10*	*2000–10*
National peak season, male	1.92	1.92	2.78	0	45	44
National lean season, male	1.53	1.52	2.21	−1	46	45
National peak season, female	1.32	1.22	2.02	−8	66	53
National lean season, female	1.10	1.02	1.62	−7	58	48
India	*2000/01*	*2005/06*	*2012/13*	*2000–05*	*2005–12*	*2010–12*
National agricultural labour, male	2.13	2.15	2.91	1	35	36
National agricultural labour, female	1.59	1.61	2.21	1	37	38
Pakistan		*2007*	*2012*			*2007–12*
National agricultural worker, male		3.36	2.97			−12
National agricultural worker, female		1.68	1.46			−13
Nepal		*2003/04*	*2010/11*			*2003/04–2010/11*
National agricultural worker		1.73	2.22			29
Sri Lanka		*2007*	*2012*			*2007–12*
National agricultural daily work		2.24	3.08			38

Source: Wiggins and Keats (2014).

been used to estimate indices real wages of all workers and workers in agriculture and manufacturing for the period 2011–12 to 2015–16. These indices are presented in Table 4.7.

It is clear from Table 4.7 that in Bangladesh, after 2010–11, there has been a secular decline in the real wages of workers as a whole and for workers in both agriculture and manufacturing. The rise in real wages that took place during 2008–10 was short-lived.

What happened to real wages in urban areas and in industry in India is not so clear. One study, using data from the National Sample Survey, shows that urban wages increased (from 1983 to 2011/12) but at a lower rate compared to rural wages. And within urban areas, the rate of growth of wages in the secondary sector has been lower than in the primary sector (IHD, 2014).[16] But another study, using data from the Annual Survey of Industries, points out that real wages in registered manufacturing declined during the

Table 4.7 Bangladesh, Indices of Real Wages (2010–11 = 100)

Year	All Workers	Agriculture	Manufacturing
2011–12	97.75	97.49	98.02
2012–13	97.04	97.16	96.78
2013–14	95.38	95.89	96.20
2014–15	94.06	94.93	94.09
2015–16	94.59	95.95	93.89

Sources: The nominal wage indices are from BBS (2016) while the consumer price indices are from Government of Bangladesh (2017).

Note: For all workers, the national consumer price index has been used while for workers in agriculture and manufacturing, rural and urban consumer price indices have been used to convert nominal wages into real wages.

second half of the 1990s and remained stagnant after that (Chandrasekhar and Ghosh, 2015).[17]

From the data and analysis of trends in real wages presented above, it appears that the picture in this regard is somewhat mixed. While there have been periods during which real wages in some sectors have increased in some countries, it cannot be said confidently that real wages have been rising on a sustained basis.

Moreover, as mentioned already, even a rise in real wages can be consistent with a decline in the share of labour in total factor income. As a result, the rise in real wages can be associated with a rise in the degree of inequality in the distribution of income. This appears to have happened in the case of both Bangladesh and India.

In India, during 1983–2011, real wages on the whole rose 3.1 per cent per annum, while value added per worker rose 4.8 per cent per annum.[18] The gap between the increases in labour productivity and real wages is indicative of the decline in the share of wages in value added. Data on manufacturing industries provide some corroboration to this hypothesis.[19] Data from the Annual Survey of Industries show that the share of wages in value added declined from about 45 per cent in the early 1980s to about 25 per cent in 2010–11. During that period the share of profit rose from 20 per cent to 58 per cent. Hence it should not be a surprise that the distribution of income has worsened during that period. Indeed, estimated Gini coefficients of earnings show a rise from 0.483 in 1983 to 0.542 in 2004–05. Although the figure went down to 0.510 in 2011–12, it is clear that inequality has increased during the 2000s compared to the 1980s and 1990s.

On Bangladesh, calculations made by the present author (using data from the Survey of Manufacturing Industries of various years)[20] show that the temporary rise in real wages fell short of the increase in labour productivity. In the manufacturing sector, for example, growth of employment cost per worker (a proxy for wages) during the entire period of 2001–02 to 2012 fell short of the growth of value added per worker (proxy for labour productivity). The share of employment cost in total value added stagnated around 25 per cent during 2000–05 and then increased to 36 per cent in 2012.

An important aspect of inclusive development is how women fare in the employment field, and one indication of that is provided by the male-female differences in wage rates. Data presented in Table 4.8 may be used to throw some light on that aspect – although this set of data are limited to rural workers only. Figures in this table show a few interesting patterns and trends. First, irrespective of the season (i.e., whether peak or slack), the male-female differences are of the same order of magnitude. Second, the data indicate a stubborn persistence, over time, of the gender gap in wages. And that applies to all the three countries of South Asia (viz., Bangladesh, India, and Pakistan) for which data are presented in Tables 4.6 and 4.8. This shows that despite sustained economic growth (at least in Bangladesh and India) and an overall rise in real wages (at least in India), the male-female difference in wages has not only remained but there are no signs of any convergence.

Data on wages of workers as a whole (as opposed to rural or agricultural workers) presented in Tables 4.9A and 4.9B are generally in line with the data on rural/agricultural workers presented earlier – with some differences. As for trends, there was some worsening of the gap for rural regular workers between 1983 and 2004–05. Although there was a recovery after that year,

Table 4.8 Gender Difference in Real Wages in Selected Countries of South Asia

Country and Category	Ratio of Female to Male Wages		
Bangladesh	*2000*	*2005*	*2010*
National Peak	0.69	0.64	0.73
National Lean	0.72	0.67	0.73
India	*2000/01*	*2005/06*	*2012/13*
National Agriculture	0.75	0.75	0.76
Pakistan		*2007*	*2012*
National Agriculture		0.50	0.49

Source: Calculated from data presented in Table 4.3.

Table 4.9A India: Average Daily Wages of Male and Females, 1983 to 2011–12 (Wages in Rs.)

Category	1983		1993–94		2004–05		2011–12	
	Male	*Female*	*Male*	*Female*	*Male*	*Female*	*Male*	*Female*
RR	17.6	12.8	58.5	34.9	144.9	85.3	320.2	202.8
RC	7.8	4.9	23.2	15.3	55.1	34.9	150.4	104.6
UR	25.7	19.5	78.1	63.3	203.3	153.2	462.8	368.8
UC	11.1	5.6	32.4	18.5	75.1	43.9	185.0	114.9

Source: IHD (2014).

Note: RR = rural regular, RC = rural casual, UR = urban regular, UC = urban casual.

Table 4.9B India: Ratio of Female Wage to Male Wage

Category	1983	1993–94	2004–05	2011–12
RR	0.73	0.60	0.59	0.63
RC	0.63	0.66	0.63	0.70
UR	0.76	0.81	0.75	0.80
UC	0.50	0.57	0.58	0.62

Source: Calculated from data in Table 4.9A.

Note: RR = rural regular, RC = rural casual, UR = urban regular, UC = urban casual.

the gap remained worse in 2011–12 compared to 1983. Looking at differences between different categories of workers, one finds that the situation is worst for urban casual female workers. They earned about half their male counterparts in 1983. In 2011–12 their situation improved somewhat, but they still earned less than two-thirds of their male counterparts.

The main points emerging from the data presented in this section may be summarized as follows. One good news about the trends in real wages of workers is that except in the case of rural workers of Pakistan, there have been periods of improvement. This could have a positive impact on the incidence of poverty because labour income is a major source of income of the low-income households. Moreover, as the incidence of poverty is generally higher in rural areas, a rise in wages of rural workers may have made a positive contribution to poverty reduction. However, the good news almost ends there – especially if one focusses on the longer-term trend and if the contribution of wages to inclusive development is considered in a broader framework to include inequality in the distribution of household incomes and gender inequality. Since wages have not moved in tandem with increases in labour productivity and since the share of wages in value added has declined, the rise in real wages failed to make any contribution to improving the distribution of income. In fact, inequality in income has risen in the countries of South Asia. Likewise, there has been very little impact of rising wages on the gender gap in wages.

Concluding observations

The present chapter has looked at a number of labour market outcomes that have a bearing on inclusive development. They include employment intensity of economic growth, social protection, and real wages. Using data on countries of South Asia (and comparing with countries of ESEA), the chapter has pointed out the following.

- In South Asia, employment intensity of economic growth has generally been low and has declined over time. Of course, there have been exceptions like the manufacturing sector of Bangladesh during 2000–10. But the growth of manufacturing employment in the country could not be sustained in subsequent years.

- As a result of the slow growth of employment in the modern sectors of the economies, growth of formal sector employment has been rather low despite sustained and high growth of output (especially in India and Bangladesh). And the share of informal employment in total employment continues to remain high.
- That, in turn, poses a challenge for social protection, and the level of coverage of social protection is generally rather low.
- While the level of social protection is positively correlated with the level of income, the relationship is not linear – indicating that high income or economic growth is not a sufficient condition for the expansion of social protection.
- A positive labour market outcome witnessed in some countries (except Pakistan) is rise in real wages, especially in agriculture and in rural areas. But the rise has not been sustained in recent years. Moreover, growth of wages has lagged behind that of labour productivity. As a result, the rise in real wages has not been able to make an impact on growing income inequality. Gender differences in wages have also persisted.
- On the whole, it seems that labour market outcomes in South Asia have not moved in a direction needed to make economic growth more inclusive.

In order to gear labour market outcomes towards attaining the goal of inclusive development, action will be required on a number of fronts. Consider the issue relating to employment, especially the growth of productive and remunerative jobs. It is clear that economic growth attained during the past two decades has not delivered the desired employment outcome. And that shows that conventional policies are not working. A re-thinking of development strategy and policies is required in order to pursue this goal. A major issue in this regard is to get out of the conventional approach of treating employment policy as synonymous with labour market policies. The typical argument there is that labour market rigidities are responsible for low employment growth, and hence, higher employment growth can be achieved by making labour markets more flexible. This approach is too narrow and does not recognize the importance of economic policies in promoting a pattern of growth that would be more conducive to employment expansion. Employment policy has to be broad-based, and a combination of economic and labour market policies will be needed to address the various factors that are responsible for growth not leading to desired job creation – an issue to which we shall return later in this book.

As for social protection, an easy option may be to take the view that with economic growth, the coverage of social protection will also expand. This does happen to some extent, but the relationship is not linear. Hence, the expansion of the coverage of social protection cannot be expected to continue automatically. Public policy including legislation would be necessary, achieving real continuous progress in this respect.

A major challenge in the area of social protection is that economic growth has not led to an increase in the growth of formal employment at the desired rate. Given the persistence of high proportion of informal employment, it is necessary to consider ways and means of extending social protection to workers in the informal economy. India's Unorganized Sector Workers' Social Security Act of 2008 provides a good example of moving in that direction.

The experience of East and South East Asian countries during their period of high growth shows that formal sector employment may not be a guarantee to access to social protection. Some of those countries started to look at it seriously only in the wake of the economic crisis that hit the region in 1997–98. In the countries of South Asia also, social protection is not universal for workers in the formal sector. But rather than waiting for a crisis, a better way would be to develop strategies and plan of action for extending social protection to all workers.

In some countries, e.g., in India, improvements have happened with regard to wages of workers. However, since the rate of increase has not matched that of labour productivity, the share of wages in output has declined. As a result, the rise in wages has not been able to stem the rise in income inequality. In order to address these challenges, action would be needed on several fronts. First, since one of the variables influencing real wages is labour productivity, efforts to raise productivity continuously would be important. However, as growth in real wages has fallen short of growth in productivity, public policy, and legislation would be necessary to address the issue. Although the debate on the impact of minimum wage legislation on employment and poverty is a continuous one, there is no convincing evidence to point to a negative impact on employment. Apart from legislation, there may be other ways of supporting the growth of real wages. The experience of India shows that employment guarantee programmes like the Mahatma Gandhi National Rural Employment Guarantee Programme (MGNREGP), by providing alternative sources of employment, could improve the supply price of labour and thereby have a positive impact on wages.

Notes

1 This chapter draws from a paper presented by the author at an international seminar on Growth, Disparities and Inclusive Development in Uttar Pradesh organized by the Giri Institute of Development Studies, Lucknow during 23–25 September 2016 (Islam, 2019).
2 See, for example, the country studies in Islam (2006b) and the chapter in that book summarizing those experiences.
3 For a detailed discussion of this aspect of employment-intensive growth, see Islam and Islam (2015), Chapter 2.
4 A synthetic analysis of the results of those studies can be found in Khan (2007).
5 This project was called South Asia Research Network on Labour Market (SARNET).
6 The study on Pakistan (Amjad and Yusuf, 2014) does not provide such figures. But it was possible to estimate them by using the figures for growth of output and employment available in the chapter.

7   The employment situation in India seems to have worsened after the survey of 2011–12. At the time of writing this book, there were reports in the media that unemployment rate in India had risen to 6.1 per cent in 2017–18 (compared to 3.6 per cent in 2011–12). Of course, the official report of the 2017–18 survey has not yet been released, and the media report mentioned above was based on data obtained unofficially. That gave rise to a controversy in the country – with independent experts demanding the release of the official report and the government saying the data were still being processed and the report was not yet ready. See *Business Standard*, February 6, 2019, https://www.business-standard.com/article/economy-policy/unemployment-rate-at-five-decade-high-of-6-1-in-2017-18-nsso-survey-119013100053_1.html, accessed on 6 June 2019. Meanwhile, a report of the All India Manufacturers' Association (AIMO) released in 2018 claimed that 3.5 million jobs were lost between 2014 and 2018 in the trading, micro, small and medium enterprise sector. See *Business Standard*, December 15, 2018. https://www.business-standard.com/article/economy-policy/traders-msme-sector-lost-3-5-mn-jobs-in-4-5-yrs-over-note-ban-gst-survey-118121500645_1.html, accessed on 6 June 2019. The disappointing employment growth in India came in a period when economic growth was quite high, thus indicating that the employment intensity of growth must have declined.

8   Amjad and Yusuf (2014) call the former a period of "high growth" and the second half a period of "low growth".

9   For example, according to data presented in OECD Employment Outlook 2006, GDP growth in the USA during 1993–2003 was 3.2 per cent per annum compared to 2.3 per cent for the 15 EU countries and the OECD average of 2.7 per cent per annum. During 2004–07 also growth in the USA has been higher than that achieved by EU-15. Unemployment rate in the USA has been much lower (5.3 per cent on an average during 1993–2003) than in EU-15 (8.8 per cent during the same period).

10   In 2004, according to OECD (2006), the duration of unemployment benefit was six months in the USA compared to 30 and 12 months in France and Germany, respectively, and an average of 34 months in Nordic countries (Denmark, Finland, Norway, and Sweden). Likewise, public expenditure as percentage of GDP was much lower in the USA (0.55 per cent in 2002) compared to 1.39 per cent and 2.1 per cent in France and Germany, respectively (Auer et al., 2005).

11   A more detailed analysis of this aspect is taken up in the next chapter. See also Islam (2008).

12   This, of course, is not to say that it is impossible for the self-employed to organize social protection for themselves. For a description of some such efforts, see ILO (2014).

13   The idea of Social Protection Index has been developed by the Asian Development Bank and is defined as the ratio of total social protection expenditure and total intended beneficiaries. Three categories of social protection expenditures have been included (i) social insurance, (ii) social assistance, and (iii) labour market programmes. For further details, see ADB (2013).

14   It may be noted in this context that the 2006 report of National Commission for Enterprises in the Unorganized Sector (NCEUS) had made a set of recommendations social security for unorganized workers. Researchers are of the view that the Unorganized Workers' Social Security Act of 2008 does not adequately reflect the recommendations of the NCEUS. On this and the implementation of various programmes of social security for the poor in India, see Kannan and Breman (editors) (2013).

15   On India, there are studies that show real wages in rural areas rising consistently since the 1980s, although the rate of increase varied between sub-periods and for

different categories of workers, e.g., regular and casual workers. See, for example, Jose (2013) and IHD (2014).

16 Studies that cover up to 2004–05 show an acceleration in the growth of urban wages during 1993–94 and 1999–90 (compared to the period of 1983 to 1993–94), but the rate of increase declined after that (ILO, 2009).

17 It may be mentioned in this context that data presented in that study (in Figure 8) seems to show that real wages in 2010–11 and 2011–12 were higher than in 2009–10. But the key question is whether that represented the beginning of a rising trend in subsequent years.

18 These and other data presented in this paragraph are from IHD (2014).

19 Despite high growth of real wage rates (six to seven per cent per annum during the 2000s), the share of wages in value added has declined in China as well. See ILO (2015).

20 Data are from BBS (2013, 2014).

Bibliography

Amjad, Rashid and Anam Yusuf (2014): *More and Better Jobs for Pakistan: Can the Manufacturing Sector Play a Greater Role?* Monograph Series, Graduate School of Development Studies, Lahore School of Economics, Lahore.

Arif, Ghulam Muhammad and Shujaat Farooq (2011): "Poverty, Inequality and Unemployment in Pakistan". Background paper prepared for the IDB group MCPS Document for Pakistan. PIDE and IDB.

Asian Development Bank (2013): *The Social Protection Index: Assessing Results for Asia and the Pacific.* ADB, Manila,

Auer, Peter, Ümit Efendioğlu and Janine Leschke (2005): *Active Labour Market Policies around the World.* ILO, Geneva.

BBS (Bangladesh Bureau of Statistics) (2013): *Survey of Manufacturing Industries 2012.* BBS, Dhaka.

———— (2014): *Statistical Yearbook of Bangladesh 2013.* BBS, Dhaka, 2014.

———— (2015): *Report of Labour Force Survey 2013.* BBS, Dhaka.

———— (2016, August): *Consumer Price Index (CPI), Inflation Rate and Wage Rate Index (WRI) in Bangladesh.* BBS, Dhaka.

Chandrasekhar, C.P. and Jayati Ghosh (2015): "Growth, Employment Patterns and Inequality in Asia: A Case Study of India". ILO Asia-Pacific Working Paper Series, Bangkok.

Chandrasiri, Sunil (2014): "Towards Inclusive Growth through More and Better Jobs: Can the Manufacturing Sector Play a Greater Role in Sri Lanka?" Paper prepared for the SARNET project. IHD, Delhi.

Department of Statistics Malaysia (2016): "Informal Sector Workforce Survey Report, Malaysia, 2015". Kuala Lumpur.

GOB (2016): *Bangladesh Economic Review 2015–16* (in Bengali). Ministry of Finance, Government of Bangladesh.

Ghose, Ajit K. (2014): "India's Services-Led Growth". Working Paper No. 01/2014. Institute for Human Development, New Delhi.

———— (2015): "India Needs Rapid Manufacturing-Led Growth". Working Paper No. 01/2015. Institute for Human Development, New Delhi.

Government of Bangladesh, Ministry of Finance (2017): *Bangladesh Economic Review 2017.* Dhaka.

Heintz, James (2010): "Defining and Measuring Informal Employment and the Informal Sector in the Philippines, Mongolia, and Sri Lanka". ESCAP Working
Paper No. 3. ESCAP, Bangkok.

Institute for Human Development (2014): "Growth, Labour Markets and Employment: India". IHD, New Delhi.

International Labour Organization (2009): "Towards and Employment Strategy for
India". Report prepared for the Government of India. ILO, Delhi.

———— (2012): *Statistical Update on Employment in the Informal Economy*. ILO, Geneva.

———— (2014): *World of Work Report 2014: Developing with Jobs*. ILO, Geneva.

———— (2015): *Global Wage Report 2014/2015: Wages and Income Inequality*. ILO,
Geneva.

International Labour Organization and GOC (2013): *Cambodia Labour Force and Child
Labour Survey 2012, Labour Force Report*. ILO and National Institute of Statistics,
Cambodia, Geneva and Phnom Penh.

Islam, Rizwanul (2006a): "The Nexus of Economic Growth, Employment and Poverty Reduction: An Empirical Analysis", in Islam (2006b).

———— (ed.) (2006b): *Fighting Poverty: The Development-Employment Link*. Lynn
Rienner, Boulder and London.

———— (2008): "Has Development and Employment through Labour-Intensive Industrialization Become History?" in Basu, Kaushik and Ravi Kanbur (eds.): *Arguments for a Better World: Essays in Honour of Amartya Sen*. Oxford University Press,
Oxford.

———— (2010a): "Pattern of Economic Growth and Its Implication for Employment"
in Banerjee, L., A. Dasgupta and R. Islam (eds.): *Development, Equity and Poverty:
Essays in Honour of Azizur Rahman Khan*. Macmillan India and UNDP, Delhi and
New York.

———— (2010b): "Addressing the Challenge of Jobless Growth in Developing Countries: An Analysis with Cross-Country Data". Occasional Paper Series No. 01.
Bangladesh Institute of Development Studies, Dhaka.

———— (2014a): "The Employment Challenge Faced by Bangladesh: How Far Is
the Lewis Turning Point?" *The Indian Journal of Labour Economics*, Vol. 57, No. 2,
pp. 201–225.

———— (2014b): *Nepal: Addressing the Employment Challenge through the Sectoral Pattern
of Growth*. ILO Country Office, Kathmandu.

—— (2015a): "Structural Transformation and Alternative Pathways to the Lewis
Turning Point". Paper presented at the International Seminar on Labour and Employment Issues in the Emerging Rural-Urban Continuum: Dimensions, Processes and Policies, 12–14 March 2015, National Institute of Rural Development,
Hyderabad, Hyderabad.

———— (2015b): Employment and Labour Market in Bangladesh: An Overview of
Trends and Challenges. Paper prepared for the ILO and ADB, Dhaka.

———— (2017): "Bangladesh 2041 Study: Employment and Labour Market Policies
for a Maturing Economy". Paper prepared for the Planning Commission, Government of Bangladesh, Dhaka.

———— (2019): " Labour Market Outcomes and Inclusive Development: Experiences
of South Asian Countries" in Mamgain, Rajendra P. (ed.): *Growth, Disparities and
Inclusive Development in India*. Springer, Singapore, pp. 75–102.

Islam, Rizwanul and Iyanatul Islam (2015): *Employment and Inclusive Development*.
Routledge, London.

Jose, A.V. (2013): "Changes in Wages and Earnings of Rural Labourers", *Economic and Political Weekly*, Vol. XLVIII, No. 26–27, pp. 107–114.

Kannan, K.P. and Jan Breman (eds.) (2013): *The Long Road to Social Security: Assessing the Implementation of National Social Security Initiatives for the Working Poor in India.* Oxford University Press, Delhi.

Khan, A.R. (2006): "Employment Policies for Poverty Reduction" in Islam, R. (ed.): *Fighting Poverty: The Development-Employment Link.* Lynn Rienner, Boulder and London.

——— (2007): *Asian Experience on Growth, Employment and Poverty: An Overview with Special Reference to the Findings of Some Recent Case Studies,* ILO, Geneva and UNDP, Colombo.

Khanal, Dilli Raj (2014): "Employment Challenges in Nepal: Trends, Characteristics and Policy Options for Inclusive Growth and Development". Paper prepared for the SARNET project, IHD, New Delhi.

Lee, Eddy (1998): *The Asian Financial Crisis: The Challenge for Social Policy.* ILO, Geneva.

OECD (2006): *OECD Employment Outlook 2006.* www.oecd.org/employment/ emp/oecdemploymentoutlook2006.htm.

——— (2008): *OECD Employment Outlook 2008.* www.oecd.org/employment/ emp/oecdemploymentoutlook2008.htm.

Rahman, Rushidan I. (2014): "Employment for Inclusive Growth and Development in Bangladesh". Paper prepared for the SARNET project, IHD, New Delhi.

Wiggins, Steve and Sharada Keats (2014): *Rural Wages in Asia.* Overseas Development Institute, London.

World Bank (various years): *World Development Indicators.* https://data.worldbank.org/ indicator/sl.gdp.pcap.em.kd.

5 Economic fluctuations and vulnerability of labour markets[1]

Introduction

Fluctuations in economic activities are quite normal in market-based economies. But such fluctuations may become severe and take the form of crisis. Indeed, both the volatility of economic growth and the frequency of severe fluctuations in growth that warrant the use of the term crisis, appear to have increased during the decades of 1980s, 1990s, and 2000s compared to the earlier decades. An ILO report (ILO, 2004) shows that during 1980–2000, the degree of volatility of GDP growth and per capita GDP growth has been higher than in the earlier two decades. Lustig (2000) mentioned that during 1990–98, there were over 40 cases in Latin America alone in which per capita GDP fell by four per cent or more.

The Asian economic crisis of 1997–98, the Peso crisis of Mexico in 1994, the economic crisis in Argentina during 2001–02 are only some examples of the many different crises that were witnessed during the last few decades. The global economic crisis of 2008–09 came as a reminder that apart from crises affecting a single country or groups of countries in a region, the entire global economy can be affected. Given the growing integration of the global economy, this is only natural. It is also important to remember that crises emanating from the financial world often spread quickly to the real economy which then transmits the impact to the social field. Once that happens, people's lives and livelihoods get affected, resulting in an adverse effect on progress in achieving social goals like the SDGs.

Labour markets face risks and vulnerabilities arising out of economic fluctuations and crises. And it has been observed that recovery in labour markets tend to take longer than economic recovery. Given the low coverage of social protection in developing countries, their workers are more exposed to vulnerabilities faced by their labour markets. Unless an economy builds resilience to respond to such fluctuations and crises and to protect workers who are adversely affected, their lives and livelihoods are likely to be seriously hit. Several questions need to be addressed in this context.

- What is the nature of risks and vulnerabilities faced by workers in different segments of developing economies?
- How do labour markets respond to economic fluctuations and crises?

- Why do labour markets respond to economic recovery with a lag?
- What kind of instruments and measures can be used to build resilience in the labour markets so that they can better absorb the shocks and the adverse effects on workers can be minimized?

This chapter attempts to address the above questions. It is organized as follows. The second section discusses some relevant concepts like vulnerability, risk, and resilience with particular focus on labour markets. That is followed by an analysis of how labour markets respond to economic fluctuations and cries. The fourth section addresses the question why labour market recovery takes place with a lag after economic recovery starts. Instruments and measures that can be used to build resilience of labour markets in facing economic crises are outlined in the fifth section. A few concluding observations are made in the last section.

Vulnerability and risk in labour market analysis: some concepts

Vulnerability[2]

The concept of vulnerability is multidimensional and is used to describe situations or conditions influenced by a variety of factors like environment, natural calamities, economic fluctuations, etc. In development discourse, the term is usually used to indicate the possibility of individuals, households, or nations slipping into difficult situations. It is basically an *ex ante* indicator of well-being, reflecting not so much the current situation but the future prospects – especially in the face of unforeseen difficulties. One way of looking at it is through the probability of an entity (e.g., an individual, a household, or a country) falling below a socially accepted norm, e.g., the poverty line.

The term vulnerability is quite general – and is often used in the analysis of poverty. But it can also be applied to the analysis of labour markets because they may also face uncertain situations like fluctuations in economic activities and their adverse effects on the demand for labour. An individual's situation in the labour market – whether one is in wage employment or self-employment – may be subject to changes due to a variety of factors. They can range from individual contingencies like unforeseen illness affecting the ability to work, natural calamities like floods and droughts damaging crops and thus affecting work relating to production, sharp fluctuations in the demand for the goods and services, and so on. In the analysis of vulnerability of labour markets, the counterpart of poverty line would be income-generating work. And vulnerability of individuals and households could be conceptualized in terms of one's continued access to such work.

Risk

Two elements that are closely related to vulnerability are risk and exposure. Whether applied to the analysis of poverty or labour markets, vulnerability reflects the degree of exposure to difficult and uncertain situations and the risk that is faced. The term risk may be conceptualized in terms of the likelihood of an undesirable outcome – be it in terms of loss of income or a source of livelihood. It describes a state of uncertainty where the possibilities include losses and undesirable outcomes.

Two broad categories of risks are mentioned in the literature: (i) idiosyncratic risks and (ii) covariant risks. The former refers to risks that an individual or household may face due to factors like ill health, disability, death of the main wage earner, a failure of business, localized crop failure, etc. The latter (i.e., covariant risk) refers to more generalized risks, e.g., an overall economic downturn, drought, floods, war, etc. which might lead to declines in average employment and income that affect a country as a whole or a region or large numbers of households.

The risks associated with a looming economic crisis are mainly (but not only) of covariant type. For example, the loss of competitiveness of a country's exports may lead to a reduction in its exports and thus cause a decline in its foreign exchange reserves which, in turn, may put pressure on the exchange rate of its currency. A precipitous depreciation of the currency may lead to inflationary pressures as well as an increase in the burden of external debt. In extreme cases, the chain of events may contain the risk of default on external debt. Another example of covariant risks associated with economic crisis is provided by a synchronized decline in demands in major economies of the world (as it happened during the global economic crisis of 2008–09 and the Great Recession that took place) which may adversely affect exports from the exporting countries with a chain effect on their economies and labour markets. Export-oriented economic activities may face the risk of severe downturns in the demand for their products, and workers engaged in them may face the risk of retrenchment or a decline in their earnings or both. The enterprises in such sectors may face the risk of a decline in markets or prices of their products, and hence, profits and earnings.

The second example provided above of risks associated with an economic crisis should serve to indicate that risks associated with an economic crisis may start from the national level and quickly spread to the household level through a variety of channels. For example, when an export-oriented industry, plantation or a mine is faced with sharp declines in the demand for their products, workers engaged in them face the risk of job loss or declines in earnings due to a reduction in wages and/or hours of work. Smallholders engaged in the production of export-oriented crops like coffee often face the risk of a collapse in their prices. In such situations, they face the risk of direct adverse effects on their livelihoods.

Resilience

The notion of resilience can be conceptualized as the mirror opposite of vulnerability. It refers to the ability of a nation, household, or an individual to cope with the adverse effects of external shocks that may arise from various sources like environmental hazards, natural calamities, conflicts and war, economic crisis, etc. If vulnerability refers to shortage of resources and exposure to shocks and risks, resilience is about augmenting and diversifying the resource base and reducing exposure to shocks and risks. In situations where the latter are unknown and difficult to influence, building resilience would require a greater focus on augmenting, strengthening, and diversifying the resource base.

The term resilience may also be applied at the macroeconomic (or national) level and at the micro or household level. Likewise, it is possible to distinguish the purely economic dimension of resilience from a broader social dimension. Economic resilience at the macro level could be conceptualized as the ability of a country's economy to withstand shocks of a macroeconomic nature, e.g., a sharp decline in the demand for exports, a sharp deterioration in the exchange rate, a sudden outflow of capital, etc.[3] Likewise, the economic resilience of households (or individuals) could be conceptualized as the ability to absorb and recover from the adverse effects of shocks that may be caused by factors like crop loss due to a natural calamity, job loss due to an economic downturn, sharp increases in the prices of major consumer goods, e.g., food grains, etc.

Resilience of the labour market could be conceptualized in terms of its ability to cope with shocks like sharp fall in the demand for workers arising out of a collapse of the export demand or domestic demand or both. The degree of resilience could be indicated by the ability of a country to prevent a sharp rise in unemployment or to enable the workers to maintain a minimum level of living, even in periods of unemployment. The last section of this chapter will deal with the issue of how the labour market of a country can be made more resilient so that it can minimize the adverse effects of economic fluctuations on the level living of workers.

The term resilience also has a broader social dimension which would capture the ability of a system to utilize its social capabilities to cope with and recover from the external shocks that it may face. For example, a village community may be able to draw on its societal strength (represented by its cohesiveness, the existence of community-based organizations, and willingness to mobilize self-help) to cope with a crisis caused by a natural calamity. Likewise, an economy faced with an external economic shock may be able to draw on or develop a harmonious labour relation to cope with the adverse effects of economic downturn.

How do labour markets adjust to economic downturns and crises?

The impact on labour market

An economic crisis, especially if there is a sharp economic downturn, can adversely affect the employment and labour market situation of a country in at least two broad ways. First, a decline in economic activity can lead to decline in the demand for labour in the domestic economy. Second, for labour exporting countries, a decline in economic activities in the receiving countries can lead to a decline in the demand for expatriate workers, which, in turn, could create additional pressure on the domestic labour market. In this book, we shall deal with the domestic economy.[4]

Output and employment can be expected to move together, although there may not be a one-to-one relationship between the two variables. Indeed, measured unemployment is usually observed to be less volatile than output growth because the labour market responds in a variety of different ways to a decline in output. The relationship between unemployment and the decline in output growth is usually conceptualized in terms of Okun's law which is due to Arthur Okun's observation on the relationship between the decline in output growth and unemployment in the USA.[5] However, in developing countries, the impact of a decline in output (or its growth) may not remain confined only to increases in unemployment. The labour markets in such countries may adjust in different ways – through variations in quantity (viz., increases in unemployment), changes in the type of employment (e.g., moving towards more flexible type of labour arrangements, shift of workers to informal segments of the economy, etc.), and adjustment in wages.

As for the adverse effect of a decline in output growth on employment in the domestic labour market, different groups may be affected in different ways and in varying degrees. For example, depending on the sectors that are more seriously affected, the levels of education and types of skills of the affected workers may also vary. If the adverse impact is more on the financial service sector, more educated workers may be expected to be more seriously affected. On the other hand, if manufacturing and constructions sectors are affected, workers with lower education and skills may be more seriously affected. In many developing countries, export-oriented industries employ women in large numbers. So, if such sectors suffer a decline in growth, women workers may be disproportionately affected. So, an analysis of the impact of the economic crisis on employment would have to start from the manner in which and the degree to which the various sectors of an economy were affected.

Depending on the seriousness of the situation, public policy aimed at stimulating the declining economies may also include measures to minimize the adverse impact on labour markets. But such measures are usually time-bound, and once an economy starts recovering, macroeconomic considerations of inflation and budget deficit lead to the termination of and even reversal of anti-cyclical measures. What is often not noticed is that while the impact of economic downturns quickly gets transmitted to the labour markets, recovery in the labour market usually comes with a lag.

There is a debate in the development literature on the relative importance of the various ways in which labour markets adjust to a decline in labour demand caused by economic downturns. While some studies (e.g., Fallon and Lucas, 2002; McKenzie, 2004) argue that the major mechanism is price adjustment (i.e., wage flexibility), data and analysis presented in this chapter (see below) show that in reality, a variety of mechanisms work. Even when wages are flexible, quantity adjustments (e.g., increases in unemployment and under-employment) are found to take place. The latter could also have different variants. For example, rather than a simple reduction in the level of employment, an economy (and its enterprises) may resort to measures like changing the nature of contracts (e.g., from regular to temporary), hours of work, and so on. Adjustment could also be made through changes in the structure of employment, e.g., through a shift from formal/modern sectors to informal/traditional sectors, or a shift from regular wage employment to self-employment. Some of the latter could also have implications for the level of earnings (if not the wage rate as such) of workers. In addition, adjustment could be made through a combination of the different means mentioned above.

Mechanisms for adjustment: quantity, price or both?

Let us first analyze two broad ways in which the labour market of a country can adjust to economic downturns that cause sharp declines in labour demand: by lowering wage rates and by reducing the level of employment (which, respectively, could be referred to as price adjustment and quantity adjustment). At the risk of oversimplification, we adopt a Lewis-type framework (Lewis, 1954) which assumes a dualistic economy consisting of a modern sector and a traditional sector.[6] We, however, consider situations with or without the existence of surplus labour. It is assumed that labour demand in the traditional sector is not directly affected by the downturn, but the sector plays the role of absorbing workers who may be retrenched from the modern sector.

Figure 5.1a–d provide a stylized description of how the adjustment mechanisms through variations in wage and employment levels could work. While Figure 5.1a and b represent the modern sector (respectively, with and without surplus labour in the economy), Figure 5.1c and d represent the traditional sector (respectively, with and without surplus labour).

Consider the modern sector of an economy with the existence of surplus labour which is depicted in Figure 5.1a. D_1 and S_1 represent demand and supply of labour before the fall in demand for labour while D_2 represents the demand curve after the fall in labour demand due to economic recession. If wages are rigid at OW_0, the decline in demand would lead to a contraction of employment from OL_0 to OL_2. However, if wages are flexible and decline to OW_1, employment does not have to fall to OL_2, it would fall to OL_1. In this case, the labour market adjusts through a combination of wage and employment reduction rather than employment reduction alone. The same is shown in Figure 5.1b for the modern sector of an economy where there is no surplus labour. The supply curve is upward sloping throughout, and depending on the existence of wage flexibility, adjustment could be entirely through the employment route or through a mix of employment and wages.

Figure 5.1c and d depict the situation of the traditional sector as a result of the fall in labour demand in the modern sector. As mentioned above, employment in the modern sector is likely to decline even if wages are flexible

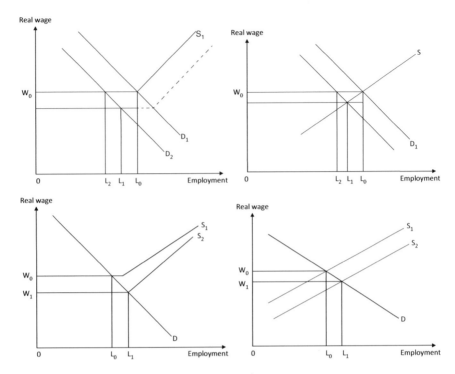

Figure 5.1 (a) Labour Market Adjustment to a Fall in Labour Demand: *Modern Sector* in an Economy with Surplus Labour. (b) Labour Market Adjustment to a Fall in Labour Demand: *Modern Sector* in an Economy without Surplus Labour. (c) Labour Market Adjustment to a Fall in Labour Demand: *Traditional Sector* in an Economy with Surplus Labour. (d) Labour Market Adjustment to a Fall in Labour Demand: *Traditional Sector* in an Economy without Surplus Labour.

and some part of the adjustment takes place through the wage route. In the absence of social protection measures like unemployment benefits, those who lose jobs in the modern sector are most likely to end up in the informal parts of the economy. As a result, supply curve for labour in the traditional sector shifts to the right as shown by S_2. Employment in the traditional sector increases from OL_0 to OL_1, but wages decline to OW_1.

To sum up, with or without surplus labour in the economy, the result of a fall in labour demand in the modern sector is likely to be a combination of declines in wages and employment (unless one of them is rigid). The impact of the fall in labour demand is likely to spill over to the traditional sector where supply of labour would increase, and an increase in employment is likely to be accompanied by a decline in wages.

It needs to be mentioned here that the Lewisian framework mentioned above does not take into account many other ways in which labour markets in developing countries adjust to a sharp fall in the demand for labour. The other mechanisms include shift to part-time work, change in the composition of employment type (e.g., from wage employment to self-employment), change in the type of contract (e.g., from regular to fixed-term), migration from urban to rural areas and from one region of a country to another, and dropping out from the labour force.[7]

What happens in reality can be illustrated with examples from countries that were affected by economic downturns and crises. Some such examples based on the experiences of the Asian economic crisis (1997–98) and the Great Recession (2008–09) are presented in a summary form in Table 5.1. A general point that needs to be noted is that while the Great Recession

Table 5.1 How Labour Markets Adjust to Economic Crisis/Downturns: Some Examples

Mechanism of Adjustment	Country and Period of Economic Crisis/Downturn
Quantity Adjustment	
Rise in unemployment	i Indonesia, Republic of Korea, Malaysia, Philippines, and Thailand during the Asian economic crisis (1997–98)
	ii Korea, Mauritius, Philippines, Singapore, and Thailand during the Great Recession (2008–09)
	iii China during the Great Recession (urban unemployment)
Increase in the retrenchment of workers in manufacturing or slowdown in employment growth	Bangladesh, Cambodia, Indonesia, Malaysia, and South Africa during the Great Recession
Job losses in the formal sector	India during the Great Recession
Price Adjustment	
Decline in real wages	i Indonesia, Republic of Korea, Malaysia, Philippines, and Thailand during the Asian economic crisis
	ii India during the Great Recession
Adjustment through Change in the Composition of Employment	
Reverse migration to rural areas and a rise in rural employment	i Indonesia and Thailand during the Asian economic crisis
	ii China during the Great Recession
Decline in wage employment and increase in self-employment	i Indonesia, Korea, Malaysia, and Thailand during the Asian economic crisis
Higher rate of retrenchment of contract workers compared to regular workers	i Bangladesh and India during the Great Recession

Source: Constructed by the author on the basis of data and information in Betcherman and Islam (2001), Huynh et al. (2010), and Islam (2011).

affected a large number of developed countries, some of the major developing economies were affected only indirectly – through the effect of their linkage with the global economy. While most of the latter were able to escape outright recession (see Table 5.2), they experienced moderate economic downturns. In contrast, the countries of East and South East Asia (ESEA) who were affected by the Asian economic crisis were severely affected by the crisis, and as a result, they experienced sharp declines in output and negative growth. The labour markets of those countries were also more seriously affected compared to the impact of the Great Recession.

Be that as it may, what is clear from the summary presented in Table 5.1 is that multiple adjustment mechanisms were at work in most countries that experienced economic downturns and crises. Decline in employment growth, rise in unemployment rate, and fall in real wages took place simultaneously. A second point to note is adjustment through change in the composition of employment. Given the absence of social protection measures like unemployment benefits in many developing countries and the incidence of poverty, being unemployed is not an option for most. In such circumstances, eking out a living through engagement in the informal economy and sharing of work

Table 5.2 The Great Recession 2008–09: Periods when Different Countries Were Affected

Countries/Region	Period of Recession
EU (28 countries)	Q2-2008 to Q2-2009
	Q4-2011 to Q2-2012
	Q4-2012 to Q1-2013
Eurozone (17 countries)	Q2-2008 to Q2-2009
	Q4-2011 to Q1-2013
France	Q2-2008 to Q2-2009
Germany	Q2-2008 to Q1-2009
Japan	Q2-2008 to Q1-2009
	Q4-2010 to Q2-2011
	Q2-2012 to Q3-2012
OECD (34 countries)	Q2-2008 to Q1-2009
Republic of Korea	None
U.K.	Q2-2008 to Q2-2009
U.S.A.	Q3-2008 to Q2-2009
Argentina	Q4-2008 to Q2-2009
	Q1-2012 to Q2-2012
Brazil	Q4-2008 to Q1-2009
	Q1-2014 to Q4-2016
China	None
India	None
Indonesia	None
Malaysia	Q3-2008 to Q1-2009
Philippines	Q4-2008 to Q1-2009
South Africa	Q4-2008 to Q2-2009
Thailand	Q4-2008 to Q1-2009

Source: Wikipedia: http://en.wikipedia.org/wiki/Great_Recession Accessed on 11 June 2018.

in family farm (through reverse migration) are mechanisms that are found to be operational. Increase in the proportion of employment in the informal economy, in own-account work and in unpaid family work are manifestations of such mechanisms.

Why does labour market recovery follow economic recovery with a lag?

There are some easily understandable reasons for which recovery in labour markets follows economic recovery with a lag. One such reason is the uncertainty that prevails for a period when an economy recovers from recession. During that period, it would be natural for enterprises to respond to increased demand for products by raising productivity rather than by adding to the workforce. The deeper the recession, the more uncertain the initial period of recovery is likely to be, and hence the longer the time before firms start hiring again may be.

Another reason for the lag in labour market recovery could be the change in the approach to enterprise management that is made possible by a recession. In modern market-based economies, where volatility in economic activities has increased, enterprises may be looking for opportunities to change the structure of operations, and a recession may offer them that opportunity. For example, an enterprise may opt to shift towards a leaner structure in terms of regular staff and depend more on temporarily hired staff for meeting demand, so that it has more flexibility in terms of payroll size. Every recession creates an opportunity for enterprises to introduce changes in management style that is considered to be more in line with the prevailing economic environment. Indeed, the experience of post-Asian crisis labour market transformation in countries of ESEA indicates this kind of changes in the labour market resulting in a slower growth of employment than witnessed before the economic downturn.[8]

Third, countercyclical measures adopted during economic downturns usually involves expansionary monetary policy, one of whose major mechanisms is reduction in interest rates. That may lead to a change in the relative prices of factors of production in favour of capital, thus creating an incentive for entrepreneurs to adopt capital deepening measures. That, in turn, may reduce the requirement for labour and cause a decline in labour requirement during the period of recovery.

Apart from the reasons mentioned above, there could be factors that are more fundamental to an economy and the downturn that it experiences which could have implications for the speed with which the labour market would respond. One such factor requires an understanding of the nature of the adjustments that are likely to take place in an economy and its labour market during a recession. Adjustments required and made by an economy (and its enterprises) during a recession can be of two types: cyclical and structural.[9] The cyclical adjustments refer to changes that are made when the fall in demand simply reflects the downward phase of a business cycle and are expected to be reversed as the economy recovers. In such a situation, enterprises simply adjust quantity of output; retrenchments of workers are temporary, and re-hiring is expected to start when the volume of production rebounds. In contrast, structural adjustment refers to changes that are required when the decline in economic activities is not only a matter of quantitative adjustment to the falling segment of the business cycle, but one that is more fundamental, reflecting a change in the *pattern* of demand, technological change, and reorganization of production. The latter kind of change could lead to a permanent fall in demand and warrant a reallocation of factors of production including labour. When this kind of adjustment takes place in an economy, retrenchments are likely to be of a permanent kind because even when the economy comes to an upturn, production and hiring may not resume in the same lines of activities. Old industries may decline, and new ones may come up; hiring may take place in new industries, and hence the same workers may not be re-hired.

It should be clear from the above distinction between cyclical and structural adjustments that while job losses during the former are likely to be temporary, they are unlikely to be so in the second type of situation. There may, of course, be a lag between resumption of production and that of hiring even when adjustment is cyclical for reasons mentioned earlier, but the lag could be longer when the nature of adjustment is structural. And the overall lag with which labour markets recover would be a function of the relative weight of the structural vs. cyclical adjustments in various sectors of an economy. Labour market recovery would be slower if more layoffs are structural (and hence, permanent) in nature. On the other hand, if much of the layoffs are cyclical (and hence, temporary) in nature, the labour market recovery could be quicker. Hence, from the point of view of explaining the lag in job recovery during economic recovery, it would be important to examine the type of adjustment that is taking place in an economy during the recovery period.

The points made above can be illustrated by using the experiences of countries where labour markets responded to economic downturns through a variety of mechanisms like rise in unemployment, decline in real wages, and recovery in the labour market took place with a lag after economic recovery started. This is done below by using the examples of (i) Indonesia which suffered from sharp economic downturn during the Asian economic crisis of 1997–98 and (ii) the Great Recession of 2008–09 during which many developed countries went into recession and several developing countries suffered from the adverse indirect effects of such recession.

Indonesia's experience with economic downturn and labour market recovery

It may be recalled that the East Asian economic crisis started in Thailand with sharp devaluation of the currency and collapse of equity prices and stock markets that followed massive reverse flows of foreign capital.[10] The contagion effect of those developments quickly spread to several countries of ESEA, including Indonesia, Republic of Korea, Malaysia, and the Philippines. In Indonesia (as well as in the other affected countries), in 1997, economic growth declined, and in 1998, the economy contracted sharply – GDP declining by 13.13 per cent. Open unemployment increased significantly, and employment growth, especially in manufacturing, declined sharply in those years. Even when economic recovery started (i.e., after 1999), it took several years before the level of employment – overall and in manufacturing – went back to the pre-crisis level (see Figures 5.2 and 5.3). In fact, employment growth never went back to the kind of growth achieved by the economy during the 1980s and early 1990s.

Of course, real wages also declined very sharply in Indonesia in 1998 (Figure 5.2). But that can be ascribed more to the hyperinflation experienced by the economy in that year than to an adjustment in actual wages. It may be recalled in this context that the consumer price index for workers rose to 213 in 1998 (compared to the base of 100 in 1997).[11] The decline in real wages witnessed in 1998 was therefore hardly surprising. However, as prices started stabilising, real wages also started to rise and returned to the pre-crisis level by 2000 (Figure 5.2).

The story of labour market adjustment to the economic crisis in Indonesia will not be complete without the mention of other important mechanisms

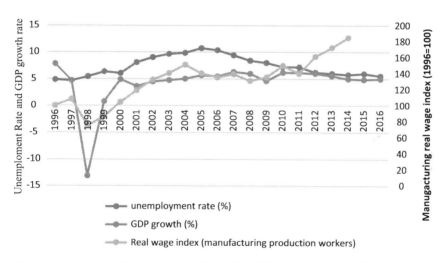

Figure 5.2 Indonesia Unemployment Rate (%), GDP Growth Rate (%), and Manufacturing Real Wage Index (1996 = 100).

Sources: (i) Unemployment rate and real wage indices are from the website of the Central Bureau of Statistics, Government of Indonesia at www.bps.go.id (Accessed on 13 June 2018), (ii) GDP growth rate figures are from the World Bank's World Development Indicators data available at http://data.worldbank.org/indicator/NY.GDP.MKTP.KD.ZG?locations=ID (Accessed on 13 May 2018).

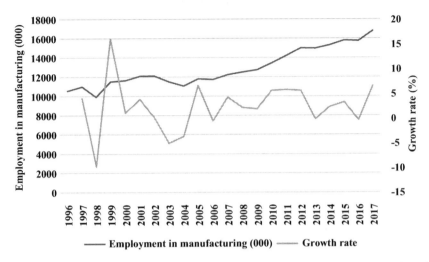

Figure 5.3 Indonesia Employment in Manufacturing (Number in Thousand and Annual Growth in Percentage).

Source: Constructed by the author by using data available on the website of the Central Bureau of Statistics, Government of Indonesia at www.bps.go.id (Accessed on 13 May 2018).

that came into play. The structure of employment changed significantly. For example, employment in agriculture increased by about five million (which was six per cent of the labour force),[12] and much of that was supply driven. Indeed, in the areas where total employment increased, much of that increase was accounted for by the increase in employment in agriculture. Second, the share of wage employment declined. This share which was rising gradually before the crisis (thus indicating a trend towards formalization of the economy) and had reached 35 per cent in 1997 declined to 32 per cent in 1998. Correspondingly, the share of self-employment and informal forms of employment increased. These adjustments helped preclude the possibility of a bigger decline in the open unemployment rate. Another adjustment mechanism operating in the Indonesian labour market was reverse migration of workers from urban to rural areas (which was reflected in the rise in employment in agriculture).

The conclusions (regarding labour market adjustment to a sharp economic downturn) that follow for Indonesia are as follows. First, labour market adjusted through both the quantity (i.e., employment/unemployment) and price (i.e., real wages) mechanisms.[13] Indeed, given that the decline in real wages was a reflection of hyperinflation experienced by the economy, it may even be argued that quantity adjustment was more dominant. Second, Indonesian labour market also adjusted through structural change – from non-agriculture to agriculture and from formal to informal sectors. A third observation that can be made on the basis of the Indonesian data concerns the lag with which the labour market recovered. Although the economy returned to healthy growth in 2000 (GDP growth was 4.92 per cent), employment growth was much slower (only 1.14 per cent). And the low and fluctuating employment growth continued throughout the period of economic recovery and growth in Indonesia. In fact, in some years (2003, 2004, and 2006), the manufacturing sector recorded negative employment growth although output in the sector had healthy growth of 5.33 and 4.59 per cent, respectively, in those years. Thus, the experience of Indonesia during the recovery from the Asian economic crisis can be described as a classic case of jobless recovery and substantial lag in labour market recovery.

But how does one explain the lag with which employment recovery followed economic recovery in Indonesia? At least a tentative explanation can be found in terms of the distinction drawn above between structural as opposed to cyclical types of adjustment that might take place in an economy during recession. A closer look at what happened in Indonesia's economy (especially in its manufacturing sector) just before, during, and immediately after the economic crisis of 1997–98 throws useful light on this issue. A few points may be worth noting in that regard.[14]

First, significant changes have been taking place in the structure of manufacturing industries of Indonesia even before the crisis erupted in 1997. For example, growth in output of major labour-intensive industries like textiles and wood had declined sharply during 1993–97 compared to 1989–92. And that trend continued even when the economy started its recovery in 2000. During 2000–04, growth of textiles, wood, and food industries were way below the growth rates achieved in the 1980s and 1990s. In fact, the only industry that attained double-digit growth rate during 2000–03 was chemical (which is not a labour-intensive industry).

Second, the decline in the growth of labour-intensive industries in Indonesia is a reflection of the decline in the growth of exports of their products. The shares of labour-intensive industries like food, textiles, wood, etc. in total exports declined during 2000–03 compared to 1993–97. On the other hand, the share of chemical, transport equipment and machinery, and miscellaneous manufacturing increased. Thus, the structure of Indonesia's exports had undergone a significant change away from labour-intensive manufactures.

Third, Indonesia's major labour-intensive industries (e.g., textiles, garments, and footwear) suffered a decline in the growth of labour productivity which, in turn, led to the loss of international competitiveness[15] and decline in export growth in these sectors.

In sum, economic crisis and downturn experienced by Indonesia during 1997–98 was associated with major structural changes in the economy (especially in the manufacturing sector). As a consequence, a large part of the job loss that took place must have been structural in nature (rather than cyclical). As traditional labour-intensive industries like textiles, garments, footwear, wood products, etc. were no longer growing at nearly the same rate as before the crisis, workers who lost jobs from those sectors were finding it difficult to get re-hired.

The Great Recession 2008–09

How labour markets in developing countries have been affected by the Great Recession of 2008–09 can be gauged by the figures on unemployment and their changes during those years. Although such data are not available for many countries, monthly data on unemployment and changes therein are available at the ILO website for "developing countries".[16] Figure 5.4, which is based on that data, shows interesting trends.

First, unemployment rate continued to rise till December 2009, although the rate of that rise declined after May of that year. It may be recalled here that the global economy (especially the US economy) had already come out of recession towards the middle of 2009. And yet, unemployment rate continued to increase.

Second, although it is often feared that women would be hit harder by retrenchments during economic downturns, the situation seems to have been different during the Great Recession of 2008–09. It is clear from Figure 5.4 that increase in unemployment rate has, by and large, been greater for men than women.

Figure 5.5 shows the monthly change in total employment in developing countries – for men and women together as well as separately. This figure also shows that employment growth continued to decline till September 2009 and started to rise in October 2009. The decline in employment growth was sharper for men and when it started to rise, the rate was higher for women. Thus, data presented in Figure 5.5 corroborate that in Figure 5.4 regarding both the temporal pattern of change and its gender differential.

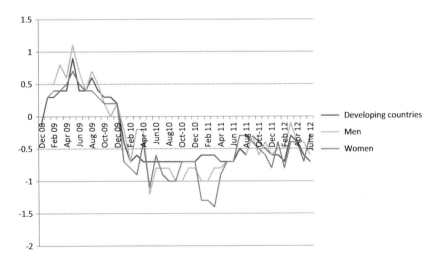

Figure 5.4 Unemployment Rate in Developing Countries: Percentage Point Change from Previous Period.

Source: Prepared by using data from ILO website: http://laborsta.ilo.org.

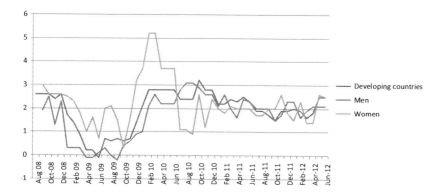

Figure 5.5 Percentage Change in Total Employment in Developing Countries (From the Corresponding Period in the Previous Year).

Source: Prepared by using data from ILO website: http://laborsta.ilo.org.

Building resilience

To recapitulate, labour markets are vulnerable to economic downturns and crises because the adverse effects of a decline in output growth get transmitted to the labour market. Moreover, labour markets often follow economic recovery with a lag. Vulnerability of labour markets affect the livelihoods of people. For the poor and vulnerable who are dependent on their labour for a living, loss of jobs or a fall in real wages can mean falling deeper into poverty. Labour market shocks may also push some of the non-poor to poverty. In order to prevent such adverse effects on levels of living, it would be important to build resilience of labour markets so that they can withstand shocks caused by economic downturns.

As mentioned already, the notion of resilience can be conceptualized as the mirror image of vulnerability. Hence, building resilience should be about undertaking measures to reduce vulnerability. That, in turn, implies augmenting the resource base, reducing exposure, increasing preparedness to manage and cope with risk and shocks, and build up the capacity to cope with crises. Once the causes of vulnerability are understood, it should be possible to identify measures and instruments needed for building resilience corresponding to the causes of vulnerability. Table 5.3 provides a stylized description of possible instruments/measures for building resilience that correspond to major sources of labour market vulnerability.

For reducing exposure in the face of an economic crisis, a country would do well to include employment as an important element in its development strategy. A country that is firmly on a growth path conducive to employment generation would be less exposed to vulnerability than a country where economic growth is not employment-intensive. Likewise, at the household level, investment in education and health is likely to yield dividend at the time of

Table 5.3 Instruments for Building Resilience of the Labour Market

Sources of Vulnerability	Instruments for Building Resilience

Exposure
  i High level of poverty and concentration of people around the poverty line
  ii High degree of unemployment and underemployment
	i An employment-focussed development strategy

Lack of Preparedness
  i Absence of automatic stabilizers and labour market programmes (e.g., severance benefits, retraining programmes) to respond to crisis
  ii Absence of social protection and safety nets
	i Automatic stabilizers in the form of unemployment benefits, employment guarantee programmes, etc.
	ii Active labour market programmes (including retraining and redeployment programmes and employment generation programmes)
	iii Introduction/strengthening of social protection and SSNs

Lack of Capacity to Cope/Respond
  i Lack of fiscal space
  ii Lack of institutional capacity
  iii Resource limitation at the household level
  iv Absence of livelihood diversification
	i Build up fiscal space before crisis by raising revenue
	ii Strengthen institutional capacity before crisis by implementing programmes of the kind mentioned above
	iii Pro-poor programmes for augmenting the asset and resource base of the poor
	iv Adopt strategies for diversifying livelihoods

economic difficulty because the better educated are often seen to be less affected by or better able to cope with an economic crisis (although the reverse cannot be ruled out, depending on the nature and cause of the crisis).

A country without any automatic stabilizers and social safety net programmes would be ill-prepared to face a crisis. The degree of preparedness to face an economic crisis can be increased in various ways. Possible instruments related to the labour market would include introduction of automatic stabilizers in the form of unemployment benefits, other social protection and social safety net measures, and active labour market programmes.

The importance of automatic stabilizers and the degree of preparedness can be illustrated with the experiences of the Great Recession and the Asian economic crisis. When the Great Recession hit various countries, the share of unemployed workers not receiving unemployment benefits was as high as 57 and 40 per cent in the USA and the UK, respectively, compared to 18 and 13 per cent in France and Germany (ILO, 2009). Moreover, those with access to unemployment benefit in the USA were entitled to shorter periods of such benefits compared to France and Germany. The immediate fall in income due to the absence of (or short duration of) unemployment benefits was exacerbated by the loss of non-cash benefits like employer-provided health care. As a result, workers in the USA were much more vulnerable to their counterparts in France and Germany. It is not surprising that the USA had to undertake measures to extend the period of unemployment benefits during the Great Recession.

During the Asian economic crisis, countries like the Republic of Korea, Indonesia, Malaysia, and Thailand were not prepared to provide protection to unemployed workers through unemployment benefits. As a result, large numbers of workers in those countries suffered sharp declines in incomes (and even falling into poverty), and the countries had to scramble for measures for protecting the workers.

However, the ability of countries to respond during economic crises may be constrained at the macro level by a limited fiscal space and institutional capacity. While it is often said that developing countries lack the necessary fiscal space for undertaking programmes for improving preparedness and crisis coping measures, a bit of investigation would demonstrate that such space can be created in various ways, e.g., by augmenting revenues and improving efficiency. Improvement of resource and asset base at the household level would require pro-poor policies and programmes directly aimed at that goal. Diversification of the sources of livelihood at the household level is one way of building resilience at that level.[17] Public policies and programmes can play a role in that regard as well.

Concluding observations

Labour markets usually suffer from an exposure to risks of a sudden decline in labour demand, and hence unemployment, associated with economic fluctuations. Livelihoods of individuals exposed to such risks are often vulnerable, and episodes of poverty even among the non-poor are not uncommon. The degree of vulnerability depends on the degree of exposure of an economy, its labour markets and individuals and the extent of their resilience. The extent of resilience is indicated by the ability of a country to prevent sharp increases in unemployment, underemployment, and precarious forms of employment, and fall in real wages and to enable workers to maintain a minimum level of living even during sharp economic downturns.

It has been analytically argued and empirically demonstrated in the present chapter that labour markets in developing economies adjust to economic downturns through a variety of mechanisms including increases in unemployment and underemployment and precarious forms of employment, declines in real wages, increases in informal employment, etc. Moreover, labour markets respond to economic recovery with a lag, and workers continue to suffer from the adverse effects for a longer period than other groups in the economy. And hence the importance of building resilience of the labour markets so that such adverse effects can be minimized.

The mechanisms for building resilience of labour markets range from a general employment-friendly development strategy to raise the degree of preparedness to face crisis by introducing social protection measures; unemployment benefits; and active labour market policies, including special employment programmes. Fiscal space necessary for such measures as well as institutional capacity to implement them need to be created during times of economic prosperity so that an economy is not caught unprepared when a crisis hits it.

Notes

1 This chapter draws on Islam (2011).
2 There is a large body of literature on vulnerability and risk relating to poverty and livelihoods. One could see, for example, Alwang et al. (2001), Cafiero and Vakis (2006), Chambers (1989), Chaudhury (2003), and Dercon (2001, 2002, 2009). On measuring vulnerability, see Lignon and Shechter (2003), Naude et al. (2009), and Zhang and Wan (2009).
3 For a more detailed discussion on the notion and measurement of economic resilience, see Briguglio et al. (2009).
4 This does not mean that the impact of economic downturn in labour receiving countries on labour migration from other countries is not important. In fact, experience with previous crises (e.g., the Asian economic crisis of 1997–98) shows that when a country is hit by sharp economic downturn, it is the foreign workers who suffer the first brunt of retrenchment (Betcherman and Islam, 2001). Likewise, during the Great Recession of 2008–09, a number of labour importing countries either retrenched foreign workers or reduced the intake of such workers (Verick, 2010). An adverse effect on international migration of workers can create serious problems for countries that are dependent on this channel for employment as well as remittances sent by the workers.
5 In Okun's original work (Okun, 1962), a 3 per cent increase in output is associated with a 1 per cent decline in the rate of unemployment in the USA. Subsequently, Okun's Law has been quantitatively expressed as 2 per cent decline in GDP is associated with a 1 per cent increase in the rate of unemployment. For an empirical application of Okun's Law to the global economic crisis of 2008–09, see IMF (2010) and Verick and Islam (2010).
6 For use of similar frameworks, see Fields (1994) and Manning (2000).
7 These other mechanisms of labour market adjustment may operate in developed countries as well. For example, during the economic recession of 2008–09, recourse to part-time employment and irregular contracts, and dropping out of labour market were common in developed countries as well.
8 In Republic of Korea, for example, during the economic crisis of 1997–98, the number of "daily workers" started rising soon after the decline in the first quarter of 1998, while the number of "regular workers" continued to decline throughout 1998. The proportion of part-time workers increased significantly (from 7.2 per cent to 9.3 per cent) during 1997–98. See Kang et al. (2001).
9 This distinction was made by Groshen and Potter (2003) in the context of their analysis of jobless recovery in the USA from the recession of 2001.
10 There is a large body of literature on the causes of the crisis. A good analysis is provided by Lee (1998).
11 These data and data on real wage index are from ILO (1999).
12 This figure and other data mentioned in this paragraph are from Islam et al. (2001).

13 Betcherman and Islam (2001) came to the same conclusion based on the experience of Indonesia and other countries of ESEA.
14 The observations made in the next three paragraphs are based on data presented in Islam and Chowdhury (2009).
15 It may be worthwhile to mention here that one study points out that "External factors rather than internal factors such as rising wage rates were responsible for the declining competitiveness of traditional Indonesian exports" (Dhanani, 2000, p.5, quoted in Islam and Chowdhury, 2009).
16 The data presented in Figure 5.4 are based on figures from 25 to 37 countries.
17 There is a sizeable literature on the determinants of diversification and on how diversification improves the capabilities of households and individuals to improve livelihood security. For a good review, see Ellis (1998).

Bibliography

Alwang, J., P.B. Siegel and S.L. Jorgensen (2001): "Vulnerability: A View from Different Disciplines". Social Protection Discussion Paper Series No. 115, Social Protection Unit, Human Development Network, World Bank, Washington, D.C.

Asian Development Bank (2002): *Handbook of Integrated Risk Analysis in the Economic Analysis of Projects*. ADB, Manila.

Betcherman, Gordon and Rizwanul Islam (eds.) (2001): *East Asian Labour Markets and the Economic Crisis: Impacts, Responses and Lessons*. World Bank and International Labour Organization, Washington, D.C. and Geneva.

Briguglio, Lino, G. Cordina, Nadia Fargugia and Stephanie Vella (2009, September): "Economic Vulnerability and Resilience: Concepts and Measurements", *Oxford Development Studies*, Vol. 37, No. 3, pp. 229–247.

Cafiero, C. and R. Vakis (2006): "Risk and Vulnerability Considerations in Poverty Analysis: Recent Advances and Future Directions". Social Protection Discussion Paper No. 0610, World Bank, Washington, D.C.

Chambers, R. (1989): "Editorial Introduction: Vulnerability: Coping and Policy", *IDS Bulletin*, Vol. 20, No. 2, pp. 1–7.

Chaudhury, S. (2003, June): *Assessing Vulnerability to Poverty: Concepts, Empirical Methods and Illustrative Examples*. Department of Economics, Columbia University, New York.

Dercon, S. (2001): "Vulnerability to Poverty: A Framework for Analysis". Paper prepared for DFID. www.economics.ox.ac.uk/members/stefan-dercon/ (Accessed on October 2001).

——— (2002): "Income Risk, Coping Strategies and Safety Nets", *The World Bank Research Observer*, Vol. 17, No. 2, pp. 141–166.

——— (2009): "Risk, Poverty and Human Development: What Do We Know and What Do We Need to Know?" in Fuentes-Nieva, Ricardo and Papa A. Seck (eds.): *Risk, Shocks and Human Development: On the Brink*. Palgrave Macmillan, New York.

Dhanani, S. (2000): Indonesia: Strategy for Manufacturing Competitiveness. UNIDO, Jakarta. Quoted in Islam and Chowdhury.

Dhanani, S. and I. Islam (2002): "Poverty, Vulnerability and Social Protection in a Period of Crisis: The Case of Indonesia", *World Development*, Vol. 30, No. 7, pp. 1211–1231.

Ellis, Frank (1998, October): "Household Strategies and Rural Livelihood Diversification", *The Journal of Development Studies*, Vol. 35, No. 1, pp. 1–38.

Fallon, Peter R. and Robert E.B. Lucas (2002): "The Impact of Financial Crises on Labor Markets, Household Incomes, and Poverty: A Review of Evidence", *The World Bank Research Observer*, Vol. 17, No. 1, pp. 21–45.

Fields, Gary S. (1994): *Changing Labor Market Conditions and Economic Development in Hong Kong, the Republic of Korea, Singapore, and Taiwan, China*. The International Bank for Reconstruction and Development/World Bank, Washington, D.C.

Groshen, Erica L. and Simon Potter (2003): "Has Structural Change Contributed to a Jobless Recovery?" *Current Issues in Economics and Finance*, Vol. 9, No. 8, pp. 1–7.

Huynh, Phu, Steven Kapsos, Kee Byom Kim and Gyorgy Sziraczky (2010): *Impact of the Current Global Economic Crisis on Asia's Labour Market*. Asian Development Bank Institute Working Paper, Tokyo.

International Labour Office (ILO) (1999): *Indonesia: Strategies for Employment-Led Recovery and Reconstruction*. Report of the Employment Strategy Mission, ILO, Jakarta, 26 April to 7 May 1999.

——— (2004): *Economic Security for a Better World*. ILO, Geneva.

——— (2009): *The Financial and Economic Crisis: A Decent Work Response*. ILO, Geneva.

International Monetary Fund (2010, April): "Unemployment Dynamics During Recessions and Recoveries: Okun's Law and Beyond" in IMF (ed.): *World Economic Outlook Rebalancing Growth*. IMF, Washington, D.C.

Islam, Iyanatul and Anis Chowdhury (2009): *Growth, Employment and Poverty Reduction: The Case Study of Indonesia*. ILO, Geneva.

Islam, Iyanatul and Sher Verick (eds.) (2011): *From the Great Recession to Labour Market Recovery: Issues, Evidence and Policy Options*. ILO and Palgrave Macmillan, Geneva and London.

Islam, Rizwanul (2011): "The Employment Challenge in Developing Countries during Economic Downturn and Recovery" in Islam, I. and S. Verick (eds.) (2011).

Islam, Rizwanul, Gopal Bhattacharya, Shafiq Dhanani, Max Iacono, Farhad Mehran, Swapna Mukhopadhyay and Phan Thuy (2001): "The Economic Crisis: Labour Market Challenges and Policies in Indonesia" in Betcherman, G. and R. Islam (eds.) (2001).

Kang, Soon-Hie, Jaeho Keum, Dong-Heon Kim and Donggyun Shin (2001): "Korea: Labor Market Outcomes and Policy Responses after the Crisis" in Betcherman, G. and R. Islam (eds.): *East Asian Labour Markets and the Economic Crisis: Impacts, Responses and Lessons*. World Bank and International Labour Office, Washington, D.C. and Geneva.

Lee, Eddy (1998): *The Asian Financial Crisis: The Challenge for Social Policy*. ILO, Geneva.

Lewis, W.A. (1954): "Economic Development with Unlimited Supplies of Labour", *Manchester School of Economic and Social Studies*, Vol. 22, No. 2, pp. 139–191.

Lignon, E. and L. Schechter (2003): "Measuring Vulnerability", *The Economic Journal*, Vol. 113, No. 186, pp. C95–C102.

Lustig, Nora (2000): "Crises and the Poor: Socially Responsible Macroeconomics", *Economía: The Journal of the Latin America and Caribbean Economic Association*, Vol. 1, No. 1, pp. 1–30.

Manning, Chris (2000, April): "Labour Market Adjustment to Indonesia's Economic Crisis: Context, Trends and Implications", *Bulletin of Indonesian Economic Studies*, Vol. 36 No. 1, pp. 105–136.

McKenzie, D.J. (2004): "Aggregate Shocks and Urban Labor Market Responses: Evidence from Argentina's Financial Crisis", *Economic Development and Cultural Change*, Vol. 52, No. 4, pp. 719–758.

Naudé, Wim, A.U. Santos-Paulino and Mark McGillivray (2009, September): "Measuring Vulnerability: An Overview and Introduction", *Oxford Development Studies*, Vol. 37, No. 3, pp. 183–191.

Okun, Arthur (1962): "Potential GNP: Its Measurement and Significance", in *Proceedings of the Business and Economic Statistics Section of the American Statistical Association*. American Statistical Association, Alexandra, VA, pp. 89–104.

Verick, S. (2010): "Unravelling the Impact of the Global Financial Crisis on the South African Labour Market", Employment Working Paper No. 48. ILO, Geneva.

Verick, Sher and Iyanatul Islam (2010): "The Great Recession of 2008–2009: Causes, Consequences and Policy Responses", IZA DP No. 4934, Institute for the Study of Labour, Bonn.

World Bank (2009): *The Global Economic Crisis: Assessing Vulnerability with a Poverty Lens*. PREM, World Bank, Washington, D.C.

Zhang, Y. and G. Wan (2009, September): "How Precisely Can We Estimate Vulnerability to Poverty?" *Oxford Development Studies*, Vol. 37, No. 3, pp. 277–287.

6 Has employment-intensive growth become history?[1]

Introduction

In Chapter 2, reference was made to models of economic development in dual economies (e.g., Lewis, 1954; Ranis and Fei, 1961) that describe economic development in countries with surplus labour as a process of economic transformation towards modern sectors and the transfer of surplus labour from traditional sectors to modern sectors until such surplus is exhausted and real wages start rising. Indeed, development in several countries of East Asia (viz., Republic of Korea, Taiwan-China, Hong Kong, and Singapore) during the 1970s and 1980s followed that general pattern. A number of the countries of South East Asia, especially Malaysia and Thailand, and to a lesser extent, Indonesia and the Philippines, were also making good progress in their journey towards the so-called "Lewis turning point" – at least until the time they were hit by the economic crisis during 1997–98.

The basic characteristics of the so-called East Asian model include export-oriented industrialization based on their abundant and cheap labour, high rate of investment – including in human capital, and flexible labour market. It has often been argued that flexibility in the labour market helped investment, economic growth, and expansion of employment.[2] Rapid economic growth of an employment-intensive nature, in turn, led to impressive rates of poverty reduction.

The model of economic development described above became so influential that it was widely regarded as something to be emulated by other developing countries. However, as early as in the eighties, questions were raised about the difficulty of replicating some of the initial conditions of success and the extent to which such a model could be emulated by other countries (Lee, 1981). Nearly four decades have passed since then. There are many countries in the developing world which are still characterized by surplus labour and are at various stages of development. They are often advised to pursue open (or export-oriented) economic and trade-policies – the expectation being that such strategies would enable them to achieve development, absorb their surplus labour, and reduce poverty.

The empirical analysis presented in Chapters 2 and 4 has shown that the countries of South Asia have not been able to attain the same degree of success attained by countries of ESEA in terms of the level or pattern of growth required for absorbing surplus labour and reaching the Lewis turning point. And that was despite their shift from inward-looking economic policies towards outward-looking and export-oriented policies. Such experiences, in turn, raise the question whether a repeat of the type of employment-intensive economic growth through industrialization achieved by the countries of ESEA is at all possible. This question becomes even more pertinent in the context of two recent strands of discussions. The first concerns the possibility of premature de-industrialization while the second is a concern arising out of the availability of new technology that is regarded as the hallmark of the fourth industrial revolution. If de-industrialization starts before a country's economy has absorbed all its surplus labour, the task of further labour absorption would become correspondingly difficult. Likewise, a premature spread of new labour-saving technologies may make it difficult to attain the Lewis turning point.

The purpose of the present chapter is to address the two issues mentioned above. It starts with a brief outline of the notion of employment-intensive growth and the role of industrialization in achieving such growth. That is followed by a recapitulation of the East Asian experience from the perspective of the employment intensity of economic growth that was achieved. Then the issues of de-industrialization and of new technology acting as a brake on employment growth are examined with particular focus on countries of South Asia. The concluding section points out the difficulties faced by contemporary developing countries of Asia in achieving development and employment through labour-intensive industrialization.

Employment-intensive growth and industrialization

Elasticity of employment growth with respect to output growth can provide a summary indicator of employment intensity of economic growth, and it can be used at the level of an economy as well as at the sectoral level. It needs to be noted, however, that employment elasticity is the mirror image of labour productivity, and hence the relationship between the two is likely to be negative. So, if the goal is to improve labour productivity alongside high economic growth, a decline in the employment intensity of economic growth – by the measure of employment elasticity – may be the result.

But employment growth may result not only through high elasticity of employment with respect to output but also through high output growth – as long as the effect of the latter can outweigh any negative effect of a decline in employment elasticity. This is demonstrated below by using a procedure outlined by Osmani (2010). The method involves splitting employment growth into two components: the "output effect" and the "elasticity effect". The former refers to

> the amount by which the rate of employment growth changes from one
> period to the next in response to the change in the rate of output growth,
> assuming the elasticity of employment with respect to output to remain

constant. The elasticity effect is defined as the amount by which the rate of employment growth changes from one period to the next in response to change in the elasticity of employment, assuming the rate of growth of output to remain the same.

(Osmani, 2010, p.301)

The decomposition equation[3] showing the change in employment growth between two periods is:

$$E_2 - E_1 = \eta_2(Y_2 - Y_1) + Y_1(\eta_2 - \eta_1)$$

E_1 and E_2 represent employment growth in periods 1 and 2, respectively, Y_1 and Y_2 represent output growth in periods 1 and 2, respectively, and η_1 and η_2 represent elasticity of employment with respect to output in periods 1 and 2, respectively.

The first part of the right-hand side of the above equation shows how much of the employment growth can be said to be due to output growth with employment elasticity remaining unchanged at η_2. And the second part represents the part of employment growth that is due to a change in employment elasticity if output growth remains unchanged at Y_1.

If both the output and elasticity effects on employment are taken into consideration, employment-intensive growth can be looked at in a broader perspective where both output growth and the pattern of growth would play a role. Consider the rate of growth first. By referring to Kaldor's analysis of economic growth, the role of manufacturing in attaining growth has already been mentioned in Chapter 2. As for employment, there are industries which, by their nature, are labour-intensive, and when their weight in the total manufacturing sector is high, the elasticity of employment in the sector can also be expected to be higher than in agriculture. With higher output growth and employment elasticity, the rate of growth of employment in manufacturing is also likely to be higher than in agriculture. In fact, at some stage of development, especially when surplus labour is exhausted, agriculture may experience negative employment growth. Hence, manufacturing industries can play an important role in attaining employment-intensive growth – especially during the early stages of economic growth.

However, the manufacturing sector may fail to perform this role for at least two reasons. First, the sector as a whole may fail to grow at the required/expected rate due to a variety of reasons. When growth of output is low, the growth of employment can also be low, unless growth is associated with low productivity – in which case growth will be inefficient. Second, even with high growth, the manufacturing sector may fail to generate employment at the required rate if the composition of the manufacturing sector is such that sectors with low labour intensity assume higher weights. In such a situation, elasticity of employment in the sector will be low, and the output effect may not be strong enough to generate a decent growth of employment.

How the two forces relevant for employment growth are working in countries of South Asia are illustrated below with examples from Bangladesh and India. Table 6.1 presents data on output growth and employment elasticity in the manufacturing sector of Bangladesh for different sub-periods during 1999–2000 to 2015–16.

Based on data presented in Table 6.1, the output effect on the difference in employment growth – η_2 ($Y_2 - Y_1$) – between the first and third periods works out to be 1.62 per cent, while the elasticity effect works out to be −2.34 per cent. Thus, the net effect on employment growth works out to be −0.72 per cent. This implies that the negative elasticity effect was so large that the positive output effect could not neutralize its effect to produce a positive change in employment growth. In reality, growth of employment in manufacturing declined from 5.82 per cent per annum during the first period to 5.12 per cent during the third period.

Table 6.2 presents data on output growth and employment elasticity for the manufacturing sector of India.

In this case, the output effect on the difference in employment growth between the first and second periods works out to be 0.53 per cent, while the elasticity effect works out to be −1.34 per cent. Thus, the net effect on employment growth works out to be −0.81 per cent. Clearly, the negative elasticity effect was so large that even a substantial increase in output growth was not sufficient to produce a positive change in employment growth. Growth of employment in manufacturing declined from 2 per cent per annum during the first period to 1.5 per cent during the second period.

Table 6.1 Bangladesh: Annual Growth of Output and Employment Elasticity in Manufacturing

	1999–2000 to 2005–06	2005–06 to 2010	2010 to 2015–16
Growth of output (%)	7.48	7.52	10.95
Elasticity of employment with respect to output	0.7807	0.8697	0.4676

Source: Islam (2017a).

Table 6.2 India: Annual Growth of Output and Employment Elasticity in Manufacturing

	1983/84 to 1993/94	2004/05 to 2011/12
Output growth (%)	4.8	8.9
Elasticity of employment with respect to output	0.41	0.13

Source: Institute for Human Development (2014).

The upshot of the two illustrations provided above is that unless output growth is very high in manufacturing, its positive effect on employment growth may not be adequate to counteract any negative effect of a decline in employment elasticity. In such a situation, the overall employment growth in the sector is likely to decline. And unless other sectors, e.g., services are characterized by high employment growth, the overall employment growth in the economy may run short of what is required for absorbing surplus labour.

Labour-intensive industrialization and development in East and South East Asia: a recapitulation[4]

Amongst the late industrializers, four countries of East and South East Asia (henceforth referred to as ESEA), viz., Republic of Korea, Hong Kong, Singapore, and the Taiwan province of China (henceforth referred to as Taiwan), are regarded as having succeeded in achieving development through export-oriented industrialization. However, in terms of possible emulation by other developing countries, the latter three are often considered to be non-representative because of their small size and other special characteristics. Therefore, the present chapter will use the experience of Korea as a success story and see how far the other developing countries of Asia have been able to develop along the path trodden by that country.

On growth experience in the region as a whole, one would notice several features. First, Korea and some other countries of the ESEA region achieved high and sustained rate of economic growth over several decades (Korea starting in the 1960s and some others starting from the 1970s). The rate of economic growth (measured by annual compound rate of GDP growth) has been consistently higher in the ESEA countries compared to the South Asian countries (see Table 6.3).

The second and an important aspect of the growth experience (which also comes out of the data presented in Table 6.3) has been the high rate of growth of manufacturing industries, especially in Korea and also in some ESEA countries. Indeed, the elasticity of growth of manufacturing with respect to overall GDP growth was over 2 in Korea in the 1960s and dropped to just below 2 (1.9, to be precise) during 1970–80. It dropped to below 1.5 only during the 1980s. In Malaysia also, the elasticity of manufacturing output growth with respect to overall GDP growth has been between 1.5 and 2 for almost three decades (during 1970–96). Indonesia and Thailand also had similar experience. On the other hand, this figure has been in the range of 1.3–1.4 in India and lower in Pakistan. In Bangladesh and Sri Lanka, there has been a considerable degree of fluctuation in the elasticity of manufacturing growth with respect to GDP growth. On the whole, it is quite clear that not only has overall economic growth been higher in Korea and a few other countries of ESEA (Philippines being an exception) than in South Asia, the manufacturing sector has been the major (and a more important) driver of growth in the former. And that enabled Korea (and other countries of

Table 6.3 Growth Rate of GDP and Manufacturing Output in Selected Countries of Asia (Annual Compound Rate of Growth in Percentage)

Country	1960–70			1970–80			1980–90			1990–96			2000–17		
	GDP	Man	Em	GDP	Man	Em	GDP	Man	Em	GDP	Man	Em	GDP	Man	Em
Bangladesh	n.a.	n.a.	n.a.	2.3	5.1	2.2	4.3	3.0	01.4	4.3	7.3	1.7	6.0	8.7	1.5
Cambodia	n.a.	n.a.	n.a.	n.a.	n.a.	n.a.	n.a.	n.a.	n.a.	6.5	7.8	1.2	7.5	9.5	1.3
China	n.a.	n.a.	n.a.	5.5	10.8	1.96	10.2	11.1	1.1	12.3	17.2	1.4	9.7	n.a.	n.a.
India	3.6	4.8	1.3	3.4	4.6	1.4	5.8	7.4	1.3	5.8	7.5	1.3	7.5	8.3	1.1
Indonesia	3.5	3.3	0.9	7.2	14.0	1.9	6.1	12.8	2.1	7.7	11.1	1.4	5.5	4.6	0.8
Republic of Korea	8.5	17.2	2.02	10.1	17.7	1.8	8.9	12.1	1.4	7.3	7.9	1.1	3.8	5.5	1.5
Malaysia	6.9	n.a.	n.a.	7.9	11.7	1.5	5.3	9.3	1.8	8.7	13.2	1.5	4.9	4.2	0.9
Nepal	n.a.	n.a.	n.a.	2.0	n.a.	n.a.	4.6	9.3	2.0	5.1	12.0	2.4	4.1	1.7	0.4
Pakistan	6.7	9.4	1.4	4.9	5.4	1.1	6.3	7.7	1.2	4.6	5.5	1.2	4.2	5.4	1.3
Philippines	5.1	6.7	1.3	6.0	6.1	1.0	1.0	0.2	0.2	2.9	2.6	0.9	5.3	4.9	0.9
Sri Lanka	4.6	6.3	1.4	4.1	1.9	0.5	4.0	6.3	1.6	4.8	8.8	1.8	5.9	5.5	0.9
Thailand	8.2	11.0	1.3	7.1	10.5	1.5	7.6	9.5	1.3	8.3	10.7	1.3	3.9	3.7	0.95
Vietnam	n.a.	n.a.	n.a.	n.a.	n.a.	n.a.	4.6	n.a.	n.a.	8.5	n.a.	n.a.	6.3	7.2	1.1

Sources: World Bank, World Development Indicators (1998, 2004, 2007, 2018), available at: http://data.worldbank.org/products/wdi and http://wdi.worldbank.org/table/4.1; World Bank, World Development Reports (1998 and 1999).

Notes: (i) Man = manufacturing output; Em = elasticity of manufacturing growth with respect to GDP growth. n.a. denotes "not available".
(ii) A number of countries of East and South East Asia suffered from the Asian economic crisis of 1997–98 and its aftermath. As the figures for 1997–99 are affected by sharp declines in overall economic growth as well as export growth, those years have been excluded from this table.

ESEA in varying degrees) to achieve structural change in their economies of a kind that is in line with the Lewis model. Of course, not all countries of ESEA succeeded in achieving such transformation, especially of their labour markets – an issue to which we shall turn in the next section.

The third important aspect of economic growth in the countries of ESEA compared to South Asia has been the superior export performance of the former and greater openness of their economies (Lee, 1981; World Bank, 1993). Indeed, the share of exports in total GDP has been consistently much higher in the countries of ESEA compared to those in South Asia. Even after the economic reforms introduced in the 1980s and the 1990s and the gradual opening up of these economies, the share of exports in GDP in Bangladesh, India, and Pakistan has remained below 25 per cent, whereas it has ranged between 40 and 130 per cent in the countries of ESEA (Islam, 2003). More important from the point of view of industrialization, the growth rate of manufacturing exports has been much higher in the countries of ESEA compared to South Asia (Lee, 1981; Table 6.4 below).

From the point of view of labour–intensive industrialization, it is important to look at the composition of industrial exports. And in that regard, the experience of Korea in particular is noteworthy. During the 1960s (i.e., the early stages of export-led development) the share of "light industries" in manufactured exports remained at high levels – ranging from 83 per cent in 1964 to 89 per cent in 1968. Only in the 1970s, this share started declining and went down to 60 per cent in 1978 (Park, 1981).[5] Between 1960 and 1970, direct employment in exports in Korea increased by more than 18 times, or at an average annual rate of 34 per cent. As a result, the share of export industries in total employment expanded from 5 to 22.5 per cent during the same period (Hsia, 1981). In fact, the degree of capital intensity (measured by capital-labour ratio) of Korean manufacturing declined during the 1960s till about the early 1970s (Little, 1981).[6] Capital intensity of Korean manufacturing and of exports in particular started rising only in the early 1970s.

The labour–intensive character of Korea's early stages of industrialization is also illustrated by the high employment intensity of growth in the manufacturing sector. While estimates for the 1960s is difficult to come by, according to one estimate (Khan, 2006), the elasticity of employment with respect to output growth in manufacturing was 0.69 during the 1970s, and declined to 0.49 during the 1980s. It is thus clear that even after almost a decade of industrialization with high rates of output growth, the manufacturing sector in Korea remained highly employment-friendly. And there was a decline in the elasticity of employment only after surplus labour was exhausted. It should be added here that with an employment elasticity of 0.69, there was still considerable scope for labour productivity to improve, and that is what happened in reality. The high rate of growth-induced expansion in employment was accompanied by high growth in productivity as well as earnings of workers (Storm and Naastepad, 2005; Khan, 2006).

Table 6.4 Growth of Total Exports and Manufactured Exports of Selected Countries of Asia (Annual Compound Rate of Growth in Percentage)

Country	1980–90		1990–96		2000–05		2005–14	
	Total Exports	Manufactured Exports	Total Exports	Manufactured Exports	Total Exports	Manufactured Exports	Total Exports (2000–17)	Manufactured Exports (2005–14)
Bangladesh	7.6	8.4	12.7	n.a.	8.6	7.2	13.4	14.1
Cambodia	n.a.	n.a.	n.a.	n.a.	6.7	n.a.	12.9	14.4
China	11.0	18.0	14.3	18.7	26.7	26.2	n.a.	13.6
India	6.5	10.0	7.0	10.5	19.2	14.8	10.9	12.9
Indonesia	2.8	35.2	21.3	19.0	7.1	2.7	6.1	6.5
Republic of Korea	12.8	14.5	7.4	11.1	12.9	10.5	8.2	7.5
Malaysia	10.3	18.0	17.8	28.9	8.8	6.1	3.2	3.5
Nepal	4.5	17.1	22.1	19.8	1.1	0.3	0.9	0.5
Pakistan	9.0	11.8	8.8	12.1	12.7	10.9	3.0	3.9
Philippines	2.5	9.7	10.2	21.2	1.7	0.1	5.5	3.2
Sri Lanka	6.8	18.7	17.0	21.0	4.1	2.9	3.4	7.0
Thailand	13.2	23.2	21.6	18.5	11.1	10.1	5.7	8.0
Vietnam	n.a.	n.a.	n.a.	n.a.	17.7	n.a.	12.5	23.5

Sources: (i) World Bank: World Development Report (various issues including 1992, 1995, 1997, 1999/2000); (ii) World Bank: WDI, 1997, 2002, 2007, and 2018; (iii) UNCTAD (2006, 2015).

Notes: (i) A number of countries of East and South East Asia suffered from the Asian economic crisis of 1997–98 and its aftermath. As the figures for 1997–99 are affected by sharp declines in overall economic growth as well as export growth, those years have been excluded from this table.
(ii) The total export growth figures for 1990–96 are for 1990–95 as available in WDI 1997.
(iii) Manufactured export growth figures have been calculated from UNCTAD data available in various issues of UNCTAD Handbook of Statistics, including UNCTAD (2006, 2015).

Is South Asia facing the possibility of premature de-industrialization?

In the course of the discussion of structural transformation in Chapter 2, reference has been made to the phenomenon of de-industrialization – a term that is used to describe the decline of the share of manufacturing in the total output and employment of an economy.[7] In the analysis and experience of economic growth, this was considered normal for an economy as it attained a certain level of income. For example, in the UK and the USA, the share of manufacturing employment rose to 35 and 36 per cent, respectively, before it started to decline. The level of per capita income at which it happened in those countries as well as in some other developed countries of Europe varied between US$9,000 and US$11,000 (at 1990 prices).

In contrast with de-industrialization experienced by developed countries, some developing countries are facing it at a much lower level of development – a phenomenon that is being referred to as "premature de-industrialization".[8] While there may be different explanations for this in different countries, the impact, especially on the generation of productive employment through structural transformation of the economy is likely to be negative. It is, therefore, important to see whether developing countries, especially those with surplus labour and have not yet succeeded in attaining the Lewis turning point are facing the danger of this happening. It is in that context that the question becomes particularly important for the countries South Asia.

A number of studies (e.g., Tregenna, 2011; Rodrik, 2013) point out that there are developing countries where de-industrialization started much below the levels of per capita income at which this happened in the developed countries. Rodrik (2013) mentions India alongside Brazil and China among countries that have already experienced such premature de-industrialization. On India, he says:

> Manufacturing employment there peaked at a meager 13% in 2002, and has since trended down.

On the other hand, Tregenna (2011) mentions India alongside Bolivia, Indonesia, Malaysia, and Thailand as five countries (out of 28 countries included in the study) where the share of manufacturing in total employment did not decline. In fact, data on the share of manufacturing in total employment presented in Table 6.5 below show that between 1993–94 and 2004–05, it increased a bit (from 10.5 per cent to 12 per cent). Furthermore, between 2004–05 and 2011–12, the share increased to 12.9 per cent. The share of manufacturing in India's GDP also shows a small increase during 2000–14 – from 15 to 17 per cent. While these figures do not signal a spectacular increase in the share of manufacturing either in employment or output, they do not warrant the conclusion that India has already experienced premature de-industrialization.

Table 6.5 Share of Manufacturing in GDP and Total Employment in Selected Countries of South Asia

Country	Share in GDP (%)	Share in Total Employment (%)
Bangladesh	15 (2000)	9.5 (1999–2000)
	17 (2014)	11.0 (2005–06)
		12.5 (2010)
		14.4 (2016–17)
India	15 (2000)	10.5 (1993–94)
	17 (2014)	12.0 (2004–05)
		12.9 (2011–12)
Nepal	9 (2000)	5.8 (1998–99)
	6 (2014)	6.6 (2008–09)
Pakistan	15 (2000)	13.8 (2005–06)
	14 (2014)	13.7 (2010–11)
		15.3 (2014–15)
Sri Lanka	17 (2000)	24.1[a] (2004)
	18 (2014)	24.0[a] (2011)

Sources: Data on share in GDP are from World Bank, World Development Indicators. http://data.worldbank.org/products/wdi and http://wdi.worldbank.org/table/4.2.

Notes: Data on share in employment are from (i) Bangladesh: Bangladesh Bureau of Statistics: Labour Force Survey, various years; (ii) India: IHD (2014); (iii) Nepal: GON (2009); (iv) Pakistan: Amjad and Yusuf (2014); and Government of Pakistan (2016); (v): Sri Lanka: Department of Census and Statistics (2013, 2017).

a These figures are for "Industry" not manufacturing. The figures within parentheses refer to the year of the data.

Out of the other countries of South Asia, Bangladesh witnessed a rise in the share of manufacturing in both GDP and employment. During 2000–14, the rise in the share of GDP was small. But the rise in the share of employment during 1999–2000 to 2016–17 was substantial – from 9.5 per cent to 14.4 per cent. The country has been able to attain this mainly through high growth one labour-intensive export-oriented industry, viz., ready-made garments.[9]

The situation in the other countries of South Asia, especially in Nepal and Pakistan is less clear with respect to industrialization. In Nepal, the share of the sector in GDP declined (2000–14) while that in employment increased slightly (1998–99 to 2008–09). In Pakistan, the share in GDP declined while that in employment remained virtually unchanged up to 2010–11. However, data from the labour force survey of 2014–15 reported in Pakistan Economic Survey 2015–16 (Government of Pakistan, 2016) show that the share rose to 15.33 per cent. In Sri Lanka, the share of the sector in GDP increased slightly – from 17 to 18 per cent. But in the absence of data for manufacturing employment (it's available for industry which is broader than manufacturing), nothing can be said what has happened to its share in employment.

Further light on the question of de-industrialization can be thrown by data on growth of employment in the manufacturing sector (Table 6.6). A couple of points may be noted on the basis of this data. First, in all the four countries for which data are available for two periods, there has been a decline in

Table 6.6 Growth of Manufacturing Employment in
Selected Countries of South Asia

Country	Annual Growth of Manufacturing Employment (%)
Bangladesh	
1999–2000 to 2005–06	5.82
2005–06 to 2010	6.34
2010 to 2016–17	5.12
India	
1993–94 to 2004–05	3.2
2004–05 to 2011–12	1.5
Nepal	
1998–99 to 2008–09	3.42
Pakistan	
2001–02 to 2005–06	3.93
2005–06 to 2011–12	1.00
Sri Lanka	
1999–2000 to 2005–06	4.41
2005–06 to 2014–15	3.46

Sources: (i) Bangladesh: Bangladesh Bureau of Statistics: Labour Force Survey, various years; (ii) India: IHD (2014); (iii) Nepal: GON (2009); (iv) Pakistan: Amjad and Yusuf (2014); (v): Sri Lanka: Department of Census and Statistics (2013, 2017).

the rate of employment growth in the sector. Second, the decline has been particularly sharp in the case of India and Pakistan. And during the 2000s, the rate of growth of employment in both those countries has been very low −1.5 and 1 per cent respectively. In Bangladesh also, there has been a decline, although the extent has not been so much. But even in this case, the decline has been quite sharp in recent years – to 2.33 per cent between 2015–16 and 2016–17 compared to the annual average of 5.12 during the previous five years.

What can be said to conclude this discussion on the danger of premature de-industrialization in the countries of South Asia? If the shares in GDP and employment are used as indicators, India and Bangladesh clearly have not entered the phase of de-industrialization. But the same cannot be said so confidently about Nepal, Pakistan, and Sri Lanka. This, however, should not be taken to imply that Bangladesh and India are firmly positioned on the path of industrialization, and manufacturing will be able to perform the role of absorbing the surplus labour in those countries. The share of the sector in total employment was way below that attained by the peak share of 23 per cent attained by both Republic of Korea and Malaysia (both in 2000).

In India, the share rose from 10.5 per cent to 12.9 per cent over a 15-year period. In Bangladesh, the rise was from 9.5 per cent to 14.4 per cent over a 17-year period. Whether the figures in these countries will ever cross the 20 per cent mark, and if so, when, remain open questions. Given the pace and pattern of industrialization in the countries of South Asia, even if they are not showing signs of de-industrialization in a technical sense (i.e., decline in the share of manufacturing in GDP and employment), they may remain prone to this possibility. And this possibility is becoming increasingly real with the availability of labour-saving technologies associated with the fourth industrial revolution – an issue to which we now turn.

Technological change, automation, and implications for employment in developing countries

If one looks at the history of evolution of human society, one would note that technological progress has been a continuous process, and such progress has been associated with automation of various degrees and kinds. That, in turn, had significant implications for employment and the world of work. If the issue of development is looked at from a longer-term perspective, it would be necessary to take this into account and see how the employment situation in developing countries may be influenced by technological changes that are likely to take place.

The world is currently witnessing the fourth industrial revolution, the basic characteristics of which include the use of robots, artificial intelligence, nanotechnology, and biotechnology. A common perception in that respect is that this is going to threaten employment of human beings. Robots are making inroads even in countries that are still characterized by the existence of surplus labour. And if one takes a long-term perspective of several decades from now, one could imagine the following scenarios: (i) in factories producing textiles, garments, shoes, etc., instead of human beings, robots are performing major tasks; (ii) instead of the numerous retail stores of different types, there are only huge stores where robots arrange merchandise on shelves, customers pick up their needed items and go out through automated checkout points; (iii) online retailers have replaced most of the retail stores and their warehouses are run primarily by robots, and so on.

If the above scenario becomes a reality even before millions of underemployed workers find good jobs characterized by high productivity and incomes, there will be serious problems of mass unemployment and underemployment. And it would be logical for policymakers to take steps to prevent such a scenario. But how realistic would it be to paint such a scenario for the future – even if one considers a period of several decades?

This question is not new to human society; it dates back to the early nineteenth century when the so-called Luddites (in Britain) had attacked weaving machines because they were thought to be causing destruction of jobs in textile factories. And the question has resurfaced in the wake of several reports published in 2017 by influential institutions including renowned private companies like McKinsey (2017), PWC (2017), and international agencies like the United Nations (UN–DESA, 2017) and the World Bank (Raja and Christiaensen, 2017). In the context of the Fourth Industrial Revolution currently under way, these reports analyze activities and occupations that are "automatable" and develop scenarios of job losses if such automation does indeed take place. While most of these reports focus mainly on developed countries, the analysis is not limited to them.[10] As if to repeat the attack of Luddites to destroy weaving machines, measures like taxing robots are being proposed in developed countries.[11]

If the concern can be so serious in developed countries, for countries like Bangladesh and India, a development of the kind mentioned above can really spell doom. Shouldn't policy discourse take a serious view of it? However, before starting with a pessimistic and doomsday scenario, it is necessary to take a careful look at what one is talking about. In doing so, one should also distinguish between prospects that are likely to be faced by countries at different stages of development. At the risk of saying the obvious, the concern cannot be the same in the USA, the UK, China, Vietnam, and Bangladesh.

What does the history of automation tell us?

It may be useful to refresh our memory with the history of technological progress vis-à-vis employment, and a few facts may be worth recounting in that regard. First, automation during the first industrial revolution was associated with an increase in jobs – not decline. Between the early nineteenth and early twentieth century, the number of textile jobs increased (Bessen, 2017). Second, although jobs were lost in the steel and textile industries in countries like the UK and the USA during the twentieth century, it's important to understand whether that was due to automation or globalization leading to these industries moving offshore. Third, the spread of IT in recent decades has been associated with a rise in employment (Bessen, 2017). Except during economic downturns, the US economy has not faced a problem of shortage of jobs. Fourth, even in recent years, automation has not been associated with a decline in overall employment. The example of Amazon is often cited in this context where there has been a sharp increase in the number of robots used, but hiring of workers has also continued (Kessler, 2017). Fifth, if one takes a longer-term view, one would see that fears of mass unemployment have, by and large, been proven unfounded. Employment-population ratio has increased during the twentieth century (UN–DESA, 2017).[12]

So, what happens when technological progress takes place and activities and occupations are automated? As Acemoglu and Restrepo (2016) have pointed out, there can be two types of technological changes: "automating technology" that can replace labour, and "labour augmenting technology" that can, by creating new tasks, create new jobs. For example, automation may be associated with new jobs in the spheres of supervision, repair, and maintenance. The net impact on employment would depend on the relative strength and magnitude of the two effects.[13]

Yes, the first and immediate impact may be the loss of jobs as machines may indeed replace some human jobs. But in addition to this immediate impact, technological progress leads to changes that may have a positive effect on employment. For example, one positive impact is often a rise in productivity leading to a decline in prices and a rise in the demand for products. That, in turn, leads to growth of output and employment.

Second, technology replaces certain tasks rather than complete occupations. Of course, new jobs that are created are likely to require different types and levels of education and skills compared to the jobs that may have been lost. We shall get back to this issue in a moment.

Third, automation, by raising the productivity of workers, creates a necessary condition for wage increases. Moreover, by reducing the drudgery of manual jobs, machines may lead to improvement in the quality of jobs.

What is also important to note is that only in a small proportion of occupations, jobs are completely automated. Machines often work together with human beings – thus creating positive complementarity and raising productivity.

Of course, there would be winners and losers as automation creates differentiation in the labour markets with implications for relative wages and incomes. While some jobs will be lost, new job opportunities will be created in sectors (e. g., services) and occupations that are difficult to automate. So, it is difficult to predict whether the net impact on employment will be positive or negative. The nature of jobs is likely to change with greater demand for workers with higher levels of education and skills, thus creating conditions for accelerated wage increases in certain jobs. And that can unleash forces for a rise in inequality in income.

Regarding individual workers, it is the less educated who are likely to be more affected and those with higher and more specialized education who are likely to gain. Public policy will have an important role to play in ensuring that the potential gains from automation are shared more widely and the brunt of the negative effects can be minimized.

Possible scenario for South Asia and policy implications

What kind of scenario can be expected for countries of South Asia if one takes a long-term perspective like the middle of this century? How likely is it that a doomsday scenario would become a reality? In addressing this question, it might be useful to refer to the so-called "flying geese model" of development where one lead goose is followed by a few more flying in formation, and comparative advantage in the production and export of labour-intensive industrial goods shifts from one group of countries to another. In the original version of the model, Japan was the lead goose who was followed by countries like South Korea, Taiwan, and Singapore in the second tier and with Malaysia, Indonesia, and Thailand completing the formation. That model could be extended to include China in the second tier and countries like Vietnam and Bangladesh following the third-tier countries.

The flying geese model mentioned above seems to have been reflected in the development pattern that unfolded in Asia and can be expected to characterize the sequence in which countries at different levels of development progress in their journey towards higher level of development. A moot question in the context of the debate on the impact of automation on employment in the countries of South Asia is whether the flying geese formation will be broken by the latest technological development. Can countries like China and Malaysia, for example, prevent their loss of comparative advantage in certain product lines by resorting to automation? If that happens, are countries of South Asia going to follow suit and adopt automation on a large scale in order to match the competitiveness of the geese flying ahead of them?

The Mckinsey report mentioned above does mention the possibility that emerging economies with younger population may have to worry about generating new jobs in an age of automation, and points out the possibility that automation could upend some prevailing models of development. This is because low-cost labour may lose some of its edge as an essential development tool for such economies.

While predicting the future is a tricky business, it may be worth noting a few points. First, even for developed countries, reports like the ones mentioned above express considerable degree of uncertainty. For example, the time frame in the McKinsey report is 2055, and it concedes that the kind of automation it is looking at could happen a decade earlier or a decade later than predicted by them. In fact, automation depends on a variety of factors – technical, economic, and social; and it is difficult to predict how the relevant factors will unfold in a particular country. But the past experience and the present situation of a country can provide useful insights.

A number of questions would be important. How feasible would automation be in the various sectors of the economy – present as well as those that are likely to grow? If technically feasible, would it be economically viable – especially in the context of the relative prices of the important factors of production? How would the acquisition of new technology be financed? What proportion of enterprises would have access to necessary finance?

Considering factors and questions mentioned above, it is possible to identify opportunities that countries of South Asia could have as well as concerns, threats, and challenges it could face. They are outlined in Table 6.7.

What could be said by way of conclusion? Although it is difficult to say anything firmly about a distant future, it would not be unrealistic to conclude that the concern about large-scale job losses arising out of automation

Table 6.7 Impact of Automation on Employment: Opportunities, Concerns, and Challenges

Opportunities	Dangers/Concerns	Challenges
• When surplus unskilled labour is exhausted, selective automation can help overcome the constraint created by shortage of labour. • New jobs, e.g., in supervision, repairs, and maintenance, can be associated with automation. • New technology, by raising overall productivity and efficiency, may make it possible to lower prices of products. That could result in a rise in demand, and hence in output and employment. • Increase in labour productivity can create a necessary condition for a rise in wages, which in turn could augment demand, output, and employment. • Automation can reduce drudgery of work in certain lines. • Automation can bring about positive change in the structure of the economy towards sectors and activities characterized by higher productivity and incomes.	• Ill-conceived policies like artificially lowering prices of machines through fiscal measures may lead to premature automation and thus to job losses even before surplus labour is exhausted. • By reducing costs, automation may give competitive edge to countries at higher levels of development – thus jeopardising the export-led development efforts of countries at lower levels of development. • Competition in the international market may tempt governments to adopt such policies mentioned above. • Competition may also lead enterprises who are capable of adopting automation to go for it – resulting in adverse effect on employment. • While demand for skilled workers increases, unskilled workers may face problems. This may lead to faster increases in wages of workers in the former category and accentuate the trend of rising income inequality.	• Designing appropriate macroeconomic policies taking due account of a country's economic and labour market situation. • Designing policies to ensure that automation does not lead to exclusion of certain enterprises. • Designing policies for education and skill development in a way that the country can adjust smoothly to new technologies.

Source: Author's elaboration.

is probably overblown. A good deal will depend on how policies are geared and the process is managed. A few points would be relevant in that context.

• Public policy, especially fiscal and trade-policies and legal and regulatory measures, can be used to steer the pace and direction of automation in such a way that its net benefits exceed costs associated with it. It would be particularly important to prevent premature automation and when appropriate, create an incentive structure to facilitate selective automation so that gains can be made in raising productivity.[14]

• Automation will of course be associated with changes in the type of jobs that the economy will have, and hence the education and skill development system of the country will face the challenge of adjusting to the changes. While the overall level of education of the workforce has to be raised, attention will need to be given to ensure that the type of education and skills imparted by the education system can meet the requirements of a knowledge economy.

There is a danger that the change in the nature of jobs and the education and skills that will be required for them will accentuate the degree of economic inequality. This is because automation will benefit workers with higher level skills with creativity and problem-solving ability. Access to higher education and skills needed in a knowledge economy is already skewed in favour of the upper-income groups. When access to the labour market and returns associated with different types of jobs will depend more and more on education and skills, inequality in the distribution of incomes is naturally going to rise. In order to prevent that possibility, the system of education and skill training will have to be more inclusive and broad-based.

Concluding observations

The major features of the experience of countries that were successful in achieving economic growth and the absorption of surplus labour included a combination of high rates of economic growth and high rates of growth of export-oriented labour-intensive manufacturing industries. It is by now well known that such success has remained limited to a small number of developing Asian countries. How does one explain this? One well-known answer was that the laggards had been pursuing inward-looking economic policies that constrained their growth prospects. However, this argument may no longer be as valid as it was during the nineteen sixties, seventies, and the early part of the eighties. Most countries of developing Asia have now switched over to more outward-looking strategies of development and have been undertaking market-oriented economic reforms. Some have also been able to narrow down the differences in the rate of economic growth. Among the countries of South Asia, India has achieved growth rates that are comparable to those achieved by the successful countries. Others like Bangladesh and Sri Lanka have also succeeded in getting out of the low growth regime. And yet, success in achieving the kind of industrialization and labour absorption seen in the pioneer countries has been elusive.

Not only has been the growth rate of manufacturing relative to GDP growth lower in the countries of South Asia, but they are also facing the possibility of premature de-industrialization. Although they have not experienced clear declines in indicators like the share of manufacturing in GDP and total employment, there have been substantial declines in the growth of manufacturing employment. With the share of employment stagnating at much lower levels than the peak shares attained historically by successful countries like Korea and Malaysia and growth rates of employment falling sharply, it does not look like that such success can be repeated.

In addition to lower rates of output growth and lower (and declining) employment elasticity, countries of South Asia – like other countries – are facing the prospect of automation in manufacturing that is associated with the fourth industrial revolution. Although the danger of employment declining due to automation is sometimes overblown, if the manufacturing sector does indeed embrace automation on a large scale, the ability of the sector to generate employment may decline further.

Difficulties in replicating some of the conditions of success (e.g., prior industrialization, role and ability of the State in administering complicated incentive schemes, and flexible labour markets) achieved by the front runners of labour-intensive and export-oriented industrialization were noted in some writings in the early 1980s. The possibility of late-starters facing a greater intensity of competition in the international market or in attracting foreign investment was also noted (Lee, 1981).

If emulation of success achieved by the front runners was already difficult in the eighties, it must have become much more so in more recent years. The global context for trade and industrialization has changed substantially in various respects. First, competition based on cheap labour has become much more intense with the emergence of new late-starters like Bangladesh, Cambodia, Laos, and Vietnam. In addition, there are large countries like China and India who not only have the advantage of cheap labour but also fulfil one of the basic preconditions for success, namely, a prior degree of industrialization. Given this scenario, the quest for productivity growth has resulted in a greater focus on technology (and hence, capital) than was the case with front runners like Korea and Taiwan. Instead of declining capital-labour ratio (Korea in the sixties) and the use of lower level technology including second-hand machines (e.g., in Taiwan), the recent experience has been one of capital deepening and continuous efforts to be at the frontier of technology. However, even the countries with a stronger initial industrial base have not been able to achieve the same level of elasticity of manufacturing output growth rate with respect to GDP growth as was achieved by Korea or Malaysia. Moreover, the degree of employment intensity has also been lower (and falling).

The second respect in which the global context has changed is the functioning of labour markets. What has been referred to as "superior labor market performance" in ESEA (World Bank, 1993, p. 242) basically refers to a situation in which there was labour repression either in the form of wage repression (euphemistically referred to as "wage restraint") or rights repression and absence of union power. In the current global context, both seem to have become more difficult – given greater union power and international pressure for compliance. If labour market flexibility implies labour repression of either kind, it is neither desirable nor feasible.

The overall policy environment may get further tilted in favour of excessive use of capital in situations where measures that are introduced in the name of creating incentives for investment result in artificially lowering the price of capital (India, for example). In the absence of any such incentives for the use of labour, the relative factor price gets distorted and results in excessive use of capital (either in the form of investments in capital-intensive products or technologies). Given the changed international context mentioned above and the kind of policy environment prevailing in the economies of late-starters in labour-intensive industrialization, it is not surprising to see a much lesser degree of success in such countries than in the front runners.

Notes

1 Parts of this chapter draws on Islam (2009a).
2 There is a large body of literature on the East Asian experience of economic development. Good accounts are provided by World Bank (1993), Lee (1981), and Storm and Naastepad (2005).
3 Osmani (2010) shows how this equation is derived.
4 This section draws on Islam (2009a).
5 There is a body of literature documenting the labour-intensive character of Korea's export-led industrialization during the 1960s. For references, see Park (1981).
6 The experience of Hong Kong and Taiwan also provides good examples of exports of labour-intensive manufactures. In Taiwan, the manufactured exports were more labour-intensive than overall manufacturing. During the early phase of its industrialization, Taiwan also utilized a variety of means (e.g., the use of labour-intensive technology and even second-hand machines and multiple shift operation) to make their production labour-intensive. Korea also followed similar practices in the 1960s. See, for example, Little (1981) and Ranis (1973) for descriptions of the experiences of Taiwan and Korea, respectively.
7 Both these indicators were used by Tregenna (2011).
8 There is a growing body of literature on this subject. See, for example, Dasgupta and Singh (2005), Tregenna (2011, 2015), Rodrik (2013, 2015), and Chaudhury (2015).
9 This, however, should not be interpreted to imply that the country is firmly on a path of export-oriented industrialization like those in ESEA. The manufacturing sector as well as the exports of the country remain highly concentrated on one item.
10 For example, the McKinsey report divides the countries covered by it into three categories: (i) advanced economies, (ii) emerging economies with ageing populations, and (iii) emerging economies with younger populations. The countries in the last category include India, but Bangladesh is not included.
11 No other than Bill Gates has proposed this.
12 For some highlights of the potential for automation in different sectors and countries, see Islam (2017b).
13 In a subsequent chapter, the same authors showed that in the USA, the impact of the use of robots during 1990–2007 has been negative.

14 An example of such fiscal incentive is the provision of subsidy on the cost of combine harvester in Bangladesh. According to newspaper reports (Bonik Barta, 26 November 2017, https://bonikbarta.net/bangla/fbs/2017-11-26/139505/#. WhuMLZSdfgM.gmail), there is, currently, a hefty subsidy of 50–60 per cent on this capital equipment that is intended to assist farmers in overcoming bottlenecks created by a "shortage" of workers during the harvesting season. There are at least two questions surrounding this issue. First, seasonal tightening of the labour market in monsoon-dependent agriculture is not an entirely new phenomenon, although the shortage of workers during peak seasons may have become more prominent as the economy has grown. Second, if the price of labour has risen to such an extent that a substitution of labour by capital is economically justifiable, the market should provide that signal. By introducing a subsidy on capital equipment, the relative price of capital and labour is being distorted and an artificial incentive for mechanization is being created.

Bibliography

Acemoglu, Daron and Pascual Restrepo (2016): "The Race between Machine and Men: Implications of Technology for Factor Share and Employment". NBER Working Paper No. 22252. Cambridge.

——— (2017): "Robots and Jobs: Evidence from US Labour Markets". NBER Working Paper No. 23285, Cambridge.

Amjad, Rashid and Anam Yusuf (2014): *More and Better Jobs for Pakistan: Can the Manufacturing Sector Play a Greater Role?* Monograph Series, Graduate School of Development Studies, Lahore School of Economics, Lahore.

Bangladesh Bureau of Statistics (various years): *Labour Force Survey*, 1999–2000, 2005–06, 2010, and 2016–17, Dhaka.

Bessen, James (2017): "Bill Gates is Wrong That Robots and Automation Are Killing Jobs". *Fortune*, 25 February 2017.

Central Bureau of Statistics, Government of Nepal (2009): *Report on the Nepal Labour Force Survey 2008*. Kathmandu.

Chaudhury, Sudip (2015): *Premature Deindustrialization in India and Re-Thinking the Role of Government*. HAL Archives Ouvertes. https://halshs.archives-ouvertes.fr/halshs-01143795.

Dasgupta, Sukti and Ajit Singh (2005): "Will Services be the New Engine of Indian Economic Growth?" *Development and Change*, Vol. 36, No. 6, pp. 1035–1057.

Department of Census and Statistics, Government of Sri Lanka (2013, 2017): *Sri Lanka Labour Force Survey*, Annual Report, 2012 and 2016. Colombo.

Driemeier, Mary Hallward and Gaurav Nayyar (2018): *Trouble in the Making? The Future of Manufacturing-Led Development*. World Bank, Washington, D.C.

Government of Pakistan (2016): *Pakistan Economic Survey 2015–16*. Ministry of Finance, Government of Pakistan, Islamabad.

Hsia, R. (1981): *Technical Change, Trade Promotion and Export-Led Industrialization*. In Lee, 1981.

Institute for Human Development (2014): *Growth, Labour Markets and Employment: India*. IHD, New Delhi.

Islam, R. (2004): *The Nexus of Economic Growth, Employment and Poverty Reduction: An Empirical Analysis*. Issues in Employment and Poverty Discussion Paper No. 14. ILO, Geneva.

———— (2003): *Labour Market Policies, Economic Growth and Poverty Reduction: Lessons and Non-Lessons from the Comparative Experience of East, South-East and South Asia.* Issues in Employment and Poverty Discussion Paper No. 8. ILO, Geneva.

———— (ed.) (2006): *Fighting Poverty: The Development-Employment Link.* Lynn Rienner, Boulder, Colorado and London.

———— (2009a): "Has Development and Employment through Labour-Intensive Industrialization Become History?" in Basu, Kaushik and Ravi Kanbur (eds.): *Arguments for a Better World: Essays in Honour of Amartya Sen Volume II Society, Institutions and Development.* Oxford University Press, Oxford.

———— (2009b): "What Kind of Economic Growth is Bangladesh Attaining?" in Shahabuddin, Quazi and Rushidan Islam Rahman (eds.): *Development Experience and Emerging Challenges Bangladesh.* BIDS and UPL, Dhaka.

———— (2017a): "Bangladesh 2041 Study: Employment and Labour Market Policies for a Maturing Economy". Paper prepared for the Bangladesh Planning Commission, Government of Bangladesh.

———— (2017b): *Is Automation Going to Destroy Jobs of Human Beings?* Policy Note, Centre for Development and Employment Research, Dhaka.

Kessler, Sarah (2017): *The Optimist's Guide to the Robot Apocalypse. Quartz,* 9 March 2017. https://qz.com/904285/the-optimists-guide-to-the-robot-apocalypse/ (Accessed on 31 October 2017).

Khan, A.R. (2006): *Employment Policies for Poverty Reduction.* In Islam, 2006.

Lee, E. (ed.) (1981): *Export-Led Industrialization and Development.* Asian Employment Programme. ILO, Bangkok.

Lewis, W.A. (1954): "Economic Development with Unlimited Supplies of Labour", *Manchester School of Economic and Social Studies,* Vol. 22, No. 2, pp. 139–191.

Little, I.M.D. (1981): *The Experience and Causes of Rapid Labour-Intensive Development in Korea, Taiwan Province, Hong Kong and Singapore, and the Possibilities of Emulation.* In Lee, 1981.

McKinsey Global Institute (2017): *A Future That Works: Automation, Employment and Productivity.* www.mckinsey.com/mgi (Accessed on 31 October 2017).

Osmani, S.R. (2010): "Accounting for Employment Outcome of Growth: A Methodology and Its Application" in Banerjee, Lopamudra, Anirban Dasgupta and Rizwanul Islam (eds.): *Development, Equity and Poverty: Essays in Honour of Azizur Rahman Khan.* Macmillan and UNDP, New Delhi and New York.

Park, Y.C. (1981): *Export-Led Development: the Korean Experience 1960–78.* In Lee, 1981.

Price Waterhouse Coopers (PwC) (2017): *UK Economic Outlook March 2017.* www.pwc.com/uk (Accessed on 2 November 2017).

Raja, Siddhartha and Luc Christiaensen (2017): *The Future of Work Requires More, Not Less Technology in Developing Countries.* Jobs Notes, Issue No. 2. World Bank, Washington, D.C.

Ranis, G. (1973): "Industrial Sector Labour Absorption", *Economic Development and Cultural Change,* Vol. 21, No. 3, pp. 387–408.

Rodrik, D. (2013): *The Perils of Premature Deindustrialization.* Project Syndicate, 11 October 2013. www.project-syndicate.org/commentary/dani-rodrikdeveloping-economies--missing-manufacturing (Accessed on 15 October 2018).

Storm, S. and C.W.M. Naastepad (2005, November): "Strategic Factors in Economic Development: East Asian Industrialization", *Development and Change,* Vol. 36, No. 6, pp. 1059–1094.

Tregenna, F. (2011): "Manufacturing Productivity, Deindustrialization and Rein-dustrialization". UNU–WIDER Working Paper No. 2011/57. Helsinki.

——— (2015): "Deindustrialization, Structural Change and Sustainable Economic Growth". Working Paper No. 2/2015, UNIDO, Vienna.

UNCTAD (United Nations Conference on Trade and Development) (2006): *Handbook of Statistics, 2006*. UNCTAD, Geneva.

——— (2015): *Handbook of Statistics 2015*. UNCTAD, Geneva.

UN-DESA (2017): "The Impact of the Technological Revolution on Labour Markets and Income Distribution". Frontier Issues, 31 July 2017. United Nations, New York.

World Bank (1993): *The East Asian Miracle: Economic Growth and Public Policy*. Oxford University Press, New York.

——— (various years): *World Development Indicators* (1997, 1998, 2002, 2004, 2007, 2018). http://wdi.worldbank.org/table/4.1 and http://wdi.worldbank.org/table/4.9.

——— (various years): *World Development Report* (1992, 1995, 1997, 1998, 1999/2000).

7 Globalization of production and the world of work

Is a race to the bottom inevitable?[1]

Introduction

Economic globalization involves trade, capital flows, and the movement of labour, and an important element in that process is the globalization of production. With the gradual dismantling of trade barriers, and capital flows becoming easier, globalization of production has flourished. It is no longer necessary to produce goods in one location. Even though a product may bear the mark of being produced in a particular country, its components may come from different locations. This is particularly the case with high-tech products for which research and development (R&D) is usually carried out in developed countries, components are made in different countries depending on their competencies, and the final assembly takes place in another country. This approach is also used for labour-intensive goods, such as garments, shoes, etc.

Globalization of production has influenced the world of work in ways not seen before.[2] While some impacts have been positive from the point of view of workers, others have given rise to serious concerns. On the positive side, new employment opportunities hitherto unknown in many developing countries have opened. On the other hand, serious pressure on the working class has come through the stagnation of real wages[3] and adverse workplace conditions. The term "race to the bottom" has come into circulation in this context. But this does not have to be the only way forward since there are useful positive aspects from which workers could benefit alongside the rest of the global community. The present chapter looks at both the positive outcomes of globalization and the pressures that workers face, and explores possible paths to better outcomes.

Globalization of production and changes in the world of work

Since the globalization of production involves the splitting of the global value chain into different components, success depends critically on several conditions, including the technical capacity of the producers of components and assembly firms, the availability of workers with necessary skills, and the ability of managers to deliver according to strict time schedules (the so-called "just-in-time delivery"). In some cases, e.g., for basic consumer goods such as garments and shoes, the skills required are rather basic, while in the case of others, such as electronics and their components, parts of capital goods, etc., higher level skills are required. But what is key in either case is the flexibility with which labour can be employed and its low cost, an arrangement that has its positive as well as negative aspects.

One major positive aspect is the location of labour-intensive (usually export-oriented) manufactures in labour-abundant countries and the absorption of surplus labour in sectors where wages and incomes may be higher than in traditional sectors. This facilitates the transformation of the structure of employment towards sectors where productivity and incomes are higher.

A related aspect is the creation of new avenues for women's employment. The early experience of export-oriented industrialization illustrates this, having created jobs in industries such as electronics and garments requiring so-called "nimble fingers", particularly in countries of East and South East Asia. More recent examples of increases in women's employment are in countries such as Bangladesh and Cambodia. Developments related to women's employment in export-oriented industries include increases in women's participation in the labour force,[4] higher growth of women's employment compared to men and a rise in the share of women in paid employment.[5]

The location of modern manufacturing in developing countries, by generating demand for skills of different types, creates one of the basic preconditions for skills development. Although R&D, design and planning are normally carried out in developed countries, and there may not be much scope for transfer of technology through locating parts of production activity, a process of "learning by doing" may be engendered, thus creating grounds for entrepreneurship development. Further, opportunities for participating in the global value chain lead to investment, both by domestic and foreign investors, and thus creates the possibility of attaining higher growth.

Participating in global value chains and the resulting growth of economies have also incurred costs in terms of negative effects on work. One feature that distinguishes industries emerging from the globalization of production is their direct link with work orders from buyers, and hence the uncertainty in the size of operation that a producer needs to maintain.[6] The risk that arises out of such uncertainty is usually borne by workers in terms of the flexible arrangements through which they are hired. Flexibility may be manifested in terms of temporary contracts, if a formal contract is even given to workers;[7] the compulsory nature of overtime work, often without appropriate compensation; the possibility of termination without notice and often without severance benefits; and so on. In fact, the workforce in such industries does not resemble the industrial labour force as it is commonly understood.[8]

Even in formal enterprises, workers are often engaged without normal benefits and allowances, e.g., those that protect against illness, old age, unemployment, etc. Thus, the boundary between formal and informal employment often blurs, and informal employment does not remain confined to the informal sector alone.

While increased women's employment has been a positive impact, this has also been associated with a host of issues including discrimination in wages and other terms of employment, a higher incidence of women in informal and casual employment, and the imperative to combine household and reproductive responsibilities with income-earning activities. Women employed in formal enterprises are usually young and unmarried, and what happens to their working life at later stages remains a question.

Competitiveness is a key word in the globalization of production, usually interpreted in the narrow and static sense of cost per unit. As costs of material inputs are often beyond the control of producers in developing countries, the onus of maintaining competitiveness in terms of cost usually falls on labour. Wage repression is a commonly used mechanism for achieving this goal. This is amply demonstrated by the decline in the share of wages in value added (or national income) that has been experienced by many developed as well as developing countries for different periods, including the 2000s (ILO, 2013, 2015); developed countries from 1980 to 2004 (IMF, 2007); developing countries from 1980 to 1994 (Jaydev, 2007); and both developed and developing countries from 1970 to 2009 (Guerriero, 2012).[9] A poor work environment and unsafe workplaces, which also characterize global value chains, provide further evidence of attempts by producers to cut costs, as exemplified by the frequency with which accidents occur in export-oriented industries.

Where workers lack formal contracts, it is a far cry to think of their right to voice grievances and demands. A very small proportion of workers enjoy fundamental rights such as freedom of association and collective bargaining. Not only is the degree of unionization very low, but the formation and joining of unions are actively discouraged in many developing countries. An additional challenge is the fractious nature of unions and their image problem in pursuing the real goal of workers' interests.

In many ways, the ready-made garment (RMG) industry of Bangladesh epitomizes the positive as well as negative aspects of globalization and the pressures created on workers. How forces of globalization can squeeze workers alongside opportunities created for them and their countries is exemplified well by this industry. The following section presents a case study, providing a description of the gains arising out of the growth of the industry as well as the squeeze that the workers face.

Supplying the global market and the squeeze on workers: the ready-made garment industry of Bangladesh

Gains made

Growth of this labour-intensive export-oriented industry started in the early 1980s. In 1984–85, there were 384 factories producing RMG for exports that fetched $116 million accounting for 12.44 per cent of total exports. The industry employed 120 thousand workers during that year. The number of factories grew to a peak of 5,876 employing four million workers in 2012–13 and fetching $21.52 billion in terms of export earnings. The latter was about four-fifths of the country's total export earnings. Since then, the number of factories has declined (to 4,560 in 2017–18), and the number of workers employed stagnated at the same level; but exports from the industry continued to increase and rose to $30.61 billion in 2017–18 – which was 83.49 per cent of total exports. The growth of the RMG industry not only provided jobs to workers – the majority of whom are women and migrated from rural areas – but also enabled the country to overcome its unfavourable trade balance and to build up a healthy reserve of foreign exchange.

The genesis and early growth of the RMG industry in Bangladesh owe much to the Multifibre Agreement that came into force in 1974 for regulating trade in textiles and garments. It imposed quotas or quantitative restrictions on the volume of exports from countries that grew at rates higher than established bilaterally by the trading partners. In Asia, Republic of Korea was one such country that faced restrictions on their exports to the USA. Entrepreneurs from such countries started to shift their production to countries whose quota remained unutilized, and Bangladesh was one such country where there were entrepreneurs willing and able to learn the trade. Their counterparts from Korea provided them with necessary help in terms of market linkage, training, etc. and the government of Bangladesh acted as the catalyst with conducive policies. The outcome was the emergence of a new industry, a new class of entrepreneurs and jobs for poor people who were desperately looking for ways to come out of acute poverty.

While the quota system was abolished by WTO in 2004, the industry had, by then, established itself to a point from where they could weather the initial competition. The international environment was conducive in that the earlier set of developing countries that specialized in labour-intensive exports were losing competitiveness because of higher labour cost. Domestically, the industry was helped by continued support from the government and the latter's willingness to overlook the conditions in which work was being carried out.

Data presented in Table 7.1 show how growth of the RMG industry in Bangladesh evolved over time. While the early years were marked by very high growth of exports as well as employment, growth slowed as the industry matured. However, dispelling projections made by many, growth of the

Table 7.1 Annual Growth (%) of Employment and Exports of the Ready-Made Garment Industry of Bangladesh

Period	Employment	Export	Export Per Worker
1984–85 to 1994–95	25.89	34.36	6.73
1994–95 to 2004–05	5.24	11.16	5.62
2004–05 to 2014–15	7.18	14.79	7.10
2014–15 to 2017–18	0	6.29	6.29

Source: Calculated from data available at the website of BGMEA (Accessed on 6 September 2018). It may be noted that total employment for all years from 2011–12 to 2017–18 is shown as four million.

industry did not suffer any decline after the termination of the MFA in 2004. In fact, growth of both exports and employment during the decade after 2004–05 was higher than during the previous decade. Of course, export per worker grew at higher rate during the post-MFA period, indicating that the industry adjusted to the situation by raising labour productivity and thus making itself more competitive.

Poor quality of jobs

The gains from globalization came at some cost involving squeeze on workers that took a variety of forms ranging from unfavourable terms of work, poor conditions in which work is carried out, and the wages they received. During the early years of the industry, employment without written contracts was the norm, and there was no concept of severance pay. Workers were hired informally and were let go when not needed. It was only in 2006 (i.e., after more than two decades of the industry's genesis) that the issue of appointment letter was agreed upon by members of the Bangladesh Garment Manufacturers' and Exporters' Association (BGMEA). And the practice has not yet become universal. In a situation where hiring is done through verbal agreements or at best through informal arrangement, provision for benefits like severance pay, protection against unemployment and old age would be a far cry. Thus, although the industry has the characteristics of formal sector, much of its employment is informal.

Conditions in which work is carried out often fall far short of requirements in terms of safety and health. In the early days of the industry, many factories were set up in rented premises which were not constructed for such purposes. Apart from overcrowding, accidents caused by fire were frequent.[10] Over time, there has been a transformation within the industry and many factories have been established in buildings designed and constructed for the purpose. And yet, many are found to be lacking in terms of standards of safety against fire and health hazards. Even though the importing companies contracted with suppliers having factories meeting safety standards, subcontracting was (and continues to remain) common in the industry. The factories of subcontractors are typically smaller where working conditions are also worse.

Although accidents in garment factories, especially fire-related ones, have been a regular feature, two accidents marked some kind of watershed for the industry. The first was fire in 2012 in a factory called Tazreen Fashions that led to the death of 112 and injury of 150 workers. The second was the collapse of a building called Rana Plaza (in April 2013) in which several garment factories were located and which caused the death of at least 1,136 workers and injury of hundreds. As these accidents involved factories that produced garments for leading global brands, they caused global uproars and brought the industry under spotlight. For the first time in the history of the growth of the RMG industry, serious action was taken jointly by the government, buyers, suppliers, and international organizations. A common approach to determining the safety of factory buildings was arrived at jointly by the National

Tripartite Committee, the Accord on Fire and Building Safety (a group of global brands and retailers, based mostly in Europe but including a few from Asia), and the Alliance for Bangladesh Worker Safety (which represents a group of North American companies representing 90 per cent of RMG exports from Bangladesh to the United States). Each of the above took responsibility for inspecting a certain number of RMG factories, for determining the work needed to remedy the problems that were detected with respect to safety of the factory premises, and for overseeing the remediation work.[11]

In addition, an initiative titled Bangladesh Sustainability Compact was taken to bring together the European Union (EU), Bangladesh, the USA and the ILO with the common goal of improving working conditions and the respect of labour rights in Bangladesh's RMG industry to ensure that the Rana Plaza tragedy is not repeated.

The work mentioned above has led to considerable improvements in many garment factories, and the number of serious accidents has declined. But the industry has not yet become free of accidents (as can be seen from Table 7.2), and one report (Barret et al., 2018) expresses the apprehension that there may be a reversal of the achievements once the foreign partners of the process leave at the end of 2018 – after a period of five years from the date of start.[12]

Wage and price repression

Another issue on the qualitative side of employment is the wage rate and earnings of workers in the industry. It is quite well known that low wage is the major factor on which the competitive edge of Bangladesh in the RMG industry is based.[13] This has remained one of the most contentious issues (although not the only one) in the labour-management conflict that has persisted in the industry since its genesis. The minimum wage which was fixed in 1994 at Tk. 930 ($16) per month was revised only in 2006 when it was raised to Tk 1,662 ($24) per month. But the revised wage was not able to compensate for the rise in the cost of living of workers, and there was widespread unrest

Table 7.2 Number of Accidents in the Ready-Made Garment Industry of Bangladesh

Year	Total Number of Accidents	Number of Significant* Accidents During the Year
2013	38	17
2014	26	2
2015	21	3
2016	34	5
2017	20	4

Source: Barret et al. (2018).

* Accidents resulting in more than five deaths and/or ten injuries have been mentioned as significant.

among workers of the industry. In the face of unrest, in 2010, minimum wage was revised upwards to Tk. 3,000 ($43) per month. Despite these revisions in wages, the issue was not satisfactorily resolved, and the industry continued to face periodic unrest and violence over the issue. The next revision of the wage came after the Rana Plaza disaster in 2013, and the monthly wage was raised to Tk 5,300 ($68) per month. In 2018, the minimum wage was raised to Tk 8,000 ($95).

Despite periodic revisions in wages, wages in Bangladesh remain the lowest among countries of Asia which are notable exporters of RMGs. Data compiled by Japan External Trade Organization (JETRO, 2017) show that in 2017, the average manufacturing wage in Bangladesh was $101 compared to $135, $170, and $216 in Myanmar, Cambodia, and Vietnam, respectively. This naturally raises the question whether there is space for a better wage deal for the workers of the RMG industry in Bangladesh.

It is also interesting to note that the negotiations on wage revision were marked by rigid position taken by the employers, their reluctance to raise wages at all and wage settlement at a level which is way below the level considered reasonable even by independent analysts. And in settling the issue, there had to be intervention either by foreign buyers or by the country's Prime Minister herself.

While the RMG industry of Bangladesh is credited as being the provider of manufacturing jobs for millions of workers, it is by now widely acknowledged that their earnings are nowhere near what is required for getting out of poverty and for a decent living. One study (by Fair Labour Association, reported in Fair Action, 2018) looking at wages of more than 6,000 garment workers at 18 factories in Bangladesh found that not a single garment worker was earning an income even close to a living wage, measured against any living wage benchmark. The average worker in that report would need an 80 per cent pay raise to begin earning wages equal to even the most conservative living wage benchmark. The report concluded, "Even though the minimum wage will be raised from €53 (BDT 5,300) to €80.5 (BDT 8,000) per month from December 2018, life will continue to be a struggle" (Fair Action, 2018, p. 33).

One argument that is often provided by employers against raising wages is that that will push up the cost of production and adversely affect the competitiveness of the industry in the export market. The mirror image of this argument is the reluctance of international buyers to raise prices. Not only are they reluctant to raise prices, but they also keep suppliers under constant pressures to reduce prices and shorten the lead time for supplying. And pressures for price reduction are exercised not because of declines in the prices of inputs, but basically for the purpose of raising the profit margin. This can be illustrated with the example of the price trend of one item of import (cotton trousers) from Bangladesh into the USA. Some data are presented in Table 7.3. It can be seen from this table that during 2015–17, import prices of cotton trousers declined despite a rise in the price of cotton.

Table 7.3 Import Prices of Cotton Trousers from
Bangladesh into the USA and Price of Cotton

Year	Price of Trousers (USD per Dozen)	Price of Cotton (USD Cents per Pound)
2013	62.26	90.42
2014	62.49	83.09
2015	60.52	70.41
2016	58.11	74.23
2017	54.29	85.99

Source: Anner (2018).

Rights at work

Another dimension of the quality of jobs in the garment industry of Bangladesh is their ability to voice their opinions and concerns on issues relating to their work. The standard mechanisms through which this is expected to be done in the world of work, viz., associations freely formed and chosen by workers and collective bargaining with employers, remained absent in the industry for decades after its start. And it is not difficult to understand why it was so. On the one hand, during the initial years, the workers were basically young women, many of whom were migrants from rural areas. For many, this was the first paid job and was a welcome transition from just being helpers in family's farm or peripheral non-farm work. For such workers, a job with a monthly salary was an attractive alternative to poverty and lack of access to even the basic needs of life. They were not aware of the concept of job quality, not to speak of bargaining for an improvement in such aspects. Many may not have even heard of mechanisms like forming associations and bargaining with employers through them. In that sense, this group of industrial workers was very different from the standard notion of industrial workers.

On the other hand, the employers, many being first-generation entrepreneurs, were attitudinally not geared towards recognizing the basic premise of worker-employer relationship – that the workers also have some rights in the places of work. They were always ready to point out that for many of the workers the alternative to the factory job was sharing work in the family farm back home and living in poverty, and hence there should not be any question on wages. Indeed, the reservation wage for many was rather low (if not zero), and employers often pointed that out whenever the question of wages came up for debate.[14] They also did not hesitate to adopt strong-arm tactics to prevent the possibility of trade unions finding a way into their factories. Measures would be taken to identify workers with links to trade unions, intimidate them, and even dismiss them.[15]

The trade union movement in Bangladesh has long faced various criticisms, and their credibility was also under question. Multiplicity of unions, politicization, frequent use of pressure tactics, and use of union power by

their leaders for personal gains raised doubts about their real role in protecting workers' rights.

Rights of workers in the industry came under real spotlight in the wake of the
Rana Plaza disaster when the issue of workers' rights came to the fore alongside
the conditions of work. As international pressure increased, the government of
Bangladesh showed some willingness to facilitate the registration of unions at
the enterprise level and some progress did take place. Data presented in Table 7.4
show that compared to only a handful of government approval for registration
of trade unions in 2011 and 2012, the number increased substantially in 2013
and in subsequent years. But two things emerge from the data. First, both the
number of applications for registration and the number of government approvals
declined sharply after 2014. It seems that after the initial period of global attention and pressure could be passed, there was a tendency to drift towards the old
ways. Second, a very high proportion of the applications (nearly 47 per cent) for
registration made during 2000–17 was rejected by the government. Although
the reasons for such a high rate of rejection are not known, it may be useful at
this point to get to the issue of labour laws of the country.

It may be recalled that the Bangladesh Labour Act 2006 was criticized for
its being anti-labour and for not conforming to a number of international
standards (especially those relating to freedom of association and collective
bargaining although the government of Bangladesh is a signatory to the relevant ILO conventions. After the Rana Plaza incident, a number of improvements were made in labour policies generally, and particularly in the RMG
industry. The main element of improvement in the overall labour policy is an
amendment to the Act of 2006 enacted in 2013, which brought about certain
improvements in freedom of association, collective bargaining, and safety in
the workplace. More specifically, registration of trade unions has been made
easier and the ban on strikes in export processing zones withdrawn. But the
amendments still fell short of international standards in a number of areas

Table 7.4 Registration of Trade Unions in the Ready-Made
Garment Industry of Bangladesh

Year	Applied for Registration	Approved by Government	Rejected by Government
2010	1	0	1
2011	10	1	7
2012	12	1	5
2013	158	84	44
2014	392	182	155
2015	150	67	148
2016	133	77	49
2017	78	57	26

Source: Anner (2018).

Note: As of 31 March, the RMG industry had 659 registered trade
unions and trade union federations. See European Commission (2018).

including the condition of a minimum of 30 per cent of the total number of workers of an enterprise for registering a trade union. It was only in 2018 that this condition was modified to bring the requirement down to 20 per cent. But the difficulties in forming and registering trade unions continue to persist, and the proportion of workers who are members of trade unions remain very low.[16]

Summing up the Bangladesh case

The RMG industry of Bangladesh provides a classic case of globalization opening up possibilities of gains in macroeconomic terms as well as in terms of jobs for the poor people. But the quality of the jobs that came remain rather low in terms of wages, terms of work, the physical condition in which work is done and the possibility of workers having a voice in the place of work. There has been some progress, especially in the areas of workplace safety and rights of workers, but it has been rather slow and small.

Is a race to the bottom the only way?

In view of the scenario outlined above, it is not surprising that there is serious concern about the danger of a race to the bottom. But given the existing and potential benefits of globalized production, this does not have to be the only outcome. The prevailing gloomy scenario is mainly due to a misplaced emphasis on a static, narrow interpretation of competitiveness in terms of financial costs per unit of production. The adoption of a slightly longer term, broader perspective could perhaps lead to a different conclusion.[17]

Why is a static view of competitiveness inadequate even from the point of view of profitability and of benefiting from advantages opened by the globalization of production? The simple reason is that a competitive edge based on low-cost, unskilled labour does not last indefinitely. Once surplus labour is exhausted, and the labour market tightens, an economy will be required to adopt other means of maintaining competitiveness. Even while surplus labour exists, and it is possible to keep production lines operational without raising real wages, there is often a cost in terms of the productivity and efficiency of workers. Unsafe and poor work environments also may have negative consequences for productivity.

Apart from economic aspects of costs and competitiveness, an important element of today's global market is perception about conditions in which goods are produced. Consumers are becoming increasingly aware of and sensitive to these, and buying intermediaries are facing growing pressures arising from ethical considerations. In such an environment, a single-minded pursuit of cost efficiency is likely to be a shortsighted strategy. That is illustrated by the global outcry caused by successive accidents in the RMG industry of Bangladesh. It is a measure of global concern about conditions along global value chains that major retailers who source their imports from factories in

Bangladesh have initiated remediation plans and are providing financial support. Although those initiatives have their limitations,[18] they nevertheless indicate that sweatshop conditions are no longer acceptable in workplaces that are part of the global value chain.

Cambodia's experience illustrates the ability of a country to maintain its export market even by keeping wage rates and conditions of work at acceptable levels. Development of the economy of that war-torn country started in the early 1990s. Right from the beginning, the country was keen to earn a reputation in export markets by maintaining minimum standards in terms of workplace rights and conditions. A key factor in Cambodia's success with this approach was an agreement with the United States in 1999. Under it, Cambodia agreed to uphold the rights of workers and the United States agreed to increase the annual quota of imports from the country. Cambodia has continued doing quite well in markets in the United States even after the quota system for garment imports was abolished, showing that low wages and poor working conditions are not essential for maintaining competitiveness.[19] Examples like this are still not common, however, and overall, the position of workers is becoming increasingly weak.

How to prevent the race to the bottom?

Despite alternative ways of attaining and maintaining profitability and competitiveness in the globalized production system, the world of work associated with this system reflects many characteristics of a race to the bottom. This is not entirely surprising, because it is not easy to see the benefits of the high road to growth, and short-term profit motives usually lead to what seems to be the more lucrative path. What then is the way out? A combination of measures will be needed.[20] Singling out a few areas should not imply that others are less important, but those mentioned below must not be compromised under any circumstances.

The first area of non-compromise is safety in places of work. The worst situation one can think of is where security of life is threatened, and that must top the list of unacceptable aspects of the work environment. Accidents like the disaster at Rana Plaza in Bangladesh should provide a wake-up call (if any was needed), and necessary measures must be adopted to prevent any such accidents in future irrespective of the level of development of a country, the type of industry and the type of contract under which a worker is working. Security of life must top the agenda of human development relating to the world of work.

The second area where improvement needs to be made on a priority basis is the wage rate – with particular focus on ending gender discrimination – and the rate's periodic adjustment. Since trade unions and collective bargaining are still exceptions, workers are often at the mercy of employers with respect to wage rates, compensation for overtime work and other allowances.

Timely payment of wages and allowances often becomes an issue. Adjustments of wages to growth of productivity and cost of living are not usually made unless there is intervention from governments. Even then, the usual arguments of jeopardizing competitiveness and inability to pay are invoked in order to keep adjustments to the barest minimum. All such practices must end and modalities of wage determination and adjustment must be straightened out.

Third, the dignity of people who work to produce goods and services for the world cannot be compromised in any discourse on development. A basic prerequisite is for them to have a voice in matters relating to their work and life, which, in turn, requires that the fundamental principles and rights at work be honoured.[21]

Coming back to measures to bring about the kind of improvements mentioned above, the basic question is how private enterprises can be encouraged to move in the required direction. They are not likely to do so on their own, and that's where public policy and governance of the labour market come in. There are two levels at which this issue needs to be addressed – national and international. At the national level, appropriate legislation is needed in areas mentioned above as well as on other relevant issues. Compliance requires not only legislation, however, but also the willingness and capacity of governments to implement it in an efficient and transparent manner.

Action to improve the terms of employment and working conditions will inevitably face resistance unless producers can find a way of passing on at least a part of the additional costs to their buyers. And that's where the role of the global community also comes in. If there is real commitment to meeting basic standards in the world of work, that would have to be reflected in the willingness to incorporate them in price negotiations. In other words, consumers in the importing countries and buyers who act on their behalf would have to underwrite, to some extent at least, the cost increases resulting from wage adjustments and improvements in working conditions. In this connection, it would be useful to remember Amartya Sen's observation: "The increasingly globalized world economy calls for a similarly globalized approach to basic ethics and political and social procedures" (Sen, 2000, p. 127). A "globalized approach" would require national action in tandem with action from beyond national boundaries.

Democracy, freedom of expression and an active media – both national and international – can play a valuable role in the implementation of ethical standards in the world of work. This has been demonstrated, to some extent at least, in the wake of the Rana Plaza disaster in Bangladesh, when both national and international media became active in bringing out the roles and responsibilities of various partners in the global value chain, viz., producers and international buyers, and putting pressures on them to adopt remedial measures.[22] The responsibility of the media should extend beyond ex post reporting, however, to embrace more proactive journalism that points out, on a regular basis, the need for interventions and improvements.

Notes

1 This chapter uses material from Islam (2015) which was prepared for the UNDP.
2 There is a sizeable body of literature on the impact of globalization on the labour market. UNDP's Human Development Report 1999 (UNDP, 1999) pointed out the negative impact of globalization on labour markets. Likewise, the International Labour Organization (2004) provides a detailed analysis. There are many more studies, and no attempt is made here to provide a full list of the relevant literature.
3 Real wages have risen in some countries such as China and India but not in many others. Further, rates of wage increases have been lower than those of labour productivity.
4 With, of course, exceptions such as India.
5 For a good discussion of the gender dimensions of the globalization of production, see Barrientos et al. (2004).
6 Of course, apart from centrally planned economies where production is usually designed to fulfil the targets of production allocated by the planning authority, production in market-oriented economies is supposed to be undertaken in response to demand, and hence, is bound to be subject to the uncertainties of the market. But in traditional industries, a workforce of a certain size is usually engaged on the basis of an ex ante estimate of the demand for a product.
7 During the early phase of the development of the readymade garment industry of Bangladesh, employment of workers without written contracts was almost universal. Even today, providing written contracts is far from universal, although issuance of appointment letters is one of the conditions mentioned in a memorandum of understanding agreed in 2006. The Bangladesh Garment Manufacturers and Exporters Association claims the rate of compliance on appointment letters among their members is 80–90 per cent. But other studies report much lower rates (Afrin 2014), for example, reports that half the employers provide appointment letters). In major industrial centres of India, unskilled production workers in the readymade garment industry are usually engaged without formal contracts, which are given only to managerial and administrative officials (Hirway, 2011). Serrano (2014) points out that except in Singapore, the incidence of "non-standard employment" has increased in other Association for Southeast Asian Nations countries during the 2000s, alongside high rates of economic growth.
8 A survey of readymade garment industries in major industrial centres of India shows that no 'permanent' employee has been recruited in the industry during the past eight years (Hirway, 2011).
9 According to standard theory, when developed countries import labour-intensive goods, their domestic industries face competition, and as their cost of labour is high, competition will result in gradual decline in such industries. The result of this process is normally a downward pressure on the wages of unskilled labour, and the share of labour in production eventually declines. On the other hand, as production of labour-intensive goods increases in developing countries, demand for labour increases, and the result is an upward pressure on wages and an increase in the share of labour in production. The result of these opposing forces in developed and developing countries should be a convergence in the wages of workers in the two sets of countries. Developments in the real world, however, do not exactly follow the theory. Although the experience of developed countries seems to be along the lines mentioned above, the experience of developing countries often diverges.
10 One study (Paul-Majumdar and Begum, 2000) reported that up to 1997, there were 58 fire-related accidents. Assuming that this figure represents a period of 12 years or so (starting from 1985), this implies nearly five accidents every year.

A list of major accidents in garment factories can be found in the Reuters report titled "Factbox: Major industrial accidents in Bangladesh in recent years", 4 July 2017. www.reuters.com/article/us-bangladesh-blast-accidents-factbox/factbox-major-industrial-accidents-in-bangladesh-in-recent-years-idUSKBN19P0JN (Accessed on 19 November 2018).
11 For details, see Labowitz and Baumann-Pauly (2014) and European Commission (2015).
12 Moazzem (2018) also expresses similar apprehension.
13 According to one estimate (Yunus and Yamagata, 2012), labour cost in the industry in Bangladesh is USD 0.22 per hour, which is lower than even in Cambodia (USD 0.33 per hour) and Vietnam (0.38). It is, of course, pointed out that low wages reflect low productivity of the workers. But the industry in Bangladesh is regarded as holding competitive advantage even after taking into account the productivity differential (Lopez-Acevedo and Robertson, 2012).
14 This attitude could be seen in the statements made by employers in public and are reported in the media.
15 On this and other difficulties of organizing trade unions in the garment industry of Bangladesh, see, for example, Paul-Majumder (2002), Kabeer and Mahmud (2004), and European Commission (2015).
16 Moazzem and Azim (2018) provide a detailed analysis of the latest situation in this regard.
17 This chapter does not go into more general issues concerning relationships between labour market flexibility and social protection, on the one hand, and economic growth and employment, on the other hand. For analysis of some of these relationships, see Islam and Islam 2015.
18 For example, even after five years of the Rana Plaza disaster in Bangladesh, the task of remediation of the factories identified for such work was not completed. Furthermore, this period was marked by periodic frictions between the various partners involved in the process – raising doubts and concerns about real commitment on the part of the stakeholders. What is also important is that conditions in factories not covered by these programmes are perhaps worse, and it is not clear whether anything was being done on that front.
19 Workplace safety and work conditions nonetheless remain a problem in Cambodia – demonstrating that it is not easy to transform them. Given the manner in which the global supply chain works and the constant focus on nominal costs, there is always a tendency to exploit the vulnerable. Without concrete leverage after the abolition of the quota regime, the long-term effectiveness of the arrangement mentioned here is coming into question (O'Keeffe, 2013).
20 The purpose here is not to elaborate a detailed agenda for decent work as espoused by the International Labour Organization.
21 In 1998, a Declaration on Fundamental Principles and Rights at Work was adopted by governments, employers' organizations, and workers' organizations at the International Labour Organization. One of these principles and rights at work is the freedom of workers to form associations and bargain collectively with their employers.
22 This is somewhat akin to Amartya Sen's argument that democracy and active media are an important factor in preventing deaths due to disasters such as famines (Sen, 1983).

Bibliography

Afrin, S. (2014): "Labour Condition in the Apparel Industry of Bangladesh: Is Bangladesh Labour Law 2006 Enough?" *Developing Country Studies*, Vol. 4, No. 11, pp. 70–78.

146 *Globalization of production*

Anner, Mark (2018): *Binding Power: The Sourcing Squeeze, Workers' Rights, and Building Safety in Bangladesh since Rana Plaza*. Research Report, Penn State Center for Global Workers' Rights (CGWR). http://lser.la.psu.edu/gwr/documents/CGWR 2017ResearchReportBindingPower.pdf (Accessed on 7 November 2018).

Barret, Paul, Dorothee Baumann-Pauly and April Gu (2018): *Five Years after Rana Plaza: The Way Forward*. Stern Center for Business and Human Rights, New York University, New York.

Barrientos, S., N. Kabeer and N. Hossain (2004): "The Gender Dimension of the Globalization of Production". Working Paper. Policy Integration Department, ILO, Geneva.

Bhorat, H. and P. Lundall (2004): *Employment and Labour Market Effects of Globalization: Selected Issues for Policy Management*. Employment Strategy Paper. ILO, Geneva.

European Commission (2015): *Bangladesh Sustainability Compact Technical Status Report*. 24 April 2015. http://trade.ec.europa.eu/doclib/docs/2015/april/tradoc_153390.pdf (Accessed on 25 November 2018).

———— (2018): *Implementation of the Bangladesh Compact – Technical Status Report*. September 2018. http://trade.ec.europa.eu/doclib/docs/2018/september/tradoc_157426.pdf (Accessed on 25 November 2018).

Fair Action (2018): *Left Behind: How Fashion Brands Turn Their Back on Women in the Bangladeshi Garment Industry*. https://fairaction.se/wp-content/uploads/2018/10/Fair-Action_Left-behind_20181003.pdf (Accessed on 23 November 2018).

Guerriero, M. (2012): "The Labour Share of Income around the World: Evidence from a Panel Dataset". Paper presented at the 4th Economic Development International Conference of GRETHA/GRES, "Inequality and development: New Challenges, New Measurement".

Hirway, I. (2011): *Restructuring of Production and Labour under Globalization: A Study of Textile and Garment Industry in India*. ILO, New Delhi.

International Labour Organization (2004): *A Fair Globalization: Creating Opportunities for All*. Report of the World Commission on the Social Dimension of Globalization. ILO, Geneva.

———— (2013): *Global Wage Report 2012/13: Wage and Equitable Growth*. ILO, Geneva.

———— (2015): *Global Wage Report 2014/15: Wages and Income Inequality*. ILO, Geneva.

IMF (International Monetary Fund) (2007): *World Economic Outlook 2007*. Washington, D.C.

Islam, R. (2015): "Globalization of Production, Work and Human Development: Is a Race to the Bottom Inevitable?" Think Piece, Human Development Report Office, UNDP, New York. http://hdr.undp.org/sites/default/files/islam_hdr_2015_final.pdf.

Islam, R. and I. Islam (2015): *Employment and Inclusive Development*. Routledge, London.

Jaydev, A. (2007): "Capital Account Openness and the Labour Share of Income", *Cambridge Journal of Economics*, Vol. 31, pp. 423–443.

Kabeer, N. and S. Mahmud (2004): "Rags, Riches and Women Workers: Export-Oriented Garment Manufacturing in Bangladesh" in *Chains of Fortune: Linking Women Producers and Workers with Global Markets*. Edited by Commonwealth Secretariat, London.

Labowitz, S. and D. Baumann-Pauly (2014): *Business as Usual Is Not an Option*. New York University Stern Business School, New York.

Lopez-Acevedo, G. and R. Robertson (eds.) (2012): *Sewing Success? Employment, Wages and Poverty Following the End of the Multi-fibre Arrangement*. World Bank, Washington, D.C.

Moazzem, Khondaker Golam (2018): "Whither Post-Accord Workplace Safety?" *The Financial Express*, 25 November 2018, Anniversary Issue Part Two.

Moazzem, Khondaker Golam and Syeda Samiha Azim (2018): *Workers' Organisations in RMG Enterprises: How to Address Institutional Challenges?* Policy Brief 2018 (13), Centre for Policy Dialogue, Dhaka.

Muqtada, Muhammed, Andrea Singh and Mohammed Ali Rashid (eds.) (2002): *Bangladesh: Economic and Social Challenges of Globalisation*. The University Press Limited, Dhaka.

O'Keeffe, K. (2013): "Garment Trade in Cambodia under Pressure", *Wall Street Journal*, 7 July 2013.

Paul-Majumder, Pratima (2002): "Organising Women Garment Workers: A Means to Address the Challenges of Integration of the Bangladesh Garment Industry in the Global Market" in Muqtada et al. (eds.) (2002).

Paul-Majumder, Pratima and Anwara Begum (2000): "The Gender Imbalances in the Export Oriented Garment Industry in Bangladesh". Policy Research Report on Gender and Development Working Paper Series No. 12. World Bank, Washington, D.C.

Safi, Michael and Dominic Rushe (2018): *Rana Plaza, Five Years on: Safety of Workers Hangs in Balance in Bangladesh*. https://www.theguardian.com/global-development/2018/apr/24/bangladeshi-police-target-garment-workers-union-rana-plaza-five-years-on (Accessed on 7 November 2018).

Sen, A. (1983): "Development: Which Way Now?" *Economic Journal*, Vol. 93, No. 372, pp. 745–762.

——— (2000): "Work and Rights", *International Labour Review*, Vol. 139, No. 2, pp. 119–128.

Serrano, M. R. (2014): *Between Flexibility and Security: The Rise of Non-Standard Employment in Selected ASEAN Countries*. Friedrich Ebert Stiftung and ASETUC, Jakarta.

UNDP (United Nations Development Programme) (1999): *Human Development Report 1999*. Oxford University Press, New York and Oxford.

Yunus, M. and T. Yamagata (2012): "The Garment Industry of Bangladesh" in Fukunishi, T. (ed.): *Dynamics of the Garment Industry in Low-Income Countries: Experience of Asia and Africa*, pp. 77–104. IDE-JETRO, Tokyo.

8 Re-thinking development strategies and policies for productive employment[1]

Introduction

Despite the importance of productive employment, development discourse at both international and national levels has tended to bypass the issue. This is reflected in the conspicuous absence of employment in influential strategies like the PRSPs (poverty reduction strategy papers) and MDGs (millennium development goals) – at least in the initial thinking on them.[2] After the MDGs were launched at the beginning of the present millennium, it took eight years to have a few indicators of employment included in the list. And even after that, there was very little thinking (let alone consensus) on how to attain the goals.[3] The situation changed when discussion started on the post-2015 development agenda. The global economy had just come out of the Great Recession that started in 2008, and a number of the major economies of the world were still suffering from high levels of unemployment. The international community was under pressure to take the issue of labour market recovery and employment into account in their deliberations on the post-MDG development agenda. The outcome was the inclusion of employment in one of the goals to be pursued (alongside economic growth).

However, it would be important to move from recognition of employment and its inclusion amongst the goals to identifying and putting in place appropriate strategies and policies for attaining the goal. As pointed out in Chapter 3, there has to be careful thinking even in terms of defining and articulating the goal of employment because this would have to take into account the level of development and characteristics of the economy. And when it comes to strategies for accelerating the growth of productive employment, one has to go beyond the conventional wisdom of suggesting that rigidities in labour markets constrain job creation, and hence labour markets should be made flexible.

Despite the recognition of the issue of employment, the debate surrounding the issue of jobs, especially on why economic growth often does not lead to job creation at an expected rate, has not been resolved. At one extreme, there is still a tendency to deny the existence of the problem of slow growth of jobs in relation to economic growth. For example, the World Bank's World Development Report on jobs (World Bank, 2012) attempts to dispel the notion of jobless growth by pointing out that economic growth is always accompanied by some growth in employment (pp. 98–99). There is, however, empirical evidence to show that there have been cases of zero growth of employment when economic growth has been positive (Islam, 2010; Islam and Islam, 2015). Moreover, the term "jobless growth" need not be interpreted in a literal sense of zero employment growth; when employment growth remains low despite substantial output growth, the situation may be termed as one of jobless growth.

A more important point to note is the approach adopted to explain the slow growth of jobs. In this respect, the conventional wisdom is to argue that distortions in the labour market and its imperfect functioning act as constraints on employment creation. This view equates employment policy with labour market policies – i.e., policies for making labour markets flexible. Influential studies like the report of the Commission on Growth (2008) and the IMF's report on job growth (IMF, 2013) are examples of this strand of work, although there are differences in details. In addition to labour market flexibility, the Growth Commission's report does talk about the need for measures to jump-start the process of job creation through encouraging the growth of new industries. Likewise, IMF (2013) talks about "selected policy interventions" that might lift barriers to private sector job creation. However, the debate on employment still seems to fall short of recognizing that growth and labour market flexibility alone cannot solve the problem of slow employment growth.

The present chapter questions the conventional wisdom of how the challenge of full employment in developing countries can be addressed and points out that a serious re-thinking of development strategies is required to pursue the goal of productive employment for all. Three elements of conventional wisdom about job creation that need questioning are (i) economic growth always creates jobs, (ii) job creation is hindered primarily by rigidities in labour markets, and (iii) education and training is key to attaining the employment goal. It may be recalled that some of the earlier chapters of this book have already dealt with the first issue mentioned above. So, the present chapter starts by recapitulating the basic evidence and arguments relating to growth and employment. After that, it addresses the question whether job creation is hindered only by rigidities in the labour market or whether there are other more important factors. Finally, an attempt is made to provide an outline of the direction in which re-thinking of development strategies is needed in order to attain the employment goals appropriate for developing countries.

Does economic growth always lead to employment?

Empirical evidence (presented in Islam and Islam, 2015 and in Chapter 4 of the present volume) has shown that employment intensity of growth (measured by the percentage change in employment in comparison with the percentage change in output) in manufacturing industries in many developing countries has been lower than what was expected on the basis of the experience of the countries of East and South East Asia who were successful in combining high rates of economic growth with high rates of employment growth. Moreover, employment intensity of growth declined during the 1990s compared to the 1980s.

Moreover, there are countries (viz., Mauritius, Pakistan, Philippines, and South Africa during the 1990s) where employment growth in manufacturing declined despite positive output growth. In fact, the number of such cases was larger during the 1990s (Islam and Islam, 2015). This provides further support to the conclusion that output growth in the second period has been less employment-intensive than in the first period. It is also clear that positive output growth is not necessarily associated with positive employment growth. Output growth in several cases has not only been "jobless" in a literal sense, but there has also been a decline in employment when output has grown.

The decline in the employment intensity of growth in developing countries as a whole continued during the 2000s. And that decline was particularly sharp in Latin American countries (Kucera and Roncolato, 2014). And the empirical evidence presented in Chapter 4 shows that employment intensity of growth declined in South Asia as well.[4]

Is job creation hindered by rigidities in the labour market?

Theoretical arguments

According to the standard neoclassical theory, output growth is supposed to lead to employment growth, and interventions in the labour market, e.g., through labour laws, trade unions, or minimum wages, distort the labour market and prevent it from producing the optimal outcome in terms of employment. It is argued on the basis of that theory that employment growth, especially in developing countries, is constrained by restrictive labour laws and trade union interventions that create rigidities in the labour market. But the debate on this issue is far from settled because there are studies pointing out that available evidence does not lend support to the hypothesis of labour market rigidities constraining employment growth. Before looking at the empirical evidence on the two sides of this debate, it may be useful to recapitulate the theoretical arguments behind this hypothesis and break it down into its major components so that the evidence on each may be systematically examined.

There are at least three aspects of labour market imperfections that, in theory, can adversely affect employment by creating rigidity and making adjustment difficult. First, minimum wage legislation may prevent wages from falling at times and in situations when downward adjustment is needed in order to clear the market. For example, even in economies characterized by the existence of surplus labour, minimum wage legislation may prevent wages from being pushed downward beyond a certain level and employment from expanding. Also, when labour demand declines during an economic downturn, one way of bringing about adjustment would be to reduce wages, but the existence of minimum wages may prevent that from taking place.

Second, regulations relating to the labour market, e.g., employment protection law (EPL), severance pay, provision of unemployment insurance and the duration of the benefit, etc. may make employers reluctant to hire when needed. For example, provisions in a country's EPL relating to firing of workers may create a perception among employers that it will be difficult to make downward adjustment in the workforce when they may have to. That, in turn, may discourage them from hiring, even when additional workers are needed during a period of economic expansion. Requirement to make severance payment for terminating workers may have the same effect mentioned above.

It is often argued that the existence of unemployment insurance and a generous duration of its benefits may discourage workers from actively looking for jobs and encourage them to remain on benefits for a longer period than is warranted by conditions in the labour market.

Third, imperfections may be created through the industrial relations route when trade union activities influence workforce adjustment or wage rates. That would imply that the level of unionization in an industry or firm may have an adverse effect on employment.

The empirical evidence

As for the impact of legislated minimum wages on employment, the available empirical evidence does not enable one to draw a definite conclusion in either direction. It would be important to note in this context that the literature on this subject is so vast that it would be almost impossible even to attempt a comprehensive review.[5] Most of these studies focus on developed countries, although there are some on developing countries as well.[6] Not surprisingly, studies differ considerably in terms of the methodologies employed and the type of data used. One study (Broecke et al., not dated) points out that the effect on employment depends on methodology and data used, and more recent (post-1995) studies are more likely to show positive effect on employment.

One review (Neumark, 2018) covering developed countries concludes that most country studies show negative effect on employment though there are some that show positive effect as well. For developing countries, the results are more mixed – studies showing both positive and negative effects and, in some cases, no impact at all. One review that covers studies on ten major emerging economies, viz., Brazil, Chile, China, Colombia, India, Indonesia, Mexico, Russian Federation, South Africa, and Turkey,[7] concludes that increases in minimum wages have minimal or no impact on employment (Broecke et al., not dated). Menon and Rodgers (2017) report positive effect for Brazil and Mexico and negative effect for Indonesia and Bangladesh. Bel-man and Wolfson (2016) mention a study on Indonesia that shows negative employment effect for small domestically owned firms and positive effects for large domestically owned farms and farms with some foreign ownership. The same review reports result from a study on China that found positive employment effect for firms that survived.

Nataraj et al. (2014) conducts meta-regression analysis of the impact of minimum wages on employment and finds that minimum wages are associated with lower formal employment and higher informal employment, and so, the impact on overall employment is ambiguous.[8] However, they admit that the study "cannot derive solid conclusions from the ... review because of the paucity of studies and the methodological difficulties encountered" (p. 556).

One study on India (Menon and Rodgers, 2017) that uses National Sample Survey Organisation's employment survey data and data on minimum wages across states and industries present interesting results. For urban areas, the study shows no impact of minimum wages on employment, while in rural areas, there was positive income effect without any negative effect on employment.

In Bangladesh, the minimum wages for the ready-made garment industry were raised in 2006, 2010, and 2013 without any adverse effect on employment. As shown in Chapter 7, employment in the industry not only increased after the 2006 adjustment, but the rate of growth was higher compared to the years before the rise (Table 7.1). Employment in the industry stagnated in the industry after 2012, but that cannot be ascribed to the rise in minimum wages in 2013. After the major accident in 2013, the industry had to face severe scrutiny on a variety of fronts including safety standards and the situation regarding rights of workers. The changes that are taking place in the industry as a result include changes in the size structure and introduction of more modern machinery. So, it is difficult to identify a single factor (be it minimum wages or structural and technological change) that has caused employment to stagnate after 2012.

The upshot of the above review of the evidence on the impact of minimum wages on employment in developing countries is that there is very little basis to argue that minimum wages (or for that matter, high wages) cause rigidity in the labour market, which, in turn, is responsible for low or negative growth in employment. The experience of Bangladesh provides a good example of flexibility in wages and yet decline in the growth of employment. Data presented in Chapter 4 show that real wages in the country – overall as well as in manufacturing – declined between 2012 and 2106; and yet, employment growth declined.

There are studies pointing out that labour market institutions in the form of EPL or unemployment benefits do not necessarily hinder the growth of employment (e.g., Bean, 1994; Nickel, 1997; Forteza and Rama, 2002; Kapsos, 2005). On Europe, a widely cited article by Bean (1994) argues that the

available evidence does not show that the existence of generous unemployment benefits was the cause of persistent unemployment. Nickel (1997) also
shows that all types of labour market rigidities do not have an adverse effect
on unemployment rates.[9] He concludes:

> Labour market rigidities that do not appear to have serious implications
> for average levels of unemployment include the following: 1) strict em-
> ployment protection legislation and general legislation on labour market
> standards; 2) generous levels of unemployment benefits, so long as these
> are accompanied by pressures on the unemployed to take jobs by, for
> example, fixing the duration of benefit and providing resources to raise
> the ability/willingness of the unemployed to take jobs; and 3) high levels
> of unionization and union coverage, so long as they are offset by high
> levels of coordination in wage bargaining, particularly among employers.
> (Nickel, 1997, p. 72)

A study by Forteza and Rama (2002) covering 119 countries (i.e., both developed and developing) shows that minimum wages and mandated benefits
do not hinder economic growth. They argue that curtailing social security
benefits might not contribute much to economic performance.

An econometric exercise undertaken by Kapsos (2005) demonstrates that
rigidities in the labour market do not have a negative effect on employment
elasticity. In his cross-section analysis with data from 100 countries, he uses
the World Bank's "employment rigidity index" (which is the average of three
indices, viz., difficulty of hiring, difficulty of firing, and rigidity of hours) and
finds that there is no statistically significant relation between employment
elasticity and employment rigidity index. Moreover, the sign of the coeffi-
cient is not in the expected direction.

One study (Chetty, 2013) addresses the question whether extending unemployment benefits increases unemployment rates in the USA. On the basis of
the results of nearly a dozen economic studies on the country, it concludes:

> ...a 10-week extension in unemployment benefits raises the average
> amount of time people spend out of work by at most one week. This
> simple, unassailable finding implies that policy makers can extend un-
> employment benefits to provide assistance to those out of work without
> substantially increasing unemployment rates.

Labour market rigidity and employment: the debate on India

The debate that took place on labour market rigidity and employment in
India during the 1990s and the first decade of the 2000s is perhaps the most
notable among such debates covering developing countries. So, it may be
useful to look at that debate, albeit briefly. The debate was basically spurred
by the decline in employment growth during the 1990s compared to the

earlier decades despite a notable rise in GDP growth, and some studies (e.g., Besley and Burgess, 2004) blaming it on labour market rigidity – especially on the difficulty of firing workers in large farms under the Industrial Disputes Act of 1947.[10] On the practical side, after the introduction of wide-ranging economic reforms in 1991, employers of India started clamouring for reforms in the labour market and trade unions took the opposite position. In order to understand this debate, it would be useful to start by looking at some numbers that lay at its background. Table 8.1 presents some numbers compiled from various studies.

A few observations may be made on the basis of the figures presented in Table 8.1. First, for the economy as a whole, growth of employment declined after 1990. Although there was some recovery after 2000, the growth rate did not go back to the pre-1990 rates. Second, growth of employment in organized manufacturing rose substantially over the decades. Except for a period of negative growth during 1997–98 to 2001–02, employment growth in the sector was higher in the 2000s compared to the 1990s and the earlier decades.[11] It was growth of employment in the economy as a whole that declined in the 1990s compared to the earlier decades. And since that happened when overall economic growth was picking up, and people started wondering whether that growth could be dubbed as jobless, a debate on the causes of low employment ensued, and the spotlight fell on labour market institutions. But if one focusses on organized manufacturing, it cannot be said that there was a secular decline in employment growth. And as the labour market rigidity argument would apply more to the organized sector, it seems that there is no prima facie case for arguing that employment growth declined in India because of labour laws causing rigidity.

However, Besley and Burgess (2004) pointed out that states which amended the Industrial Disputes Act in a pro-worker direction experienced lower

Table 8.1 Annual Growth (%) of Employment in India

Period	Annual growth (%)	Coverage	Source
1961–90	2	Whole economy	Sharma (2007)
1990–92	1.5	Do	Do
1993–2000	1	Do	Do
1983–94	1.2	Organized sector	Do
1994–2000	0.53	Do	Do
1983–94	1.78	Whole economy	ILO (2009)
1994–2000	1.12	Do	Do
2000–05	2.46	Do	Do
1973/74–1990/91	1.6	Organized manufacturing	Goldar (2004)
1990/91–1997/98	3.1	Do	Do
1997/98–2001/02	−3.3	Do	Do
1999/2000–2011/12	1.5	Whole economy	Ghose (2015)
Do	3	All manufacturing	Do
Do	5.9	Organized manufacturing	Do
Do	1.7	Unorganized manufacturing	Do

Sources: Goldar (2004), Ghose (2015), ILO (2009), and Sharma (2007).

output, employment, and investment in registered formal manufacturing.[12] And on the basis of that evidence, they argued that the balance of power is tilted in favour of workers, and that is not good for long-term growth of output and employment. Fallon and Lucas (1991) argued that faster growth of wages relative to consumer prices abetted by job security regulations resulted in the reduction of employment during 1959–60 to 1981–82. But a number of subsequent studies produced empirical evidence to argue that (i) wage increases were justified by increases in productivity (Papola, 1994), and (ii) labour market institutions play a minor role, if any, in determining employment (Sharma, 2006, 2007).

Using data from a survey of 1300 manufacturing firms across nine industrial groups, Sharma (2007) showed the following: (i) increase or decrease in labour cost did not have a significant effect on employment; (ii) a higher proportion of the bigger firms were able to lower employment, which implies that there were factors other than labour laws that played a role in the ability to adjust the workforce; (iii) both unionized and non-unionized firms raised capital intensity; and (iv) there was flexibility in the labour market irrespective of provisions in the labour laws.

Like the above-mentioned study, Ghose (2015) concludes:

> The evidence also shows that flexibility is very much there in practice. There is widespread use of regular informal and casual employees in the organized sector. ... Enterprise surveys show that most entrepreneurs view labour regulations as a minor problem.
>
> (p. 11)

Based on a review of a set of studies, Shyam Sundar (2005) concludes: (i) minimum wage laws can be and are often by-passed, so much so that this is not a source of rigidity; (ii) revisions to minimum wages are so ineffective that labour costs are unlikely to impose a burden on employers; (iii) presence of trade unions does not act as a deterrent to raising employment; and (iv) employment in the organized manufacturing sector grew in the first half of the 1990s, "despite the prevalence of unaltered statutory regulations impacting on employment decisions of firms" (p. 2276).

Although the above summary of the labour market flexibility debate on India is not intended to be a synthesis of the entire literature in this field (which is vast), it nevertheless indicates that the empirical basis for blaming labour market rigidity for low employment growth is not strong. Admittedly, the studies cited above use different indicators of rigidity in labour markets and use different methods to examine the impact on employment growth. And the results often are influenced by methods and data sources. But they should provide adequate ground to at least cast doubt on the argument that making labour markets flexible would provide solutions to the problem of low employment growth.

Despite the lack of consensus on whether labour market rigidity is to be blamed for low employment growth in India, policymaking seems to be focussing primarily on labour laws and labour market reforms – if the chapter titled "Employment and Labour Reforms" in the latest strategy document of the government (NITI Aayog, 2018[13]) is any indicator. While the document mentions a few schemes for generating employment (including the well-known Mahatma Gandhi National Rural Employment Guarantee Scheme – MGNREGS), the seven items[14] mentioned in the section on "Way Forward" does not include anything on economic policies needed to make growth more employment-intensive via a faster growth of sectors that are labour-intensive by their character. Labour law reforms seem to be the mechanism that is expected to facilitate the growth of such sectors.[15]

How helpful is education and training in meeting the employment challenge?

By preparing the workforce for the labour market, education and training should contribute to meeting the employment challenge. Better educated and trained people should have a greater probability of being employed because education and training can raise qualifications and make labour force more productive. This should be reflected in lower rate of unemployment for those with higher levels of education. But such a negative relationship between education and unemployment may hold better in situations where the labour market as a whole seeks educated people and sectors that are larger and grow at higher rates seek more educated workers. This may not be the case in developing countries where labour markets are often found to be segmented and the educated find jobs only in certain segments of the economy. For example, in a dual economy with a predominantly traditional segment that consists of agriculture and allied activities, educated workers are likely to find jobs mainly in the modern sector, which is typically small, especially at the early stages of development. Such sectors may not require much educated worker except perhaps in research, extension service, etc. Likewise, construction, traditional crafts and other informal sector activities also may not require formally educated and trained workers. As an economy grows, the modern sector is also likely to grow in size, thus raising demand for a more educated and skilled workforce. Hence, in developing countries, one may not find a clear positive relationship between education and employment in terms of the simple indicators mentioned above.

How, then, is the importance of education for the labour market of developing economies likely to be manifested? As mentioned above, with economic growth, a dual economy is likely to witness expansion of its modern sectors, which, in turn, is expected to lead to increased demand for educated and skilled labour. In such a situation education and skill training would be important to facilitate mobility of workers from the traditional to the modern segments of the economy. Likewise, developing countries are expected to witness changes in the composition of labour force in terms of the status of employment – for example, from casual workers in agriculture to regular wage and salaried workers in manufacturing and other modern sectors. This may also imply a greater demand for more educated people. All these developments are likely to mean higher wages and earnings of workers with more education.[16]

What is the relationship like in reality between education and unemployment? Two kinds of data may be used to address this question. First is country-level data on unemployment by levels of education. Figures 8.1 and 8.2 present such data for India and Bangladesh. For both countries, one can see a positive relationship between the rate of unemployment and level of education – those with higher education suffer from higher rate of

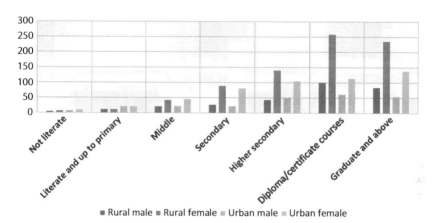

■ Rural male ■ Rural female ▨ Urban male ▨ Urban female

Figure 8.1 India: Unemployment Rate (per Thousand) by Levels of Education 2011–12.
Source: Author's construction based on data from NSSO (2014).

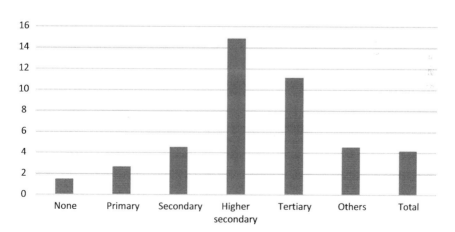

Figure 8.2 Bangladesh: Unemployment Rate (%) by Level of Education 2016–17.
Source: Author's construction based on data from the Labour Force Survey, 2016–17.

unemployment! In India, the rate of unemployment is particularly high for diploma/certificate holders. But more significantly, those with secondary and tertiary education suffer from higher unemployment rates than those who are illiterate or have only primary education.[17] The pattern is similar for Bangladesh if one ignores the inexplicably low rate of unemployment for "others".

Second, we look at cross-country data on the relationship between unemployment amongst the youth and average years of schooling (Figure 8.3). For a set of developing countries and for the period 1990–2010, the relationship is found to be positive. This apparently perverse result may not appear very surprising if one remembers the observations made above about the nature of the labour market in such countries, especially the segmented nature of the labour market and the demand for educated labour being limited mainly to the modern sectors of an economy. In such a situation, an expansion of education, especially at the secondary and tertiary levels may not correspond directly with the demand for the products.

Do the data presented above imply that education is not of much use in employment in developing countries? Why then is there so much demand for higher education? In order to understand this, it may be necessary to look at some more data relating to employment and education and returns to education. As for the latter, estimates of private rates of return to education at various levels show that there has been a change since the 1990s. In developing countries, during the 1970s and 1980s, returns used to be higher for lower levels of education. But since the 1990s, and especially in the current millennium, private rates of return to investment in higher education have been found to be higher than in primary and secondary education.[18]

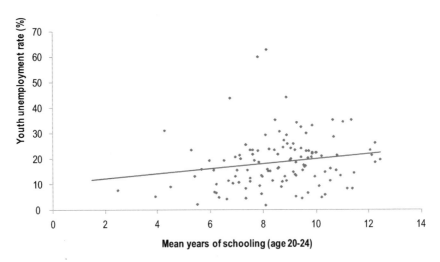

Figure 8.3 Youth Unemployment Rate and Years of Schooling (Developing Countries).
Source: Matsumoto et al. (2012).

This implies that even though educated members of the labour force may experience higher rates of unemployment, the difference in remuneration (taking into account the duration of unemployment) perhaps more than justifies the required investment.[19]

Re-thinking development strategies

Need for a multi-pronged strategy

It may be recalled that this book started by arguing the need to conceptualize the goal of full employment differently for developing countries rather than in terms of bringing down the rate of open unemployment which is anyway found to be quite low. And in that context, the importance of the pattern of growth has been pointed out. The pattern of growth has to be such that it will engender transformation of the structure of both output and employment and enable people to move from jobs characterized by low productivity and returns to ones with higher productivity and returns. The question is: why is this not happening at the desired pace and how the pace can be accelerated? Development strategies will need to address this question.

Although the development discourse at the international level is not known for its sensitivity to employment issues, the issue did get attention in the context of the SDGs and employment has been included in one of the goals and indicators have been suggested for use in monitoring progress towards the goal. But it has been pointed out in Chapter 3 of this book that in the context of developing countries the goal itself has to be conceptualized differently and indicators reflecting such conceptualization will have to be thought of. Given the diversity among the developing countries, these tasks as well as that of shaping development strategies towards attaining the goals would be best done at the country level.

A multi-pronged strategy would be needed to pursue the goal of productive employment in developing countries. Of course, the primary focus should be on growth-induced employment so that jobs are created through the process of growth. A strategy for employment-intensive growth would involve the adoption of policies for promoting the growth of sectors that are by nature labour-intensive[20] until surplus labour available in the economy is exhausted. It should be possible to identify such sectors by looking at the degree of employment intensity of various sectors and sub-sectors[21], and it would then be a matter of creating the right incentive structure for their growth.

The second part of the strategy could consist of a set of policies and programmes that can be conceptualized under the rubric of active labour market policies (ALMPs).[22] They would include programmes aimed directly at promoting employment, e.g., through entrepreneurship development and special programmes for creating wage employment,[23] as well as other programmes like skill development, retraining of workers to facilitate structural adjustment in an economy, and matching of workers and jobs. If the experience of developed countries is any guide, employment growth is positively associated with government's expenditure on ALMPs.

Another important issue that needs to be taken into account in a country's effort in attaining the goal of productive employment and decent work is the stubborn persistence of informal employment even in economies with high growth. A large proportion of those who are engaged in such work not only suffer from low productivity and incomes but also face a high degree of vulnerability. They include own account as well as wage-based workers – both in formal and informal segments of an economy. The only way the share of the informal sector can decline substantially is through a successful pursuit of the kind of employment strategy that has been outline above. However, the share of employment in the informal economy is so high in many developing countries and has shown so little response to economic growth that it may not be realistic to expect much decline in a medium-term scenario. Hence, strategies are needed for dealing with this phenomenon.

There are three aspects that need attention in the above context: (i) productivity, wages, and earnings; (ii) obstacles and barriers faced by the informal sector enterprises; and (iii) conditions of work and social protection. During the phase of labour absorption towards the Lewis turning point, more emphasis will have to be given to the first two issues, though the third should not be neglected altogether. However, as an economy attains higher levels of development, attention would have to be given to job quality issues like conditions in which work is carried out and social protection of workers. Given the unorthodox nature of the challenge, the response will also have to be innovative.[24] A two-pronged strategy may be thought of in this regard. That would involve combining the positive approach of improving the level of productivity and incomes of people engaged in micro- and small enterprises with the normative approach of applying labour standards (at least the core ones) gradually to informal segments of the labour market.

The review in the third section of this chapter indicates that the slow pace of structural transformation and growth of productive employment cannot be ascribed only to labour market rigidities. The experience of the countries that were more successful in attaining high rate of employment alongside high economic growth demonstrates that a combination of economic and labour market policies contributed to their success. On the economic front, a trading regime that does not discriminate between import substitutes and export-oriented products is important, but not sufficient, especially if there are distortions in the relative prices of factors of production. Macroeconomic policies can play an important role by ensuring that relative prices of the factors of production are not distorted and correctly reflect their relative scarcities.

In addition to trade and macroeconomic policies, sector-specific policies may be used to extend positive support to export-oriented labour-intensive industries. They may range from tax holiday, licensed warehouses for duty-free imports of inputs, assistance in developing new products and in tapping export markets, subsidy on training for R&D, etc.

Economic policies that create an enabling environment for output growth to take an employment-intensive character would have to be accompanied by policies aimed at enabling members of the labour force to attain qualifications needed to access the jobs that become available as a result of growth. Again, the experience of successful countries shows that necessary investments were made and incentives provided for the private sector to contribute to the development of human capital simultaneously with employment-intensive economic growth.

As for labour market policies, since labour market rigidities are accused of creating obstacle to employment creation, it would be useful to examine if there is solid empirical evidence in support of such arguments. Rather than blaming labour market rigidity in a blanket manner, it may be useful to look carefully at specific aspects of labour market institutions that are in need of reform.

However, the consideration of the need for flexibility in the labour markets should be combined with the need for security and protection of the workers.[25] Social protection is an important element in the concept of decent work, and hence it would be important to extend it to all workers irrespective of the segment in which they work.

Mainstreaming employment into policymaking

A broad range of actors within governments would need to be involved if the issue of productive employment and decent work were to be addressed seriously. For example, monetary policy (and hence the action on the part of central banks) is important not only from the point of view of driving the overall growth and employment generation process of an economy but also from the point of view of providing access to finance in an inclusive manner. Likewise, fiscal policies can play an important role in supporting the process of overall growth of an economy but also that of sectors that are critical in achieving the diversification and transformation that we are talking about. Similar remarks may be made about actions and policies undertaken by other government ministries like trade and commerce, industry, agriculture, labour, etc. In sum, what is required is to make employment a central element in the formulation of policies and action programmes of all relevant government agencies/institutions, and they all need to be sensitized about the centrality of employment in the fight against poverty, vulnerability, and deprivation. The tasks involved in the process will have to be delineated carefully and capacities for undertaking them strengthened.

Actual translation of the concept of mainstreaming of employment will, however, depend on the extent to which sectors with high employment potential are given importance in the overall growth strategy and how they are sought to be encouraged to grow faster. In other words, mainstreaming of employment, in the first place, would require that the pattern of economic growth favours sectors with high employment potential. In developing countries where planning is still used as a mechanism to determine the rate and pattern of economic growth, the state can play a direct role in this respect through the allocation of public investment which continues to be a significant part of the total investment, especially in infrastructure. In market economies, the incentive structure through market prices can be used to influence the direction of private investment.

The next level at which mainstreaming of employment can take place is in the framing of macroeconomic, i.e., fiscal, monetary (credit), and trade-policies. Of course, these policies have their own objectives, but employment generation could also be one of them. At least, it could be ensured that they do not militate against the objective of employment generation. For example, tax policy would have increased revenue as its main objective, but it could also include a structure of incentives for employment-intensive sectors or technologies. It could also ensure that taxation structure does not discourage employment generation by levying higher tax rates on establishments employing more people *per se*. Subsidy policy could also be used for employment creation.[26]

Given the multiplicity of actors, coordination of employment policy implementation becomes critical (more on this will be said in the next chapter). The coordination mechanism must involve major actors and stakeholders including from government, employers' and workers' organizations, and civil society institutions. Countries with a decentralized structure of administration, both horizontal and vertical coordination, will be required. The lead role, be it at a supra-ministerial level (e.g., the head of the government) or at the level of line ministry, has to be clearly articulated and mandated. The technical capacity of the coordinating institution will be important.

Summing up

High rate of employment-intensive growth and structural transformation is important for attaining the goal of full productive employment and decent work in developing countries. Employment policy cannot be equated with labour market policies; it has to be broad-based and has to focus on the rate as well as the pattern of economic growth. A combination of economic and labour market policies is needed to address the various factors that are responsible for growth not leading to desired job creation. Employment policy needs to be mainstreamed into the policymaking process, ensuring the involvement of all relevant stakeholders, e.g., various government agencies, workers' and employers' organizations, and members of the civil society. Given the multiplicity of actors in this process, a strong and effective coordination mechanism is going to be key.

Notes

1 This chapter draws on Islam (2016).
2 In fact, employment did not receive much attention even in standard theories of development – whether one talks about the early theories (e.g., those propounded by Nurkse, Hirschman, Myrdal, et al.) or models of development in dualistic economies (à la Lewis, Fei, and Ranis) and models of migration (viz. Harris-Todaro). Exceptions are the research undertaken during the 1970 and

1980s of which Sen (1975) is a good example. The latter contains references to some very good work undertaken in the context of India. Likewise, work undertaken within the ILO since the 1970s focusses on various aspects of the employment issue. However, the extent to which such work has been able to influence policy stance at the international or national level remains a question.

3 Of course, this does not mean that there has been no attempt at formulating and implementing employment policies at the country level. A number of countries have made notable efforts in this area. Some examples will be provided in the next chapter.

4 See, also, Khan (2007) which provides a synthesis of the experience of selected countries of Asia.

5 One study (Belman and Wolfson, 2016) mentions that there were 600 studies on the subject between 2000 and 2010.

6 Notable among the latter are Nataraj et al. (2014), Broecke et al. (not dated, available online, accessed on 3 January 2019), Menon and Rodgers (2017), etc. See also the review of literature in Menon and Rodgers (2017) for references to studies on a few developing countries.

7 It provides qualitative review of 74 studies and meta-analysis of coefficients and signs of 26 and 57 studies, respectively.

8 A total of 17 studies were covered by this review. They included 4 studies on low-income countries (LICs, according to the World Bank classification), 11 studies on recent LICs and 2 cross-country studies. The LICs included Bangladesh, Kenya and Zimbabwe while the recent LICs included India, Indonesia, Ghana, Honduras and Nicaragua (among others).

9 Of course, there are studies (reviewed by Nataraj et al. 2014) that support the neoclassical proposition that more stringent labour regulations are associated with lower formal sector employment and higher informal sector employment. But this review also mentions studies that challenge this view.

10 The Industrial Disputes Act of 1947 (India) provides a mechanism for securing industrial peace and harmony through a machinery and procedure for the settlement of industrial dispute. The law applies only to the organized sector. One of the most talked about provisions is the procedure to be followed for layoffs, retrenchments, and closure of factories. Chapter V-B, introduced by an amendment in 1976, requires firms employing 300 or more workers to obtain government permission for layoffs, retrenchments, and closures. A further amendment in 1982 (which took effect in 1984) expanded its ambit by reducing the threshold to 100 workers. During 1958–90, fifteen major states of India introduced a number of amendments to the Act.

11 Nath (2014) points out that the growth in employment in the organized manufacturing industries has been led more by contract and casual workers.

12 Similar results have been reported by Shembavnekar (2016).

13 This document spells out strategies to be adopted by the government during 2019–22.

14 They are enhance skills and apprenticeships, labour law reforms, enhance female labour force participation, improve data collection on employment, ease industrial relations, compliance with minimum wages, and working conditions and social security.

15 This comes out in another government document, viz., Economic Survey 2016–17 (Government of India, 2017) where various constraints on the growth of labour-intensive sectors like garments, shoes, etc. are discussed and yet the conclusion is tilted more towards labour market reforms.

16 Education may also help raise productivity and incomes in traditional sectors like agriculture. See, for example, Chadha (2003) for pointing this out in the context of India.

17 A positive relationship between the rate of unemployment and level of education is found for Sri Lanka as well. See World Bank (2012).
18 See Palmer et al. (2007) for a compilation of relevant data. See also Psacharopoulos and Patrinos (2004).
19 See Islam and Islam (2015) for a more detailed analysis of the relationship between education, training, and employment.
20 This might be interpreted as "picking winners" and hence undesirable. But what is being suggested here is a policy of ensuring the operation of market forces without distortion so that labour-intensive industries do not face obstacles and can grow. There should be no hesitation in adopting an "industrial policy" for the purpose of attaining this goal.
21 See, for example, Mitra and Bhanumurthy (2008) for estimates of employment elasticity of various industries in India.
22 ALMP may be formally defined as policies that facilitate labour market integration through purposive and selective interventions to create demand for labour, enhance employability of the workforce through training and retraining, and contribute to matching supply and demand. The measures include employment creation programmes like public works, promotion of self-employment, subsidies for providing incentives to employ special categories of workers (e.g., the youth, long-term unemployed), training and retraining, job search assistance, and employment services.
23 Programmes for creating employment could be considered to be part of the growth strategy of a country. By contributing to income generation, employment programmes could contribute to boosting domestic demand which, in turn, could be an important driver of economic growth. For this line of reasoning, see Nayyar (2014).
24 A good example of an innovative initiative to improve the quality of informal sector jobs through social protection is India's Unorganized Workers' Social Security Bill adopted by the country's parliament in 2008. Under the Act, provision was made to bring 340 million workers (out of a total labour force of 458 million) under the cover of pension, and basic health, life and disability insurance as well as group accident insurance within a span of five years. While passing of this Act has not been easy and implementation has faced obstacles, useful lessons can be learnt from the thinking and effort that have gone behind it.
25 Several countries of Europe, e.g., Denmark, Netherlands, and Sweden, provide example of models of labour market that combine flexibility in making adjustments to the workforce with protection for workers. For a discussion of the origin of the concept and its application, see Wilthagen and Tros (2004).
26 One example of how fiscal policy can be used for supporting employment is provided by the Republic of Korea, where the government has made efforts to create jobs through taxation and industrial policies. First, a "tax credit system for investment in job creation" has been instituted under which tax benefits are provided on the basis of newly created employment. Second, for SMEs that increase employment, the government has implemented a two-year tax credit system for social insurance premiums. Third, income tax for youth who are employed by SMEs is totally exempted up to three years. Fourth, earned income tax credit system has been revised to encourage work and family formation among low income households (Kang, 2014).

Bibliography

Bangladesh Bureau of Statistics (2017): *Labour Force Survey 2016–17*. Dhaka.
Bean, Charles (1994): "European Unemployment: A Survey", *Journal of Economic Literature*, Vol. 32, pp. 573–619.

Belman, Dale and Paul Wolfson (2016): *What Does the Minimum Wage Do in Developing Countries? A Review of Studies and Methodologies.* Conditions of Work and Employment Series No. 62. ILO, Geneva.

Besley, T. and R. Burgess (2004): "Can Labour Regulation Hinder Economic Performance? Evidence from India", *The Quarterly Journal of Economics*, Vol. 119, No. 1, pp. 91–134.

Broecke, Stijn, Alessia Forti and Marieke Vandeweyer (not dated, available online): "The Effect of Minimum Wages on Employment in Emerging Economies: A Literature Review". http://nationalminimumwage.co.za/wp-content/uploads/2015/09/0221-Effect-of-Minimum-Wages-on-Employment-in-Emerging-Economies-A-Literature-Review.pdf (Accessed on 3 January 2019).

Chadha, G.K. (2003): *What Is Dominating the Indian Labour Market? Peacock's Feathers or Feet?* Presidential Address, 45th Annual Conference of the Indian Society of Labour Economics, 15–17 December 2003.

Chandrasekhar, C.P. (2008): *Re-Visiting the Policy Environment for Engendering Employment Intensive Economic Growth.* Draft paper, International Labour Office, Geneva.

Chetty, Raj (2013): "Yes, Economics Is a Science", *International New York Times*, 22 October 2013.

Commission on Growth and Development (2008): *The Growth Report: Strategies for Sustainable Growth and Inclusive Development.* The World Bank, Washington, D.C.

Fallon, P. and R. Lucas (1993): "Job Security Regulations and the Dynamic Demand for Industrial Labour in India and Zimbabwe", *Journal of Development Economics*, Vol. 40, No. 2, pp. 241–275.

Forteza, Alvaro and Martin Rama (2002): *Labor Market "Rigidity" and the Success of Economic Reforms Across More Than One Hundred Countries.* Reported in ADB (2005): *Labour Markets in Asia: Promoting Full, Productive and Decent Employment.* Asian Development Bank, Manila.

Ghose, Ajit K. (2015): *India Needs Manufacturing-Led Growth.* Working Paper 01/2015, Institute for Human Development, Delhi.

GOI (Government of India, Planning Commission) (2006): *Towards Faster and More Inclusive Growth: An Approach to the 11th Five Year Plan.* New Delhi.

——— (2017): *Economic Survey 2016–17.* Ministry of Finance, New Delhi.

Goldar, Bishwanath (2004): *Productivity Trends in Indian Manufacturing in the Pre- and Post-Reform Periods.* Working Paper 137. Indian Council for Research on International Economic Relations, New Delhi.

Harris, John R. and Michael P. Todaro (1970): "Migration, Unemployment and Development: A Two-Sector Analysis", *American Economic Review*, Vol. 60, No. 1, pp. 126–142.

International Labour Organization (2009): *Towards an Employment Strategy for India.* ILO, New Delhi.

International Monetary Fund (2013): *Jobs and Growth: Analytical and Operational Conditions for the Fund.* IMF, Washington, D.C. www.imf.org/external/np/pp/eng/2013/031413.pdf (Accessed on 14 July 2014).

Islam, Iyanatul and David Kucera (2014): *Beyond Macroeconomic Stability: Structural Transformation and Inclusive Development.* ILO, Geneva and Palgrave Macmillan, Basingstoke.

Islam, Rizwanul (2006a): *The Nexus of Economic Growth, Employment and Poverty Reduction: An Empirical Analysis*, in Islam (2006b).

——— (ed.) (2006b): *Fighting Poverty: The Development-Employment Link.* Lynn Rienner, Boulder and London.

———— (2010): "The Challenge of Jobless Growth in Developing Countries: An Analysis with Cross-Country Data". Occasional Paper Series No. 01. Bangladesh Institute of Development Studies, Dhaka.

———— (2013): "Economic Growth, Employment and Poverty: Evidence and Lessons", in *Yojana, Special Issue on Growth, Employment and Poverty*, October 2013. A Development Monthly published by the Ministry of Information, Government of India.

———— (2014): "Employment Policy Implementation Mechanisms: A Synthesis Based on Country Studies". Employment Working Paper No. 161, Employment Policy Department, ILO, Geneva.

———— (2016): "Pursuing the Employment Goal: Need for Re-Thinking Development Strategies", *The Indian Journal of Labour Economics*, Vol. 58, No. 2, pp. 196–216.

Islam, Rizwanul and Iyanatul Islam (2015): *Employment and Inclusive Development*. Routledge, London.

Kang, S. (2014): "Employment Policy Implementation Mechanisms in the Republic of Korea". Working Paper, Employment Policy Department, ILO, Geneva.

Kapsos, Steven (2005): "The Employment Intensity of Growth: Trends and Macroeconomic Determinants". Employment Strategy Papers, 2005/12. ILO, Geneva.

Khan, A.R. (2007): *Asian Experience on Growth, Employment and Poverty: An Overview with Special Reference to the Findings of Some Recent Case Studies*, ILO, Geneva and UNDP, Colombo.

Kucera, D. and L. Roncolato (2014): *Structure Matters: Sectoral Drivers of Growth and the Labour Productivity-Employment Relationship*, in Islam and Kucera (2014).

Lewis, W.A. (1954): "Economic Development with Unlimited Supplies of Labour", *Manchester School*, Vol. 22, No. 2, pp. 139–191.

Matsumoto, Makiko, Martina Hengge and Iyanatul Islam (2012): "Tackling the Youth Employment Crisis: A Macroeconomic Perspective". Employment Sector Employment Working Paper No. 124, ILO, Geneva.

Menon, Nidhiya and Yana Van Der Meulen Rodgers (2017): "The Impact of the Minimum Wage on Male and Female Employment and Earnings in India", *Asian Development Review*, Vol. 34, No. 1, pp. 28–64.

Mitra, Arup and N.R. Bhanumurthy (2008): *Economic Growth, Employment and Poverty in Manufacturing, Construction and Trade in India*, Unpublished Draft, ILO, Geneva.

Nataraj, Shanthi, Francisco Perez-Arce, Krishna B. Kumar and Sinduja Srinivasan (2014): The Impact of Labour Market Regulation on Employment in Low-Income Countries: A Meta-Analysis", *Journal of Economic Surveys*, Vol. 28, No. 3, pp. 551–572.

Nath, Paaritosh (2014): "Labour Market Flexibility and Employment Growth in India's Organised Manufacturing Sector 1990–2010", *The Indian Journal of Labour Economics*, Vol. 57, No. 4, 2014.

National Sample Survey Office (NSSO), Ministry of Statistics and Programme Implementation, Government of India (2014): *Employment and Unemployment Situation in India, July 2011–June 2012, NSS 68th Round*. New Delhi.

Nayyar, Deepak (2014): "Why Employment Matters: Reviving Growth and Reducing Inequality", *International Labour Review*, Vol. 153, No. 3, pp. 351–364.

Neumark, David (2018): "Employment Effect of Minimum Wages". IZA World of Labour. https://wol.iza.org/uploads/articles/464/pdfs/employment-effects-of-minimum-wages.pdf?v=1 (Accessed on 14 January 2019).

Nickel, Stephen (1997): "Unemployment and Labour Market Rigidities: Europe versus North America", *Journal of Economic Perspectives*, Vol. XI, pp. 55–74.

NITI Aayog (2018): *Strategy for New India@75*. NITI Aayog, New Delhi.

Palmer, Robert, Ruth Wedgwood and Rachel Hayman (2007): *Educating out of Poverty? A Synthesis Report on Ghana, India, Kenya, Rwanda, Tanzania and South Africa*. Centre for African Studies, University of Edinburgh, Edinburgh and DFID, London.

Papola, T.S. (1994): "Structural Adjustment, Labour Market Flexibility and Employment", *The Indian Journal of Labour Economics*, Vol. 37, No. 1, pp. 3–16.

Psacharopoulos, George and Harry Anthony Patrinos (2004): "Returns to Education: A Further Update", *Education Economics*, Vol. 12, No. 2, pp. 111–134.

Sen, Amartya (1975): *Employment, Technology and Development*. Clarendon Press, Oxford.

Sharma, Alakh N. (2006, May 27): "Flexibility, Employment and Labour Market Reforms in India", *Economic and Political Weekly*, Vol. 41, No. 21, pp. 2078–2085.

————— (2007): "Flexibility, Employment and Labour Market Reforms in India". Working Paper No. 37, Institute for Human Development, New Delhi.

Shembavnekar, Nihar (2016): *Economic Reforms, Labour Markets and Formal Sector Employment: Evidence from India*. Department of Economics, University of Sussex.

Shyam Sundar, K.R. (2005): "Labour Flexibility Debate in India: A Comprehensive Review and Some Suggestions". *Economic and Political Weekly*, 28 May–4 June 2005, pp. 2274–2285.

Wilthagen, Ton and Frank Tros (2004, May): "The Concept of Flexicurity: A New Approach to Regulating Employment and Labour Markets", *Transfer: European Review of Labour and Research,* Vol. 10, No. 2, pp. 166–186.

World Bank (2012): *World Development Report 2013 Jobs*. The World Bank, Washington, D.C.

9 Implementation of Employment Strategies and Policies[1]

Introduction

In order to address the employment challenge, it would be important not merely to formulate strategies and policies for making economic growth more job-rich but also to implement such policies in an efficient and effective manner. Unless appropriate institutional arrangements can be put in place for coordinating policies, monitoring performance, and evaluating results, even sound policies may not produce the desired results. The other challenge is that of finding resources, especially when the question of allocating resources for active policies to be pursued by the government itself arises.

In reality, different countries adopt different approaches to the formulation and implementation of employment policies. They range from adoption of specific quantitative targets for the number of additional jobs to be created within a specified period to target rate of open unemployment. The institutional mechanisms for implementation also vary a great deal. Some countries like China and Republic of Korea have well-specified mechanisms to monitor and coordinate the process of implementation, while others (e.g., the countries of South Asia) may have lighter systems.

The purpose of the present chapter is to illustrate, with examples from selected countries[2], different approaches to the formulation and implementation of strategies and policies for employment. In doing so, attention will be given to alternative institutional approaches and modalities that can be adopted. The chapter starts by providing examples of employment policies, strategies, and targets adopted by several countries. It then describes the mechanisms for implementation of various policies and programmes and coordination among different institutions. That is followed by a description of programmes, e.g., public employment services, labour market information system, etc., which are used to provide support in implementing employment policies. Systems used for monitoring and evaluation of policies and programmes are also examined. The chapter concludes with a summary of lessons that can be drawn from the experiences reviewed in the chapter.

Employment policy: some examples

To recapitulate the discussion in the previous chapter, economic policies as well as labour market policies can influence the employment outcome of economic growth. Hence, when one talks about employment policy, it would be necessary to include both types of policies. Employment policies operate on both demand and supply sides of the equation. While some policies help augment demand for labour, others operate on the supply side (see Table 9.1). Demand-side measures include macroeconomic and sectoral policies and policies aimed at direct job creation. Expansionary macroeconomic policies help increase demand for labour by raising the rate of economic growth. On the other hand, carefully formulated monetary and fiscal policies may be helpful in influencing the pattern of growth to make it more employment-friendly. Likewise, sectoral policies are important for promoting the growth of sectors that are more employment-intensive. Similarly, direct job creation programmes (e.g., public works) are often used to create jobs.

On the supply side, policies relating to education may have both quantitative and qualitative effect on labour force. Policies aimed at raising the rate of enrolment and encouraging young people to continue with education/training can reduce the supply of labour in the market. Education and skill training can also improve the quality of labour force and help by reducing the mismatch between demand for and supply of labour. Active labour market policies (ALMPs, e.g., training and retraining of workers, employment services, etc.) play an important role in bringing about needed adjustments in the labour market and preventing unemployment.

National employment policies (NEPs) should ideally combine both kinds of policies mentioned above and should include elements ranging from macroeconomic and sectoral policies to education, training, and other ALMPs.[3] In developing countries where a very small proportion of total employment is in the formal segment of the labour market, employment policy should

Table 9.1 Possible Types and Areas of Employment Policies

Type of Policy	Areas of Policy
Demand side	*Macroeconomic policy*: (i) Growth inducing expansionary macroeconomic policy, (ii) fiscal and monetary policies to support employment-intensive sectors, (iii) subsidies for supporting job creation or for preserving jobs *Sector-level policies*: (i) policies in support of SMEs, (ii) policies in support of labour-intensive manufacturing industries *Direct job creation*: (i) programmes for creating jobs directly, e.g., through infrastructure, (ii) programmes targeted at specific groups, e.g., youth, older workers, women, etc.
Supply side	(i) Policies relating to education and training, (ii) active labour market policies (including training and retraining, employment services, etc.)

devote particular attention to macroeconomic and sectoral policies that would encourage high and sustained growth of more employment-intensive sectors of the economy, thus engendering structural transformation that would lead to high rate of employment growth. Such policies would have to be supplemented with policies on the supply side to ensure that those seeking jobs have appropriate skills required by the labour market. At the other end, in developed countries, the rate of economic growth is expected to be the main mechanism for growth of employment, and the role of macroeconomic policies should be to attain an appropriate balance between macroeconomic stability, economic growth, and employment. In such situations, it may be natural for employment policy to focus more on the labour market issues and use legislative tools and supply-side measures more vigorously to pursue the goals of ALMPs. Middle-income countries would lie somewhere in between the two types mentioned above where a judicious combination of various policies would be needed.

The priority attached to employment is reflected in different ways in different countries. In some countries, employment is given a place at the highest level of decision-making. In Brazil, for example, the Federal Constitution defines the obligations of the State with respect to employment policies. In China, employment is given priority at the highest level of decision-making, viz., the Central Committee of the Communist Party of China and the State Council. In other countries (e.g., in countries of South Asia, Republic of Korea, and South Africa), the priority attached to employment is reflected in the inclusion of employment as a goal in the country's development strategy.

The approach to employment policy and its scope also differ from country to country. While some countries adopt a comprehensive approach focussing on both demand and supply sides, as mentioned above, and attach importance to macroeconomic and sectoral policies in addition to labour market policies, there are others where the major focus is on labour market policies, and economic policies play an additional role. The summary descriptions of the approach adopted in various countries presented in Tables 9.2 and 9.3 reflect this difference to some extent, though not fully. For example, in Argentina, employment policy consists of income policy as well as policies aimed at both demand and supply sides of the labour market. However, an examination of the details does not show the presence of macroeconomic policies in the range of policies used. In addition to open unemployment, employment policies in Argentina give attention to the income aspect of employment (or the phenomenon of working poor), informal employment, social protection, and the use of child labour. On the other hand, in China, Korea, and South Africa, employment policies consist of a range of policies that include macroeconomic and sectoral policies as well as labour market policies.

Table 9.2 presents some basic information on the major elements of ALMPs adopted by the countries mentioned above. It appears from this description that while there is country-level variation in emphasis and details,

Table 9.2 Basic Characteristics of National Employment Policies in Selected Developing Countries

Country	Whether Employment Policy Incorporated into National Development Strategies	Whether a Comprehensive Approach (Combining Macroeconomic, Sectoral and Labour Market Policies) Adopted	The Major Elements of Active Labour Market Policies
Argentina	Decent work and employment included in the country's MDG issued in 2003	The employment policy encompasses income policies and policies affecting supply and demand for labour	Public employment service, vocational education and training network, and employment generation programmes
Bangladesh	Employment generation is mentioned as a major priority in both the Sixth and Seventh Five Year Plans (2010–15 and 2015–20, respectively)	The focus is on promoting productive employment through high growth of manufacturing and modern services	Skill development and entrepreneurship development programmes, and direct job creation programme for the ultra-poor
Brazil	The Federal Constitution defines the obligation of the State regarding employment policies	The government's strategy is to address the employment problem through growth-promoting macroeconomic policy. In practice, the employment policy consists of unemployment insurance, employment mediation, and skill development	Placement, training, employment incentives, and direct job creation
China	Central Committee of the Communist Party of China and the State Council attaches importance to employment as the priority strategy of the country	Employment strategy includes promoting employment through economic growth, entrepreneurship development, and skill training. Policies range from macroeconomic and sectoral policies to labour market policies	Strengthen public employment service and vocational training, Special Employment Fund for job creation, credit support for groups with difficulty

(Continued)

Country	Whether Employment Policy Incorporated into National Development Strategies	Whether a Comprehensive Approach (Combining Macroeconomic, Sectoral and Labour Market Policies) Adopted	The Major Elements of Active Labour Market Policies
India	The Twelfth Plan (2012–17) of the country made quantitative employment projections and indicated targets for job creation. But the *Strategy For New India @ 75* which is for the period 2018–23 focusses more on labour market reforms – although mention is made of employment generation and skill development programmes	Up to the Twelfth Plan, the focus was on boosting productive employment by promoting the growth of labour-intensive sectors	Mahatma Gandhi National Rural Employment Guarantee Programme (MGNREGP) is the flagship employment programme. There are skill development programmes as well
Republic of Korea	Employment rate of 70 per cent by 2017 is a policy goal of the government	Employment policies include macroeconomic (tax reforms), sectoral (labour-intensive SME) and active labour market policies	Aggressive employment support services, customized training through training voucher
Pakistan	For the 11th Five Year Plan (2013–14 to 2017–18), employment projections have been made for business as usual scenario and a scenario with policy intervention to demonstrate the need for the latter	The focus is more on programmes rather than on macroeconomic policies	Policies include skill development, entrepreneurship development, creation of a national employment fund, and the establishment of an employment bureau
South Africa	Decent employment is highlighted in the national development plan and is listed as one of the "outcomes" of the Medium-Term Strategic Framework, 2009–14	Employment policy consists of countercyclical macroeconomic policies, targeted expenditures for funding special programmes and infrastructure, policies for promoting employment-intensive sectors, and active labour market policies	Public employment service, training lay-off scheme, apprenticeship, Expanded Public Works Programme, Community Works Programme

Sources: Bertranou (2013), Dedecca (2013), Zeng, et al. (2013), Kang (2013), Marock (2013), GOI (2013, 2018), GOB (2015), and GOP (2019).

Table 9.3 Summary Information on Employment Policies in Selected Developing Countries

Country	Some Key Targets	Policy Instruments Used
Argentina	(i) Reduce unemployment rate to less than 10 per cent by 2015, (ii) reduce non-registered employment to 30 per cent, (iii) increase social protection coverage to 60 per cent of the unemployed, and (iv) reduce the incidence of working poor to less than 30 per cent	(i) Macroeconomic, industrial, social, and labour policies; (ii) wage subsidies to firms severely affected; (iii) support to SMEs; (iv) tax waivers for formalizing employment; (v) active employment policy, including PES and training
Bangladesh	(i) 2.2 million additional jobs per year during 2016–20; (ii) raise the share of manufacturing in total employment to 20 per cent by 2020	Entrepreneurship development, skill development, and direct job creation programmes
Brazil	Information not available	(i) Increased credit availability, (ii) maintenance of public investment funds, (iii) active labour market policies including PES, training, incentives for start-ups, direct employment creation, target oriented programmes, and (iv) passive measures like unemployment insurance
China	For each year, targets on the following are adopted: (i) new jobs, (ii) registered urban unemployment rate, (iii) number of re-employed and laid-off workers, and (iv) the number of disadvantaged persons employed. For 2014, the respective targets are: 10 million, 4.6 per cent, 5 million, and 1.2 million	(i) Fiscal policy for re-employment of laid-off workers and promotion of new employment, (ii) fiscal policy for creation of jobs for college graduates, and (iii) joint action mechanism between social security and employment promotion, (iv) PES, and (v) skill development
India	(i) 33.8 million additional jobs in five years from 2011–12 to 2016–17 (ii) Share of manufacturing in total employment to rise to 12.65 per cent by 2016–17 (from 10.88 per cent in 2011–12) (iii) 100 million jobs in manufacturing by 2022	Tax and tariff policies, sector-specific policies, MGNREGP, and labour law reforms
Republic of Korea	Employment rate of 70 per cent	(i) Tax reform to encourage private sector job creation including tax credit for SMEs, (ii) reform of the welfare system to enhance incentives for low-income earners to search for jobs, (iii) programmes targeted at the youth and the elderly, (iv) skill development, and (v) expansion and strengthening of PES
Pakistan	Lower unemployment rate from 6 per cent in 2013–14 to 5.7 per cent in 2017–18	Entrepreneurship development and skill development programmes, setting up of a national employment fund, and establishment of employment bureau
South Africa	National Development Plan of 2011 targets unemployment rate of 6 per cent by 2030 (implying creation of 11 million additional jobs − 5.4 per cent job growth per year)	(i) Pro-employment macroeconomic policies, (ii) Industrial Policy Action Plan to promote growth of labour-intensive industries, (iii) strategy for youth employment, and (iv) Expanded Public Works Programme

Sources: Same as in Table 9.2.

they adopted a mix of supply-side measures like training and job placement and programmes to create jobs. Direct programmes for job creation have been adopted by Argentina, Brazil, and South Africa. China has created a Special Employment Fund for NEP implementation, and in particular, for supporting innovative programmes of job creation and provides credit support to groups with difficulties (e.g., women, youth, and those with disabilities). Similarly, South Africa has created a fund to support innovative ways to address job creation (Jobs Fund).

Box 9.1: Examples of Countries that Adopted Comprehensive Employment Policies: China and South Africa

The Central Committee of the Communist Party of China and the State Council attach importance to employment as the priority strategy of the country. Employment policy in the country focusses on re-employment of laid-off workers as well as on creation of new jobs. The employment strategy includes:

- Promotion of employment through economic growth, entrepreneurship development, and skill training.
- Policies ranging from macroeconomic and sectoral policies to labour market policies

A variety of instruments are used for implementing employment policy in China which include:

- Employment Promotion Law, 2007
- Taxation policy for re-employment of laid-off workers, 2006
- Preferential fees and policies for self-employment of laid-off workers, 2002, 2006
- Policy for small loans
- Special Employment Funds designed to provide subsidies for training, job placement, interest for microcredit, etc.

In South Africa, the National Development Plan of 2011 (a long-term strategic plan) targets 11 million additional jobs by 2030. Decent employment is listed as one of the "outcomes" of the Medium-Term Strategic Framework (MTSF), 2009–14. Employment policy in the country consists of

- countercyclical macroeconomic policies,
- targeted expenditures for funding special programmes and infrastructure,
- policies for promoting employment-intensive sectors, and
- active labour market policies

In terms of sectoral policy, South Africa's MTSF (2009–14) includes:

- Support to growth of labour-intensive industries (e.g., agro-processing, clothing, tourism, biofuels, and forestry) and
- Provision for increasing finance for industrial development

The manner in which these policies should address employment is articulated in the New Growth Path (NGP) and the more detailed sectoral strategies are outlined in the Industrial Policy Action Plan (2013/14), which is moving in a direction that attempts to balance the focus between growth and employment creation.

In addition, South Africa's employment policy/programme includes a number of direct employment programmes such as the Expanded Public Works Programme.

An overview of the basic characteristics

Employment policy implementation mechanism refers to the operational system and method through which various elements of employment policies are put into practice, progress is monitored, and adjustments are made based on the experience gathered. Today, more and more countries are paying attention to employment policy implementation, monitoring, and evaluation in order to improve the effectiveness of employment policy.

The countries mentioned above have some mechanism in place for implementing their employment policies. The composition and structure of these mechanisms naturally vary depending on the characteristics of the respective NEPs. Some of them start from quantitative targets that provide specificity to the overall objectives and goals. But irrespective of the use of such quantitative targets, they all use various instruments and support mechanisms, e.g., employment services, skill development institutions, policies/programmes for boosting demand for labour, etc., for achieving their declared goals. They have some coordination mechanism and systems of accountability through which progress and success in attaining the declared goals are monitored and evaluated. The following paragraphs provide a brief account of the basic characteristics of the implementation mechanism of NEPs in the countries mentioned above.

As mentioned already, the government of Argentina adopted the MDGs including the additional target of decent and productive employment. In line with that, a number of employment-related "performance indicators" were established (with quantitative targets, e.g., reducing unemployment rate to 10 per cent), which include:

- unemployment rate (to reduce to 10 per cent),
- percentage of workers whose salary is less than the value of a market basket of consumer goods and services (to reduce to 30 per cent),

- percentage of the unemployed population that receives social protection (to raise to 60 per cent by 2015),
- the rate of non-registered employment (to reduce to 30 per cent), and
- the rate of child labour (to eradicate).

The primary mechanism for formulation and coordination of employment policy in Argentina involves entities that form part of the national, provincial, and municipal governments, and includes systems for coordination, support, and accountability.

In Brazil, NEPs are established under the 1988 Federal Constitution supplemented by the 1990 law of the Workers' Support Fund (FAT). The formulation of employment policy is the responsibility of the federal government, and every year, the Ministry of Labour prepares a Policy Action Plan (PAA) that is submitted to Council for Workers' Support Fund (CODEFAT) for approval. The PAA establishes goals for each of the planned actions according to the global budget provided by the CODEFAT. This is done in consultation with the state governments and large municipalities. The responsibility for executing the action plan lies with the state governments and large municipalities. The federal government monitors the implementation of the action plan and the use of the funds. The different modalities of implementing the employment policy are unemployment insurance, employment mediation, and labour force qualification. This, however, led to a fragmentation of the management of the employment policy.

In order to address the issue of fragmentation of the three pillars of employment policy (viz., unemployment insurance, employment mediation, and labour force qualification) and of coordination between them, a new system was agreed upon in 2005 under which the three modalities would be integrated into one public employment system with universal access and assurance of coordination of employment mediation and skill development with the unemployment insurance programme. The new structure was approved in 2006 and implementation started in 2007.

The mechanism for implementation of employment policy in China involves

- a cycle of setting targets, making policy, managing finance, monitoring progress, evaluation, adjustment, and improvement based on evaluation,
- a system of coordination at central and local levels, and
- an accountability system consisting of indicators, statistical reporting, and inspection and evaluation

The Employment Promotion Law of 2008 stipulated the employment policy coordination system at both national and local level. At the national level, The State Council established an inter-ministerial policymaking mechanism that includes 21 ministries. A key element of implementing the employment policy at the local level is the target responsibility system, under which the

National People's Congress sets the target and the State Council signs target contracts with local governments. The local governments adopt five specific objectives for the assessment of governors and relevant departments that include a net increase in jobs, the implementation of re-employment policy, strengthening of employment services, increasing re-employment of capital investment, and helping the employment of disadvantaged groups.

The employment target is set for each year by the Ministry of Human Resources on the basis of an assessment of the overall economic situation, supply of labour, and employment growth in recent years. The MOHRSS discusses the target with each province and then provides the State Council with the target of new jobs, the registered urban unemployment rate, and the number to be re-employed during the year. The specific policy measures and action programmes are formulated in consultation between central and local governments.

The Employment Promotion Law of 2008 also includes a system of carrying out assessment and supervision of the process of implementing the NEP. Once target responsibilities are agreed upon, their completion is included in the assessment of cadres. Scoring and evaluation mechanisms are established in many places.

In Korea, the mechanism for implementing the employment policy includes quantitative targets, instruments for specific policy areas, mechanism for coordinating the implementation, the system of support to employment policy and an accountability system. The major aspect of the quantitative target is to attain an employment rate of 70 per cent by 2017. Local governments are encouraged to have their own job creation targets in line with their characteristics and situation. The areas of policy focus that have been identified to pursue this goal are (i) expansion of employment through a greater attention to domestic demand, services, and small- and medium-sized enterprises (SMEs), and (ii) change in work culture with focus on promoting part-time work, shorter working hours, and a better work-life balance. The coordination mechanism provides for coordination at the national as well as local levels as well as for involving the private sector. The support system includes (i) tax and welfare systems for employment, (ii) employment insurance system, (iii) public employment service, (iv) vocational training, and (v) labour market information system. The accountability system includes provision for overall assessment of the impact of various programmes on employment, assessment of employment insurance, and assessment of local job creation strategies.

In South Africa, the mechanism for implementing the NEP involves target setting, preparation of an intervention strategy for each policy, identification of funding for various action programmes, and a coordination system that involves both horizontal (i.e., inter-ministerial) and vertical (i.e., between the federal government and administration at lower levels) interaction.

South Africa has installed a detailed institutional mechanism for implementing its employment policy. At the top is the Cabinet Committee for economic sectors, employment and infrastructure. Various "clusters" report to the

Cabinet committee. For employment, the relevant cluster is the "Economic Sectors and Employment Cluster" (ES&EC). "Implementation forums" have been established to coordinate work in different areas. For employment, the ES&EC serves as the implementation forum at the national level.

These structures are replicated, with some variance, at a provincial level, and local government participates in these forums at both provincial and national levels. In addition, the National Economic Development and Labour Council (NEDLAC) creates the space for social partners to play a role in advising with respect to these employment policies and in supporting implementation. Social Partners are also required to report progress against a number of related accords that they have signed.

A number of structures were created to fund these imperatives; one such structure is the Jobs Fund, which was set up in 2011 for three years to serve as a catalyst for innovative projects on job creation. The unemployment insurance fund also plays a key role in ensuring that individuals who are to be retrenched receive skills training and also supports employment-creating initiatives. For implementing the employment policy, an accountability system has been set up that includes setting targets, formulating intervention strategies and work plans, and monitoring, reporting, and evaluation. These are monitored through the structures with reports for review by Cabinet.

Characteristics of NEPs implementation mechanism: a summary

To sum up the above discussion, a few aspects of the characteristics of the implementation mechanisms of NEPs used in the selected countries stand out. First, most countries use quantitative targets relating to employment and labour market as benchmark for purposes of policymaking, implementing the action programmes and monitoring progress. Some use single targets (e.g., 70 per cent employment rates in Korea), while others (e.g., Argentina, China) use multiple targets. But targets are not realistic in all cases.[4]

Second, several countries have set up an elaborate system of coordinating the implementation of employment policies, with both horizontal and vertical integration. Horizontal coordination is sought to be achieved through inter-ministerial bodies at the central level, while vertical coordination is aimed through mechanisms for bringing together various actors at the central and local level. Of course, all countries have not achieved the same degree of success in these respects (more on this will be said later). In large countries where central and local-level governments are involved in implementing the employment policies, the usual pattern is the formulation of policies at the central level and the responsibility of implementation given to the local level. But in China and Korea, the central government also plays an important role in implementation.

Third, funds for implementing action programmes relating to employment policy are usually allocated by the central government, although in some cases local governments also provide supplementary funding. For example, in China the local governments are also required to allocate employment fund.

Fourth, most countries have some labour market information system (LMIS) to provide data and information for monitoring the labour market situation and evaluating the impact of employment policies. But the level of the LMIS varies substantially, and the developed countries usually have much better and more up-to-date data. Of course, it is one thing to have an LMIS providing data for monitoring the status of the labour market and another thing to have adequate data for assessing the impact of specific policies on employment.

Coordination of the implementation of national employment policies

The task of formulating and implementing employment policy cannot be performed by a single agency of the government; a range of ministries and other agencies need to get involved. That makes coordination an important aspect of implementing the policies. In general, the coordination system includes two parts which are interlinked: (a) inter-ministerial coordination system at the national level and (b) inter-departmental coordination system at the local level. The nomenclature used for the coordination system (e.g., committee, meeting, council, etc.) differs from country to country.

Coordination mechanisms employed at the country level: an overview

The countries covered by the present study have some mechanism in place for coordinating the implementation of their employment policies. However, as the framework of the NEPs varies, the corresponding coordination mechanism also varies. In this section, an analysis of these mechanisms will be provided with focus on the concept behind the approach adopted, coverage, and effectiveness. The objective will be to identify how the institutional structure provides support to the implementation of NEPs and the factors that contribute to the success of coordination. Based on this analysis, an attempt will be made to identify what has worked and what has not, so that some guidelines can be prepared for potentially effective policy coordination.

In order to understand the concept behind the coordination mechanism for implementing employment policy, the basic nature of employment policies needs to be noted. The first point to note is that depending on the approach adopted, employment policies can involve a large number of government ministries and departments. For example, policies related to subsidies or tax exemption for job creation are areas where the ministries of finance have to play a crucial role. Likewise, allocations for public expenditures aimed at job creation (e.g., in infrastructure) are made within the budgetary framework. But the actual implementation of action programmes in both the above cases is the responsibility of other ministries although in general, the Ministry of Labour, Ministry of Finance, etc. are the core members in the coordination. And social partners also play a critical role (see Box 9.2).

Box 9.2: Role of Social Partners in the Coordination of Employment Policy Implementation

The coordination mechanism for employment policy implementation assigns roles for employers' and workers' organizations in different structures. In Argentina, there are different councils and commissions within the framework of the Federal Labour Council through which coordination is provided, and these councils and commissions are tripartite bodies. Examples are the Council on Employment and Productivity and Sectoral Councils for Skill Certification and Training. The main agency responsible for employment policy in Brazil, the Workers' Support Fund Council (CODEFAT) is also tripartite in composition with equal number of participants from the government, employers, and workers (six from each). In China, the members of the Inter-Ministerial Meeting of the Central Government include representatives of employers and workers. In Korea, social partners have been playing an important role in employment policy since the Asian economic crisis of 1997–98. In 2008, an emergency tripartite committee was set up with a view to formulating agreements to overcome the adverse effects of the global economic crisis. In 2013, tripartite partners agreed on the Jobs Pact to attain 70 per cent employment.

Second, while employment is created as a result of economic activities undertaken in a large number of sectors of an economy, e.g., agriculture, manufacturing, construction, services, etc., government agencies dealing with them do not normally look at the totality of the outcome. Quite often, they do not even look at the employment aspect of the economic activities. In such situations, a coordination mechanism is needed in order to put together the whole picture.

Third, in countries with decentralized administration, implementation of programmes in a number of fields including those relating to employment may be delegated to local governments although the task of formulating the policies may be kept at the hands of the central government departments/ministries. In such cases, coordination between central and local government agencies becomes important. It is worth noting that in most cases the role of the local government is not only implementation but also to get involved in employment policy formulation, and vice versa for central government.

A look at the institutional set-up of NEP coordination in the countries under study shows that the conceptual framework mentioned above apply generally to them, although there are variations in the details.

In Argentina the institutional set-up for NEP coordination includes horizontal coordination between various ministries as well as vertical coordination between central and local-level administration. However, given the country's limited focus on macroeconomic and sectoral policies, the horizontal coordination is also limited to a small number of ministries like labour, industry, and science and technology.

The primary mechanism for the coordination of employment policy in Argentina involves entities that form part of the national, provincial, and municipal governments. The important agencies in the institutional set-up for employment policy coordination in the country include the following:

- The Federal Labour Council – an inter-jurisdictional coordinating body that includes both national and provincial governments, formed by the Ministry of Labour and labour departments of provinces.
- The Council on Employment, Productivity, and Vital and Mobile Minimal Wage – a national tripartite body, with four commissions operating under it
  - Minimum wage and unemployment benefits commission.
  - Employment commission dealing with non-registered employment.
  - Vocational Education and Training Commission dealing with training.
  - The Productivity Commission.
- Sectoral Councils for Job Skills Certification and Training.

It may be worth noting that the key areas of employment policy in Argentina include (i) the National Plan for Employment Regularization aimed at reducing the rate of informal employment and (ii) programmes for employment generation. The former uses an array of mechanisms to detect non-registered employment and then attempt to bring excluded workers into the social security system.

The programmes for employment generation focussed on improving the employability of unemployed workers and their reinsertion into the workforce. Notable among these are the Job Training and Employment Insurance Programme and the More and Better Employment Programme for the Youth. The former is a cash transfer programme consisting of money transfer in exchange for which beneficiaries must participate in different education and training activities. The latter provides help to the youth through training and guidance in job search.

The Ministry of Labour is responsible for implementing activities under both the items of employment policy mentioned above. Hence, it is not surprising that this ministry plays a key role in the institutional set-up for employment policy coordination. Of course, other entities come into play where relevant for issues relating to other sectors. One example is the National Agricultural Labour Commission – a tripartite agency charged with employment in the rural sector. Another is the coordination of the Strategic Plan for Vocational Education and Training with the ministries of industry and of science, technology, and productive innovation.

In Argentina, employment policy is implemented through a decentralized institutional set-up that involves the Regional Labour Offices (in each of the seven regions of the country) and the Agencies for Employment and Job Training that operate in the provinces. The former are responsible primarily for workplace inspection (within the framework of the national policy of employment regularization) and issues relating to labour relations including collective bargaining. The latter are charged with actions aimed at employment generation and training.

It is clear from the above description of the institutional set-up for employment policy coordination in Argentina that there are, on the one hand, national-level entities and, on the other hand, regional- and provincial-level entities that have functions relating to the formulation and implementation of employment policy. However, given the current state of the availability of information, it is difficult to judge how effectively work of these various entities are coordinated. For example, it is not clear how horizontal coordination is achieved between the Federal Labour Council and the Council on Employment, Productivity and Wage at the national level. Moreover, there is a challenge of coordinating education and training with other ministries, and the efforts to date appear to have remained ad hoc. Likewise, the division of responsibility between the Ministry of Labour and its regional offices and the provincial-level agencies for employment and job training is also not clear.

In Brazil, although the government's strategy is to address the employment problem through growth-promoting macroeconomic policy, in practice, the employment policy consists of unemployment insurance, employment mediation, and skill development. The central agency that is responsible for implementing employment policies in the country is the Workers' Support Fund Council (CODEFAT).[5] The Secretariat for Employment Policies (SPPE) of the Ministry of Labour implements provisions of employment policies approved by the Council. Key to this process is an action plan (PAA) on employment service and skill training which is submitted to CODEFAT for approval. Once the approval is received, SPPE establishes agreements with the states, large municipalities, unions, and non-governmental organizations for the execution of planned actions in the areas of employment service and skill training (unemployment insurance and wage bonus programmes are implemented directly by the federal government). These agreements allow the transmittal of funds for implementation of action programmes.

The above description of the coordination mechanism for implementing employment policy in Brazil brings out its strengths. First, the roles and responsibilities of the various actors in terms of formulation and implementation of policies are clearly defined. While the task of formulation is the responsibility of the Ministry of Labour, implementation is done at the local level. Second, since funding is allocated centrally and their use is monitored closely through a system of audit, the system contains a built-in mechanism for close coordination of the process of implementation of the policies.

There are, however, some shortcomings in the mechanism for coordination of employment policies in Brazil. First, at the level of formulation of policies, despite a recognition of the importance of macroeconomic policies influencing growth and employment, there seems to be no direct role of the relevant government agencies in the whole process of formulation and implementation of employment policies. As a result, the coordination mechanism does not include such other ministries and their organs.

Second, the list of ALMPs pursued by the country does include direct job creation and incentives for creating start-ups. The Programme for Employment and Income Generation (PROGER) aims at generating employment through support to small and micro-enterprises and infrastructure. But the institutional set-up for implementing these policies does not provide an independent mechanism for them. Funds can be allocated for such programmes only if there is an excess of funds under FAT over the minimum reserve required to be kept. Hence, funding for programmes of employment creation becomes totally dependent on the balance of FAT that is available.

Third, from the point of view of coordination of programmes of job creation, although the Ministry of Labour does have the responsibility, given the nature of activities that are envisaged under the programme, other relevant ministries need to be involved and a mechanism needs to be established for incorporating and coordinating their participation.

The coordination system of employment policy in China reflects quite well the conceptual framework of NEP implementation outlined at the beginning of this section (Figure 9.1). It is based on a recognition that employment in an economy is the result of activities undertaken in various segments, and hence policies are needed for all of them (or at least for the major ones) in order to make an impact on total employment in the economy. One key element of the coordination system in China is the inter-ministerial coordination system at the national level. Although the responsibility for this lies with the Ministry of Labour, it includes representation from key ministries (21 of them), with the Vice Premier's office providing overall supervision. This national-level coordination is provided through the inter-ministerial meeting mechanism where the Minister of Labour acts as the convener. Working under the direct leadership of the State Council, the meeting deals with formulating policies and the allocation of budgets. It also provides a forum for communication between ministries, exchange of work in progress, collection of latest information on employment, and possible solutions to problems relating to employment. In fact, the functions of the various ministries and other agencies who are members of the inter-ministerial meeting mechanism are clearly defined, thus providing a good basis for coordination of work being done by them.

An important aspect of the coordination system in China is inter-departmental coordination at the local level which, in turn, consists of two parts – a horizontal part and a vertical part. Horizontally, local governments establish an inter-departmental coordination mechanism which is similar to the inter-ministerial

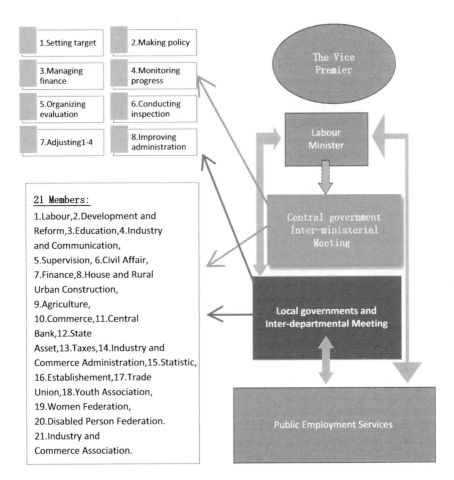

Figure 9.1 The Mechanism for Coordination of Employment Policy in China.
Source: Zeng, et al. (2013).

meeting at the national level. Vertically, the Ministry of Labour coordinates important matters of implementation to the provincial-level government. Each member of the inter-ministerial meeting issues guidelines in their own policy area, following which their provincial counterparts do the same.

A good example of how the vertical coordination (between local governments and the central government) works in China is the target responsibility system under which the State Council signs "target contracts" with local governments. The latter adopts five employment-related objectives that include a net increase in jobs, the implementation of re-employment policy, strengthening re-employment services, increasing re-employment of capital investment, and the employment of disadvantaged groups. The Employment Promotion Law requires local governments above the county level to take employment expansion as one of the major goals of economic and social de-velopment. For the implementation of the employment policy, the relevant ministries and other agencies introduce a series of policy measures which are followed up by local governments through measures for implementation.

Like in China, employment policy in the Republic of Korea also encom-passes a number of policy areas that cover both demand and supply sides of the labour market. Accordingly, the country has adopted a coordination system that reflects the need for bringing in the relevant players within and outside the government. The system also adopts the concept of vertical integration, where agencies of central and local governments work together in imple-menting employment the NEP (see Figure 9.2).

At the national level, coordination of employment policy implementation is done at two levels. The first is at the highest possible level with the President chairing the National Employment Strategy Meeting the goal of which is to deploy a coherent government-wide national employment strategy. Members of this coordinating meeting include each ministry, related government institutions like the central bank and the planning agency, political parties, etc. Research institutes and independent professional experts are also called upon to attend this meeting. The broad composition of this meeting indicates the comprehen-siveness of horizontal coordination attempted by Korea. The broad goals of the Meeting include (i) formulation of employment-friendly policies, (ii) addressing the quantitative as well as qualitative mismatch in the demand for and supply of labour through skill development, and (iii) pursuing labour market efficiency.

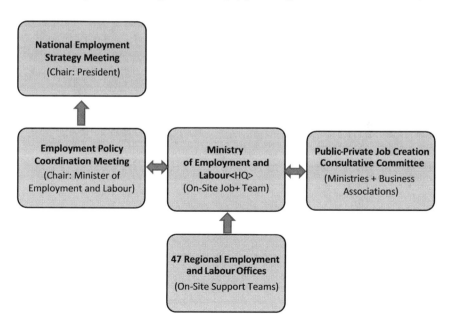

Figure 9.2 The Framework of Coordination of NEP in the Republic of Korea.
Source: Kang (2013).

The second tier of coordination at the national level is provided by the Employment Policy Coordination Meeting which is presided over by the Ministry of Employment and Labour (MOEL). This mechanism has been set up to translate the broad strategies adopted at the National Employment Strategy Meeting into policies in relevant areas of various ministries and agencies and coordinate their implementation. This meeting goes beyond government policies and addresses issues raised by the private sector with a view to improving the job creation efforts.

In addition, Public-Private Job Creation Consultative Committee has been established jointly between the government and the private sector so that the job creation efforts of the private sector could be facilitated. The Committee includes the Minister of Employment and Labour and delegates from five major business organizations (Korea Chamber of Commerce, Federation of Korean Industries, Korea International Trade Association, Korea Federation of Small and Medium Businesses, and Korea Employers' Federation). Other government ministries related to job creation efforts could participate if related issues were brought up. The Committee is chaired by the Minister of Employment and Labour.

For customized measures in response to on-site needs, MOEL began providing direct support at business sites by setting up "On-site job+ Team" – an on-site group to support job creation. These teams have been formed for providing on-site coordination by visiting workplaces to assess the difficulties that companies and job-seekers face with regard to employment issues.

In Korea, local governments pursue various job creation projects, either with support from the central government or with their own financial resources. Vertical coordination is provided by the Employment Policy Coordination Meeting, which resolves the issue relating to overlaps between the actions of central and local governments. The "On-site job+ Team" is also an important mechanism for providing support at the local level, and they work under the Regional Employment and Labour Office.

In South Africa, there are a number of actors at the national level who are responsible for implementing employment policies. At the top is the Cabinet Committee for economic sectors, employment and infrastructure development which includes key ministries and is chaired by the President. There are different "clusters" dealing with matters falling within the jurisdiction of each Cabinet Committee and for the one mentioned above it is the ES&EC. Implementation forums have been established to coordinate each "outcome" of the MTSF, and for "outcome 4" (which is the one on employment), ES&EC acts as the implementation forum. Reports covering different areas of work under outcome 4 are prepared by an implementation task team. In addition, there are coordinative structures associated with different areas of the New Growth Path[6] including infrastructure, manufacturing, agriculture, etc. They also report on matters relating to different outcomes, including outcome 4.

Three core ministries (economic development, finance, and trade and development) and various other ministries have responsibilities relating to the delivery for achieving outcome 4. The Presidency has responsibility with respect to ensuring that this coordination takes place and for monitoring the efficacy with which employment creation policies are being implemented through the Department of Performance Management and Evaluation (DPME). The Programme of Action system monitors progress in implementation.

At the provincial level, the Provincial Department of Economic Development takes responsibility for coordinating employment creation reports. The provinces engage with various employment and labour market-related policies through the Presidential Coordinating Committee (PCC), a statutory body that coordinates activities across national, provincial, and local governments.

The mechanism of coordination of employment policies in South Africa which has been briefly described above has a number of strengths. First, the concept behind the framework reflects a recognition that employment is a cross-cutting issue and actions of many government ministries and agencies have implications for the outcome. This is reflected in the various elements of the coordination structure, e.g., the implementation forum receiving reports from a variety of ministries and department, DPME (under the Presidency) coordinating the process of planning and monitoring outcome 4, etc. Another strength of the system is the existence of similar structures at the provincial level, which are integrated through the PCC and provide vertical coordination.

However, there are several problems – potential as well as real. Even from the summary description provided above, it seems that there is multiplicity of structures as well as policies in place that can give rise to challenges (if not confusion) with respect to setting priorities and reporting. The complexity of the mechanism may also cause delays in decision-making. With multiple departments responsible for single output/sub-output, there can be delays in programme formulation and implementation and confusion about responsibility and accountability.

Strengths and weaknesses of the coordination mechanisms: a comparative analysis

A comparative analysis of the coordination mechanism for implementing employment policy in the five countries brings out a number of points. First, conceptually, they reflect the basic characteristics of the employment policies adopted by the countries. It may be recalled that some countries have adopted a comprehensive approach to employment policy consisting of measures focussing on demand as well as supply sides of the labour market. Those countries have adopted a coordination mechanism that brings in a multiplicity of agencies within and outside the government. The government agencies in such cases range from ministries dealing with finance and economic affairs to production- and trade-related ones. China, Korea, and South Africa are notable amongst this group of countries.

Second, while the involvement of multiple actors and layers of administration is natural in implementing policies in an area like employment, too complex a framework may make implementation cumbersome and result in delays and confusions (see Box 9.3). South Africa is a case in point. But structures can be kept simple even with the involvement of multiple actors that are needed to be involved. China and Korea provide examples of simple structures that can provide good horizontal coordination between multiple agencies involved in formulating and implementing employment policies. On the other hand, experiences from some countries show that the capability of coordination of the Ministry of Labour and the active involvement of the ministry of finance are the driving forces of a dynamic coordination mechanism.

Box 9.3: Complexity and Simplicity in the Coordination of Employment Policy Implementation

Possible sources and illustrations of complexity

The country case studies provide examples of both complex and simple mechanisms that may be used for implementing NEPs. Complexity can start from setting of priorities and targets and identification of players for implementing and assignment of roles and responsibilities. If multiple instruments of strategy are employed, their alignment with each other can be a potential source of complexity. Complexity in coordination can arise from the need to have structures at national and local levels – unless the respective roles and responsibilities are clearly delineated. Examples of these various sources of complexity can be provided from the country case studies.

Multiple targets: Argentina, China, and South Africa are examples of countries that have adopted multiple targets and objectives with regard to employment.

Multiple priorities: The Expanded Public Works Programme of South Africa is an example of assigning multiple priorities (e.g., job creation, poverty alleviation, creation of infrastructure, skill development, etc.) to a single programme.

Alignment of various instruments of strategies: In South Africa, the alignment of various instruments, like the National Development Plan, Medium-Term Strategic Framework, New Growth Path, and Industrial Policy Action Plan, is a challenge.

Multiple centres of action: Where there is administrative decentralization and employment policy and the tasks of formulation and implementation are assigned to various levels of administration, complexities in governance can arise. The experiences of Germany and the UK provide examples of such complexities. In the UK, employment policy is formulated at the central level, but devolved administrations have responsibilities for a number of policy areas (e.g., education and skills), and usually develop employment policies. In Germany, the Federal Ministry of Employment and Social Affairs (BMAS) is responsible for policy formulation while the Federal Employment Agency is responsible for implementation. But the latter has certain policymaking competencies, especially in the area of unemployment insurance. Interaction between the employment agencies and local governments sometimes results in conflicts. The existence of different organizational forms of Job Centres (JCs) is also a source of complexity of coordination.

Simplicity in NEP implementation

Clearly defined and small set of priorities: China, for example, defines a small number of priorities on employment for each planning period.

Single or small number of targets: Korea and the UK provide examples of single targets of employment policy. China also adopts a small number of targets.

Avoiding multiple centres of coordination: In China, for example, although the Vice Premier is at the top of the coordination mechanism, the system is coordinated by the labour minister. And a single mechanism (the inter-ministerial meeting mechanism) is used for this purpose. In Korea, there are different layers in the coordination system, e.g., the National Employment Strategy Meeting presided over by the President and the Employment Policy Coordination Meeting presided over by the Ministry of Labour. But their roles and responsibilities are clearly delineated.

Third, in countries with central and local-level entities involved in implementing employment policy, vertical integration and coordination become extremely important. Most countries covered by the present study have some mechanism for achieving such coordination. Although with the information that is currently available it is not possible to fully assess how effective the systems are, it is possible to make a few remarks at least tentatively. First, in some cases, the tasks and responsibilities of local-level entities are not clearly defined. Even where such definitions exist (e.g., in Argentina) there may be overlaps in responsibilities or simple departures from laid-down rules during implementation. But there are countries where the roles and responsibilities are clearly defined, and coordination seems to be working quite well. China and Korea are examples of this category.

The task of vertical coordination becomes more complex where local governments have their own funds and can formulate and implement their own programmes. On the other hand, there are countries where local governments can implement certain programmes, but only within the budgetary framework of the central government (Brazil, China, for example).

Simplicity may be a virtue also in the context of vertical integration and coordination between national and local governments as is exemplified by the experiences of China and Korea. The "target responsibility system" of China is a good example of how local-level entities can be effectively employed to attain the broad objectives defined at the central level. Korea's "On-site job+ team" also is a good example of how problems can be resolved at the grassroots level and the goal of job creation can be achieved through such centrally formulated locally implemented action.

The country experiences show that four things are critical for the efficient operation of the coordination system:

a   While it is common for the coordination system to be led by the Ministry of Labour, it is necessary that key ministries like finance and those dealing with production activities like agriculture and industries play their due roles. Furthermore, it is important for the coordination system to be supervised by a higher level office (e.g., that of the President's or Premier's). The latter is to ensure the needed influence on the process of making and implementing policies.
b   The members of the inter-ministerial coordination system at national level include not only the relevant ministries, workers, and employers but also the local governments because the employment policies are rooted and implemented at the local level.
c   Inter-departmental coordination system at local level has the same function as the inter-ministerial coordination system at national level. It plays a pivotal role in the whole coordination system and is indispensable for implementing, monitoring, and evaluating employment policies.
d   The functions and tasks of the coordination system and of each member are clearly defined in order to avoid inefficiency that may be caused by overlapping of responsibilities across some ministries.

As for the role of the ministries of labour in coordinating NEP implementation, although they have a lead role in several countries, this is not the rule. In South Africa, for example, the labour department does not have a specific role in coordinating employment creation. On the other hand, in China, the Ministry of Labour is at the centre of the coordination mechanism. This ministry plays an important role in Argentina and Brazil as well. In Korea, coordination is done at two levels, and the labour ministry plays the coordinating role in the second tier. While the strength and capacity of the ministry are important for it to perform its coordination role effectively, that may not be the only factor in determining whether it should play that role. The latter depends to a large extent on how a country's government perceives NEP, its implementation and the respective roles and responsibilities of various actors. Employment

is a multidimensional and cross–cutting matter. Unless a country's governance structure clearly assigns the labour ministry with a lead (or coordinator's
role) role in that matter, it cannot assume the role even if it has the requisite
strength. On the other hand, if the labour ministry is assigned with that role, it
will have to perform its duties, and the appropriate strategy would be to equip
itself with necessary capacity – both technically and politically.

Supporting systems for implementing employment policies

The function of employment policy implementation, monitoring, and evaluation mechanism is supported by two systems: (a) public employment services
system and (b) labour market information system, which are inseparable parts
of the mechanism.

a   *Public employment services system*: An efficient public employment service
    plays a key role in employment policy implementation, monitoring, and
    evaluation. The Public Employment Services Centre performs functions
    of employment counselling, data collection, employment exchange, etc.
    If the public employment service network could be spread to communi-
    ties and villages, they could potentially play a role in developing countries
    as well. In developed countries, the progress and effects of employment
    policy implementation are often monitored and evaluated by the Public
    Employment Services Centre.
b   *Labour market information system*: A well-developed labour market informa-
    tion system provides strong support to employment policy implementa-
    tion. It helps to collect and analyze a number of key statistical information
    for employment policy monitoring, evaluating, and reporting.

A variety of tools may be used to support the implementation of NEPs. In
cases where the NEP is comprehensive (i.e., covering macro, sectoral and
labour market policies), the support system has to include the mechanism for
formulating and implementing all such policies, and the analysis has to start
from the process of formulating macro and sectoral policies to see how employment is being incorporated into them. However, as already mentioned,
all the countries covered by the background studies don't appear to have
adopted such a comprehensive approach to NEP. So, the present chapter will
focus on two pillars of the support system, viz., employment service and labour market information system. While the former is a tool for providing job
matching, employment policy advisory, and data collection in some countries
(which can, of course, be combined with other elements of ALMPs), the latter is a more general tool that can be used for monitoring the implementation
of NEPs as a whole.

Unfortunately, all the country studies on which the present chapter is
based do not provide information on the two elements of the support system

mentioned above. As for employment services, information is rather limited and provides only basic information. There is no analysis of the effectiveness of the services provided by those offices. The study on South Africa indicates that the Department of Labour plays a role in supporting employment creation as well as the protection of employment through its various programmes such as the Public Employment Services (PES) programme,[7] which aims to contribute to facilitating an increase in employment through its employer and work seeker services.[8] On the other hand, the study on China provides a good example not only of how employment service can be used as a tool for implementing employment policy but also what kind of data can help in assessing the actual performance of this tool of support. In the following paragraphs, an attempt is being made to present a picture of what kind of support to NEP is provided by employment services labour market information system.

Country experiences with respect to employment service and labour market information: a brief overview

In Argentina, the mechanism for support to employment policy consists mainly of three broad pillars: public employment service, workplace inspection, and the vocational education and training network. In addition, there is a mechanism for generating information and monitoring. The network of public employment offices encompasses all the Municipal Employment Offices (MEO) in the country. There are some 500 such offices covering about 70 per cent of the country's population. The aim of this network is to provide support, assistance, and occupational guidance in the process of job search as well as in generating self-employment. It also does outreach work for applicants seeking jobs in employment programmes. The MEOs work in conjunction with the vocational education and training network to provide training and occupational guidance at the local level. The network is also expected to address the needs of employers in their effort to fill vacancies and train potential employees.

Given the large number of MEOs spread throughout the country, the level of their development and capability varies greatly. And hence, strengthening the capacity of this network is a challenge that needs to be addressed.

As part of the LMIS, the Ministry of Labour in Argentina has a number of instruments that include:

- Employment Indicators Survey which contains the results of a survey of medium-sized and large businesses in all sectors except the primary sector (carried out on a monthly basis in major urban areas) which focusses on salaried employment.
- Nationwide Survey of Social Protection and Social Security (conducted in 2011) which complements the regular household survey conducted by the National Statistics and Census Bureau.
- The Labour Statistics Bulletin.

- The Collective Bargaining Report.
- The quarterly series of Employment Dynamics and Business Turnover which measures the creation and loss of employment.
- Social Security Statistics Bulletin.
- The Bulletin of Gender and Job Market Statistics.
- Child and Adolescent Labour Observatory.

It seems from the above list that they constitute Argentina's regular system of labour statistics and are not particularly geared towards assessment of the impact of specific instruments of employment policy. For example, if public employment service is regarded as a major instrument supporting the implementation of employment policy, it would be useful to be able to periodically assess how the system is functioning and what impact it is having on facilitating job matching and placement in the country.

In Brazil, public employment service is an important instrument to support its employment policy and is designed to assist unemployed workers in finding new employment as well as to become self-employed or a microentrepreneur. In some cases, the system of employment service works in coordination with microcredit policy. But there are limitations inherent in the instrument and its functioning. First, the network is concentrated mainly in large cities, although Brazil is a country characterized by regional complexity where there are a number of highly urbanized areas with high degree of population density as well as areas with small urban centres and rural hinterland. The employment service network is concentrated mainly in large cities, and as such, their coverage is limited. A few figures may illustrate this point. One-third of the total labour force of 90 million is engaged in the informal sector. In 2011, open unemployment exceeded seven million. And the number of workers supported by employment service in that year was only 943,000 workers. The second problem with employment service in Brazil is that it is not coordinated with the unemployment insurance system. The experience of developed countries (e.g., Germany) indicates that such coordination can contribute a great deal in activating job search and in reducing unemployment.

The limited impact of the employment service network in Brazil is also indicated by a comparison of the number of vacancies identified and filled in relation to the number of the unemployed. In 2011 (during which the labour market situation was better than for example in 2009), vacancies listed represented only 53 per cent of the number of unemployed workers, and the number of workers placed was only 38 per cent of the listed vacancies. These numbers indicate a low degree of participation of potential employers in the network as well as limited effectiveness of the system in placing the unemployed. The success rate of the employment service network thus appears to be rather limited.

There are two major instruments in the LMIS of Brazil: (i) the General Registry of the Unemployed Persons (CAGED) and (ii) the Annual Social

Information List (RAIS). The former compiles a monthly list of dismissals and recruitments made by companies from which an employment level index is constructed. The latter provides a consolidated list of personal information that is used for social security and has become an annual census of formal labour in the country and provides a database for the enrolment of unemployed workers in unemployment insurance. It can also be used to construct a distribution of workers by occupation and sector and a host of other characteristics of the formal sector labour market. In addition to the above two major instruments, the Ministry of Labour collects data on other aspects of the labour market including placements made through the employment service network.

Brazil has an LMIS that provides good coverage of the formal sector of the economy. But in order for it to support implementation of a broad set of employment policies (in addition to unemployment insurance, employment service, and vocational training), the system will have to extend its coverage to the vast informal segment of the economy. Even as instruments to support employment policies for the formal sector, coordination and integration of the various elements of the system, e.g., CAGED, RAIS and the labour ministry's data collection efforts will be important.

Two major tools that support the implementation of employment policy in China are: (i) the public employment service (PES) system and (ii) the labour market information (LMI) system. PES, funded by the government, provides an array of services including employment assistance, and social security service. The network of this service expanded rapidly during the 1990s and is rendering useful service to the people in finding new employment and in getting re-employed. In addition to the PES, intermediary organizations of different ownership forms – foreign as well as domestic private – have grown rapidly, especially during the 2000s.

In addition to employment assistance, the PES performs the function of monitoring and reporting of the implementation of the NEP in China. Within the framework of the Ministry of Labour's 2006 "Notification on Making Regular Report on Employment and Re-employment", the ministry, in collaboration with the National Bureau of Statistics, issues various reports covering job placement, re-employment, implementation of subsidy policies, training and skill testing, and social insurance.

The LMI of China is managed by the Ministry of Labour and provides data relating to labour market dynamics as a whole and concerning specific groups. There are four components of the data base:

i   *Management information system*: This includes (a) basic information of the employing units and individuals; (b) registration of employment information of urban residents, local and migrant workers, foreigners, and other types of personnel; (c) unemployment management; (d) re-employment management; (e) "occupation introduction" – information about PES; (f) training; and (g) labour dispatch on a variety of issues including labour relations.

ii *Employment monitoring system*: This provides employment data on various regions (currently provides LMI on 110 cities of the country).

iii *Monitoring system for transfer of rural labour*: Data on transfer of rural labour are collected in 500 counties and covers issues like rural workers going to urban areas for work, the home-going peasant-workers, and the situation of local non-farm employment.

iv *Unemployment dynamic monitoring system*: This module includes data on unemployed workers covering about 10,000 companies.

The kind of data provided by China's LMIS can be illustrated by one example, viz., data regarding placement of job applicants. Table 9.4 provides data on the number of job applicants and the number recruited by quarter for 2012.

The type of data presented in Table 9.4 not only provide the total number of applicants and recruitment and their ratios; these ratios are also indicative of the state of the labour market and how it has been changing during the period covered. For example, a figure of greater than one for the ratio of recruitment to applicants is indicative of a tight labour market on the whole. The ratio remaining more or less unchanged during the four quarters of 2012 indicates the situation has not changed much during the year. These figures are useful for purposes of monitoring the labour market and for planning future policies. It would be even more useful if such data were available on a disaggregated basis by sector and occupation. Zeng et al. (2013) provide such data for primary, secondary, and tertiary sectors which indicate that the labour market for the secondary industry tightened in three out of the four quarters of 2012, while that of tertiary industry had that experience in only one of the four quarters. This could perhaps be taken as an indication of the better employment prospects in the secondary sector. Further disaggregation of such data could help in refining and fine-tuning such conclusion.

In the Republic of Korea, Public Employment Service was initiated in 1998 through establishment of JCs, with the mandate providing employment assistance (including job intermediation and vocational counselling),

Table 9.4 China: The Number of Job Applicants and Number Recruited in 2012

	Number of Persons Recruited	No. of Applicants	Job Opening-to-Applicant Ratio	Changes Compared with Last Quarter	Changes Compared with the Same Period of Previous Year
The first quarter	5,902,890	5,462,857	1.08	+0.04	+0.01
The second quarter	6,335,394	6,037,377	1.05	−0.03	−0.02
The third quarter	6,432,960	6,099,993	1.05	−	+0.01
The fourth quarter	5,088,751	4,730,839	1.08	0.03	0.04

Source: Zeng, et al. (2013).

employment insurance management, and vocational training. During the initial years, the level of services provided by the JCs was not very high. Since 2005, the government of Korea started expanding the PES. JCs are part of the local administration office under the MOEL. In 2013, there were 82 JCs in the country.

But JCs are not the only agency providing employment service in Korea. While PES is provided by employment service agencies of local government, there are private employment service agencies as well. Although the latter are under the supervision of the JCs, the exact relationship between the private employment service agencies and the JCs is not clear.

In terms of actual services provided, there has been some innovation. Following are some examples:

- The "Successful Employment Package Programme" introduced in 2009 for low-income job-seekers.
- The Youth Employment Service started in 2011.
- Finding New Job Programme for the middle-aged and old job-seekers.

Under the above programmes, services are provided in stages. The first stage consists of career path setting when individuals receive intensive counselling. On the basis of the results of this stage, individual action plans are prepared. The second stage consists of improvement of vocational competency during which training, jobs for experience, start-up programmes, and youth internship programmes are provided. The third stage consists of intensive job matching during which the JC counsellors accompany programme participants to their job interviews for providing support. Group interview sessions are held by the participants and recruiting companies.

Efficient matching between job-seekers and potential employers is key to the success of employment services, be it public or private. Availability of labour market information plays an important role in facilitating this match. In the Republic of Korea, there is close inter-linkage between LMIS and PES. The JCs are networked by the central information centre where all information about jobs and job-seekers are gathered, classified and analyzed. The LMIS of the country covers a wide range of topics including macroeconomic aspects, labour market trends, technology and industry information, employment insurance, education, training, job counselling, etc. The information is available to the local branches of PES as well as to the public. So, the private job agencies may also use this information. On the other hand, there are private agencies providing information relating to jobs (often through the internet). Thus, the PES and private employment service in Korea complement each other.

South Africa's LMIS provides data needed to support its comprehensive NEP. It compiles data from a number of sources including the quarterly labour force survey. In addition to general data concerning the situation and trends in the labour market, data relating to specific programmes like the

Industrial Policy Action Plan (IPAP), Expanded Public Works Programme (EPWP), and the Community Works Programme (CWP) are also available. Likewise, data on the supply side, e.g., education and training, vacancies, and job placements, etc. are available. Thus, the LMIS of South Africa seems to be quite comprehensive, and it should be possible to assess the effectiveness of various employment policies and programmes that are being implemented in the country.

A few comparative remarks on public employment service and LMI

Based on the description provided above of the pillars of the support system for implementing employment policies, a few observations may be made. First, employment services can be a useful tool, especially for urban areas. In countries like China and Korea, they have demonstrated good performance. The other side of the coin is that in countries with a large proportion of workers employed in rural areas and the informal sector, it may not be a very useful tool.

Second, although this tool is conventionally applied in the case of wage- and salary-based employment, some examples (e.g., that of Argentina and Brazil) show that it is possible to extend the service to self-employment as well. This implies that with some innovation and reforms, the employment service system can become useful even in situations where large proportions of employment are in the informal sector.

Third, employment service can be particularly useful for addressing problems faced by certain groups in the labour market, e.g., the low-income groups, the young, the middle-aged, etc. This is demonstrated by the example of Republic of Korea where the tool is being used to provide support such specific groups.

Fourth, although traditionally employment service has been the domain of public service, it is gradually being opened up to the private sector. That the private sector can play a useful role in this field is demonstrated by the experience of not only a market-oriented economy like Korea but also by the experience of China. In fact, if the policy in this field is formulated carefully, the two segments can complement each other quite well.

Fifth, the effectiveness of ALMP as a tool for employment policy can be increased if employment service is combined with social service. In Brazil, an attempt was made during 2005–07 to reform the public employment system and integrate unemployment insurance, employment service and training. The basic idea was to establish a one-stop shop for public employment policies where employment service and training would be provided in coordination with unemployment insurance. However, the proposals have not been implemented fully.

Sixth, despite the usefulness of employment service as a tool for employment policy, it has important limitations, especially in developing countries with large rural and informal sector. This is illustrated by the experience of developing countries like Brazil and China (although China has made great efforts to extend PES and LMIS to villages in the last decade), where employment service is virtually limited to urban areas – thus excluding the rural areas from the service. Moreover, this tool is geared towards use in the formal sector labour market, unless its scope is widened (like in Argentina) to cover the micro- and small enterprises. The example of Brazil illustrates this point where a third of total employment is accounted for by the informal sector, and in 2011, PES provided support to only 943,000 workers out of a total unemployed workforce of seven million (or about 14 per cent of those who are unemployed).

Seventh, the use of ALMPs in general and employment service in particular needs to be accompanied by good LMIS so that the impact of the policy measures used can be assessed periodically and adjustments made accordingly. In that respect, the experiences of China, Korea, and South Africa are noteworthy. On the one hand, the labour market indicators should be sufficiently broad to cover all aspects of the labour market as for example, in Korea and South Africa. On the other hand, the LMIS should include instruments to assess the employment and labour market impact of specific employment policy support systems (e.g., with respect to PES in China). South Africa also has good examples of information available for assessing the impact of specific programmes like the IPAP and EPWP.

Accountability system for monitoring and evaluation of national employment policies

Accountability is the obligation to demonstrate that employment policy has been implemented effectively and to report on results in a timely and accurate manner. The accountability system for employment policy basically comprises six elements.

a   *Key indicators in national development strategy*: Insertion of several key indicators, such as new employment, unemployment rate into national development strategy, and macroeconomic policy, is critical for putting employment at the core of economic and social policies. It is fundamental for the accountability of employment policy implementation, monitoring, and evaluation.
b   *Annual work plan*: Such plans can be useful for employment policy implementation, monitoring, and evaluation, and should include specified employment targets, employment policies and measures, and the responsibilities of all the actors.
c   *Employment policy financing*: While the allocation of funds dedicated to specific programmes and policies is important from the point of view of implementation, cost-effectiveness is an important criterion of efficiency. Cost-benefit analysis can be applied to evaluate the efficiency of specific projects. However, there should be proper monitoring of the effective

utilization of funds that are allocated. Country experiences show that a well-functioning financial system will ensure as well as improve the employment policy implementation.

d   *Supervision, inspection, and evaluation*: Oversight of the policy implementation helps to identify ways of improving management performance of each actor by means of supervision, inspection, and evaluation. The oversight activities are conducted by the government or the third party.

e   *Statistics and reporting*: Reporting based on the statistical system and oversight activities, can not only help monitor the progress, and analyze problems and effects of employment policy implementation but can also help improve the policy framework and its implementation.

f   *Adjustment and improvement*: A functional accountability system is characterized by adaptability. Data provided by the statistical system and the evaluation (especially if it is done by independent agencies) can provide a good basis for bringing about adjustments in employment policies as well as their implementation mechanisms.

Any strategy, however well formulated, requires a sound strategy for implementation as well as mechanisms for monitoring the process of implementation. Moreover, a system of evaluation is required for assessing how well the strategy is being implemented, and for bringing about adjustments that are needed to improve the level of efficiency. Different countries have put in place different mechanisms for monitoring and evaluation. Consistent with the scope and focus of NEPs, the concept and scope of monitoring and the indicators used for the purpose vary from country to country. The accountability system also involves setting of targets, formulation of strategic plans, allocation of budgets, and the assessment of the employment impacts of policies and programmes. In this section, we first provide an overview of the accountability system that exists in the countries covered by the present study and then make a few remarks of a comparative nature.

The accountability systems in practice: some examples

In Argentina, the accountability system includes two broad phases: (i) the formulation of goals and strategic plans and allocation of budgets, and (ii) assessment of the implementation of the policies and plans. The strategic plans are formulated for three years, on the basis of which a budget is prepared. The responsibility for implementation is mainly with the Ministry of Labour who adopts results-based management methodologies in order to align strategic goals with the operational goals and performance indicators. A system for monitoring and assessment has been put in place to track the outcomes and impacts of various measures implemented.

An important element in the budget framework is the National Employment Fund (created under a law in 1991), the primary purpose of which is to provide unemployment insurance benefits. The surplus of the Fund remaining after payment of unemployment insurance is used for other employment programmes.

As for impact assessment, there is no independent unit for this purpose; the Ministry of Labour's Office of Studies and Statistics prepares assessments of specific employment policies. Two examples of such reports undertaken in the wake of the global economic crisis of 2008–09 are: (i) ways of preventing the crisis and (ii) the programme for productive recovery. In order to favour job creation, employer contribution to social security was lowered temporarily. Likewise, the scale and funding of an existing programme were expanded in 2008 with a view to supporting recovery. Those assessments provided useful insights into the performance of the programmes. But such assessments remain ad hoc.

China has a well-structured system of accountability that consists of seven parts: (i) key indicators in the national development plan, (ii) annual work plan, (iii) financial management, (iv) inspection and evaluation, (v) social supervision, (vi) statistics and reporting, and (vii) adjustment and improvement.

There are four key indicators of employment in China's National Development Plan: (i) new jobs, (ii) registered urban unemployment rate, (iii) number of re-employed and laid-off workers, and (iv) the number of disadvantaged persons employed. There are specified systems for defining and collecting information on each of these indicators. In fact, the first two indicators are integrated into the annual national plan of economic and social development.

The central and local government allocate funds (under the rubric of Special Employment Funds) for implementing employment policies. There is a well-articulated system for allocating such funds to the provinces which can be used for a variety of programmes like job placement, vocational training, social insurance, subsidies for probationary employment, interest subsidy for microcredit, etc.

The use of the Special Employment Funds is subjected to evaluation through an independent and transparent process using scientific methods. The focus of the evaluation is to relate expenditure with the relevant outputs. Indicators of performance in four aspects are used: (i) the ratio of funds raised locally, (ii) proportion of the expenditure on Special Employment Funds, (iii) a score based on new jobs promoted through subsidies for job placement, training, social insurance, interest on microcredit, and public sector jobs.

Supervision and inspection system of the law on employment promotion include three parts: (i) supervision from the organ of state power, (ii) supervision from the organ of state administration, and (iii) social supervision. The central government employs a third party to do some investigation and assessment.

As for statistics and reporting, there are four parts: (i) the labour market information system providing basic data from all levels into a database, (ii) provincial and central system, (iii) indicators of transfer of labour from rural to urban areas (collected in 500 counties), (iv) dynamic monitoring of the unemployed.

The final step in the accountability system of employment policies in China is adjustment and improvement. This is done through a series of steps in the area of employment policy. While some of these focus on overall employment (e.g., the Employment Promotion Law of 2007), there can be measures in response to specific situations (e.g., measures undertaken in 2008 in response to damages caused by the Wenchuan earthquake, and in 2009 in response to the adverse effects of the global economic crisis).

The accountability system in Korea has three major elements: (i) the employment impact assessment programme (EIAP), (ii) the local job creation strategy notice system, and (iii) the employment insurance assessment centre. EIAP was set up in the wake of the Asian economic crisis with the objective of identifying policy alternatives for job creation through analysis of policies that have a direct impact on jobs as well as of government policies that may have some impact on job creation. An Employment Impact Assessment Centre (EIAC) is designated for two years by a review board (chaired by the MOEL, and including four independent and two internal members) through an open competition. For example, in 2013, the Korea Labour Institute was selected as the EIAC. The evaluation involves examination of the relevance of the activities of a project to the goal of employment as well as the impact on employment in quantitative and qualitative terms (by using rigorous methods like input–output and computable general equilibrium models). The result of impact evaluation is sent to various ministries and other agencies relevant to the project concerned. The project entity sets up an action plan based on the assessment results which is sent to the MOEL. The progress of implementation of the action plan is reported to the Employment Policy Council and the Ministry of Finance uses the results as reference data in future budgetary allocation.

Through the Local Job Creation Strategy Notice System, local governments are encouraged to establish their own job creation targets (in line with the characteristics of the region) and formulate their employment policies which are then submitted to the MOEL for support. This has created a healthy competition among the local governments and has resulted in regionally customized job creation projects. In addition to support from the central government, the local governments are allocating budgets for such projects.

The Employment Insurance Assessment Centre functions in the same manner as the EIAC for studies on the impact of employment insurance, and the results of which are used to bring about improvements in the system.

In South Africa, the accountability system involves target setting, preparation of work plans, financing, monitoring and reporting, and evaluation and adjustment. Each policy programme area has a set of targets that are usually defined in quantitative terms. Likewise, intervention strategies are prepared for each policy to enable departments to pursue the targets. Such strategies are quite comprehensive covering macroeconomic policies, sectoral programmes, and different components of ALMPs. Each policy area and its associated strategies are supported by a financing plan which may have multiple sources. In addition to such specific financing, the government has set up a Jobs Fund which is intended to serve as a catalyst for innovative projects that can support job creation and encourage private sector investment where projects are required to raise matching funds. As was indicated previously this is also augmented by other Funds such as UIF as well as by funding allocated by Development Finance Institutions.

The monitoring and reporting system of South Africa covers the overall employment and labour market, the key sectors of the economy and various components of the ALMPs. The quarterly labour review that is based on the quarterly labour force surveys provides data relating to economic activity rate, employment, unemployment, employment in the formal and informal sectors. Thus, it is possible not only to monitor the overall situation regarding employment and unemployment but also the structure of the labour market in terms of the relative importance of the formal and informal segments of the economy. In addition to general data mentioned above, various departments of the government monitor and report employment created by their respective departments. Furthermore, each of the components of ALMPs have monitoring systems. For example, both EPWP and CWP have detailed systems of monitoring the implementation of the programmes. Likewise, the PES provides data placements. In addition to data provided by the central government, provinces and local governments take responsibility for monitoring and reporting on employment-related activities in the respective areas.

The DPME in South Africa has developed an evaluation policy, the National Evaluation Policy Framework (NEPF) which sets out an approach to establishing a National Evaluation System for the country. This, in turn, sets the basis for a National Evaluation Plan, indicating key government interventions that will be evaluated. At the macro level, the government reviews the extent to which its employment creation targets are on track, and with that end analyzes how various policy decisions may have an impact on employment creation. At the level of specific policies and programmes, ALMPs have evaluative mechanisms to provide feedback on the extent to which expected outcomes are being realized.

As for the mechanisms used for evaluation, while some work has been done by independent researchers, it is not clear whether this is the rule, especially for implementing the National Evaluation Plan.

The accountability system relating to employment policy: comparisons and a general framework

All countries covered by the present study do not have a comprehensive and well-structured accountability system that can be used to assess the working of employment policies and their effectiveness. However, those who have, e.g., China, Korea, and South Africa, appear to use frameworks that are broadly similar in structure, although the details show some variations. The starting off points generally are the national-level priorities and goals (sometimes with targets) which are translated into work plans with performance indicators associated with specific targets. The next step is to have budgetary allocations that may come from central as well as local levels (with the possibility of donor support in developing countries). Some countries have explicit performance framework with indicators of outcomes and a delivery plan. Progress and performance in implementation are monitored through a system of statistics and reporting, and evaluation is done to assess the impact of policies on various employment-related outcomes. The final stage in this process of accountability is to translate the results of monitoring and evaluation into adjustment and improvements in the programmes and policies. The process is depicted in Figure 9.3.

The above, however, is a stylized description of the accountability system followed by various countries, and there are differences in the details of implementation. One difference concerns the levels at which employment policies are pursued. Countries demonstrate differences in the definition of and approach to employment policies – some taking a comprehensive approach ranging from macroeconomic policies to labour market policies while others focus more on the latter. This is reflected in the accountability systems as

Figure 9.3 A Framework for Accountability System in Implementing National Employment Policies.

well. In South Africa, for example, the system includes examinations of the impact of macroeconomic policies as well as elements of ALMPs, while other countries may not be devoting the same degree of attention to the former.

There are differences in funding mechanisms as well. In Argentina and Brazil, for example, the main funding is linked to the unemployment insurance fund, and only the surplus that is available after meeting the needs of unemployment benefits can be used for active employment measures. This naturally limits the scope for employment policies. In other countries, e.g., China, South Africa, funds are allocated specifically for employment programmes and policies – Special Employment Funds in China, Jobs Fund in South Africa.

Differences are also found in the approach to monitoring and evaluation, especially in the degree of independence and transparency of the system. While Korea has institutionalized independent systems of evaluation, China invites a "third party" to evaluate some employment programmes.

The effectiveness of the accountability system in the implementation of employment policies depends on a variety of factors that include:

- How clearly the overall priorities are articulated and translated into measurable targets.
- Whether sound action plans and implementation strategies are put in place for each target so that the actual result/outcome can be compared with the expected ones.
- Whether budgetary allocations are made with clear indication of responsibilities and whether a transparent system of accounting is put in place.
- Whether a performance framework is defined with indicators of outcomes.
- Whether the statistical and reporting system covers the entire policy domain and how well the system performs.
- Whether there is provision for independent monitoring and evaluation system.

The above appears to be a tall order for a country to satisfy, especially when it comes to the formulation and implementation of a comprehensive NEP with action plans covering macroeconomic, sectoral, and ALMPs. Most of the countries covered by the study have a well-articulated set of priorities and have set targets clearly. However, it is in the preparation of action plans, formulation of implementation strategies and making budgetary allocations that differences occur. Likewise, the statistical systems needed for generating the required data and information vary in terms of technical as well as financial strength. While Korea, China, and South Africa have good statistical systems, for many developing countries this is a major weakness. Moreover, it is not enough to have a statistical system generating data on the labour market; it would be essential to have data that can be used to link specific policies and actions and outcomes in terms of employment generation. Data collected in South Africa with regard to the implementation of the IPAP and EPWP and in China on monitoring the re-employment of laid-off worker and the transfer of rural labour are examples of data relating to specific aspects of employment policy.

Finally, the existence of a system of independent evaluation is critical for proper and objective assessment of the outcomes in relation to the objectives set and the resources allocated for attaining them. China and South Africa are making strides in that direction.

Some lessons from the country experiences

Before making concluding remarks on the basis of the country case studies that have been synthesized in the present chapter, a general remark may be made with regard to what is often referred to as "successful experience". A country may not have achieved complete overall success in meeting the employment challenge, and yet may have demonstrated some success in one or more of the elements in the mechanism for implementing employment policies. It should be possible to draw some lessons from such experiences as well. Of course, amongst the country case studies that have been studied here, there are countries that have attained successes in several dimensions, and there would be more lessons to be drawn from them. With this preliminary remark, a few lessons drawn from the case studies are enumerated below.

First, in order for employment policies to be successful, they need to be formulated well. In that regard, an important issue is the scope and content of the policies. The policy framework should ideally include macroeconomic and sectoral policies as well as ALMPs, and there should be a balance between the demand and supply sides of the labour market. The concern for employment needs to be integrated into the process of formulating macroeconomic and sectoral policies. Although evidence in this respect in the country studies is limited, the example of Korea is worth mentioning where tax reforms included measures to create incentives for job creation. South Africa incorporated employment consideration in the formulation of macroeconomic policies and has introduced a tax incentive aimed at encouraging employers to hire young and less-experienced work seekers. Brazil also has been able to effectively use its growth strategy to overcome the adverse effects of the global economic crisis of 2008–09 on its employment and labour market situation.

Second, employment being a cross-cutting issue, coordination – both horizontal (i.e., between relevant agencies of the government and other institutions) and vertical (i.e., between various levels of implementation – central and local) is an important issue. To be effective, the responsibility of coordination has to be at a sufficiently high and influential level. Whether the labour ministry will play a lead role in that would depend largely on the governance structure of the country and the mandate given to the ministry. If it has the mandate, it would have to equip itself with necessary strength and capacity.

However, too complex a system of coordination may create additional problems, and simplicity may be a virtue in this regard.[9] China and Korea are examples of simplicity combined with clarity in the allocation of roles and responsibilities. In addition, the capacity of how to strengthen the coordination or to make the coordination more dynamic is vital.

Third, with respect to vertical coordination (i.e., between central and local levels), confusion may arise unless the mandates of formulation of policies and funding are clearly defined. This may lead to duplication of efforts and inefficiency.

Fourth, the support system for implementing employment policies needs to be as comprehensive as possible and should have a balance between demand- and supply-oriented interventions. They should also reflect the level of development and the structure of employment and labour market of a country. For example, a country whose economy is predominantly rural and the labour market is characterized by the existence of a substantial informal sector, employment services of a conventional nature may not be very useful. In such situations, greater focus would be needed on engendering high growth of an employment-intensive nature and on measures that can gradually transform the informal into formal employment. Of course, employment services and labour market information system should also be built gradually and go hand in hand with employment policy implementation.

Fifth, the accountability system for implementing employment policies needs to start from well-articulated priorities and targets that are measurable and include funding mechanisms, a plan for implementation with a clear performance framework and indicators of expected outcomes. The funding mechanism should have budgetary provision for individual policy areas. The performance framework and the expected outcomes should be linked to policies and action programmes.

Sixth, periodic monitoring of results and evaluation of policies and programmes are essential from the point of view of assessing their effectiveness and bringing about improvements. This requires, in the first place, a good statistical system which can be used to develop an LMIS needed for the purpose. In addition to a general LMIS for monitoring the overall employment and labour market situation, there should be provision for monitoring the performance of individual programmes. Developing countries need to invest resources for building up a good LMIS.

Seventh, independence of evaluation of policies and programmes is extremely important from the point of view of assessing their effectiveness and drawing lessons for possible improvements. Some countries (e.g., China and South Africa) have already incorporated independent evaluation into their systems, and it would be worthwhile to look at their experiences.

Eighth, while sound employment policies are important, the capacity to implement them is also equally important. And the issue is not only the existence of necessary institutions but also the efficiency with which they function.

Notes

1 This chapter draws on Islam (2014).
2 The study on which the present chapter is based, Islam (2014), covers Argentina, Bosnia and Herzegovina, Brazil, Burkina Faso, China, Germany, Republic of Korea, South Africa, and the EU (including two of its member states, Germany and the UK). However, this chapter leaves out Bosnia and Herzegovina, Burkina Faso, and the EU countries. On the other hand, the section on examples of employment policy includes Bangladesh, India, and Pakistan (which were not included in Islam, 2014).
3 The importance of economic policies in the context of employment has been recognized in both the Philadelphia Declaration and the Employment Policy Convention (C.122) of the ILO. According to the terms of the former, it is the responsibility of the ILO to examine and consider the bearing of economic and financial policies upon employment policy. The text of C.122 mentions that measures to be adopted for attaining the goal of full, productive and freely chosen employment (the subject of the Convention) are to be reviewed within the framework of a coordinated economic and social policy.
4 Whether targets are realistic or not depend on a variety of economic, social, and political factors relevant for each country.
5 The Council is tripartite with a total of 18 members – six each from the government, employers, and workers.
6 New Growth Path is one of the pillars of the Medium-Term Strategic Framework for 2009–14. With a medium-term perspective, it sets out the sectors that are considered critical for employment-generating growth.
7 A Public Employment Services Act has recently been passed.
8 The work currently involves: registering vacancies, disseminating scarce skills information, addressing issues relating to immigrant corporate and work permits, tracking the numbers of migrating skilled South Africans, overseeing the placements of work seekers, responding to companies in distress, facilitating a social plan aimed at companies in distress, and regulating private employment agencies.
9 In some countries (e.g., in South Africa) too many structures create confusions between the mandates and objectives set out by them as well as their areas of responsibilities. The respective country studies clearly mention difficulties encountered in achieving smooth coordination in those countries (see Box 9.3).

Bibliography

Bertranou, Fabio (2013): "Case Study on Mechanisms for the Formulation and Implementation of Employment Policy in Argentina". Draft paper, ILO, Geneva.
Dedecca, Claudio Salvadori (2013): "Case Study on Employment Policy Implementation Mechanisms in Brazil". Draft paper, ILO, Geneva.
GOB (Government of Bangladesh), Planning Commission (2015): *Seventh Five Year Plan FY 2016-FY2020*. Planning Commission, Dhaka.
GOI (Government of India), Planning Commission (2013): *Twelfth Five Year Plan (2012–17), Social Sectors, Volume III*. Planning Commission, Delhi.
——— NITI Aayog (2018): *Strategy for New India @75*. New Delhi.
GOP (Government of Pakistan), Planning Commission (2019): *11th Five Year Plan, Chapter 7 Labour, employment and skill development*. https://www.pc.gov.pk/uploads/plans/Ch7-Labour-employment2.pdf (Accessed on 28 January 2019).

Islam, Rizwanul (2014): "Employment Policy Implementation Mechanisms: A Synthesis Based on Country Experiences". Employment Working Paper No. 161, Employment Policy Department, ILO, Geneva.

Kang, Soonhie (2013): "Country Case Study on Employment Policy Implementation: Korea". Draft paper, ILO, Geneva.

Marock, Carmel and Renee Grawitzky (2013): "Employment Policy Implementation and Mechanisms: A Case Study of South Africa". Draft paper, ILO, Geneva.

Zeng, Xianquan, Yang Yumei, Yang Wang, Tian Zeng and Huining Chang (2013): "Case Study on Employment Policy Implementation Mechanisms in China". Draft paper, ILO, Geneva.

Zimmermann, Katharina and Vanesa Fuertes (2013): "Case Study on Employment Policy Implementation Mechanisms in the European Union, the United Kingdom and Germany". Draft paper, ILO, Geneva.

10 Concluding observations

Key findings and messages

Measures of open unemployment and estimates of NAIRU are of limited use from the point of view of monitoring progress in attaining full employment in developing countries

Given the standard definition of unemployment, the way it is measured through labour force and employment surveys, and the absence of social protection against loss of income during periods of unemployment in many developing countries, it is not surprising that the observed rate of open unemployment is rather low. Hence, it would not be appropriate to describe the challenge of employment in such situations merely in terms of reducing unemployment. The real issue for them is one of moving people from jobs characterized by low productivity and low incomes to ones with higher productivity and incomes. That process requires structural transformation of an economy both in terms of output and employment, and it should be an important consideration for developing countries in their pursuit of full employment.

Judging by a comparison between estimates of non-accelerating inflation rate of unemployment (NAIRU) and actual rates of unemployment, many developing countries would appear to be in a situation of full employment. On the other hand, it is well known that finding productive employment is a serious challenge for large proportions of their workforce. Indicators of progress in attaining goal 8 of the SDGs (viz., attaining full productive employment and decent work) do go beyond open unemployment and include the share of informal employment and earnings from employment. But they fall short of fully reflecting the importance of structural transformation and do not include anything that would enable one to judge the progress being made in addressing the real challenge of the growth of productive employment in developing countries.

Structural transformation led by manufacturing is key, and indicators are needed to monitor progress on that front

As for structural transformation, the contention of this book is that like the present-day developed countries and the late developers who were successful in combining economic growth with the absorption of surplus labour, in-dustrialization, and growth of labour-intensive manufacturing are key for other developing countries as well – especially for those in South Asia. Em-pirical evidence shows that alternative pathways (e.g., ICT-driven activities, tourism, etc.) do show some promise of generating employment where pro-ductivity is higher than in traditional sectors, but they are not adequate for providing jobs to the large numbers who enter the labour force every year and others who need to move from the traditional sectors.

Considering the key role of industrialization and the importance of formal sector jobs, the present book suggests, in Chapter 3, an expanded framework of indicators for monitoring the progress made by developing countries in addressing the challenge of boosting productive employment. They include (i) the share of regular salaried/wage employment, (ii) the share and the rate of growth employment in manufacturing, (iii) the share of employment in the informal economy and the rate of its decline, (iv) the proportion of the workforce who are below the poverty line, and (v) labour productivity and real wages, etc.

Progress made by countries of South Asia in attaining needed structural transformation has been slow

Using some of the indicators mentioned above, it is found that the progress made by the countries of South Asia has been rather slow. Compared to countries of East and South East Asia (ESEA), especially, China, Republic of Korea, Malaysia, Taiwan–China, Thailand, etc. they are lagging behind in terms of absorbing surplus labour and moving towards the Lewis turning point which marks an upward rise in the supply curve of labour.

Labour market outcomes in terms of employment, productivity, real wages, and social protection are extremely important from the point of view of im-proving the levels of living of workers and the distribution of income in an economy. A review of the experience of developing countries shows that the success attained by several countries ESEA in combining economic growth with employment could not be replicated elsewhere. In South Asia, employ-ment intensity of economic growth has generally been low and has declined over time. More importantly, manufacturing has not played the role of the engine of growth in the same manner as has happened in the former group of countries. As a result of the slow growth of employment in the modern sectors of the economies, growth of formal sector employment has been rather low despite sustained and high growth of output (e.g., in Bangladesh and India). And the share of informal employment in total employment continues to remain high.

Persistence of informal employment at high levels poses a challenge for social protection – the level of coverage remaining rather low. Moreover, empirical evidence shows that although the level of social protection is posi-tively correlated with the level of income of a country, the relationship is not linear – indicating that high income or economic growth is not a sufficient condition for expansion of social protection.

As for real wages of workers, there have been periods of positive trends in some countries, but that trend could not be sustained. Bangladesh is such a case. Moreover, in several instances, e.g., in Bangladesh and India, growth of wages has lagged behind that of labour productivity. As a result, even when there was a rise in real wages, it has not been able to make an impact on growing income inequality. Gender differences in wages also persist. On the whole, it may be concluded that labour market outcomes in South Asia have not moved in a direction needed to make economic growth more inclusive.

Furthermore, labour markets in developing countries are vulnerable to periodic fluctuations in economic activities, which, in turn, may be due to a variety of risks – of both idiosyncratic and covariant type. In the absence of effective coping mechanisms, the poor and the vulnerable often are the ones who suffer more; and depending on the type of shocks, recovery in the labour market may follow economic recovery with a lag. This is particularly the case with economic crises, as has been exemplified by the adverse effects of several past crises.

One may wonder whether full employment through labour-intensive industrialization has become history

On the whole, it would appear that transformation in the structure of employment towards modern sectors and success in attaining the Lewis turning point has remained confined to a small number of countries who started their journey towards development earlier than the currently developing countries. This experience gives rise to the question whether employment-intensive economic growth driven by high growth of labour-intensive manufacturing has become history that cannot be repeated. In that context, two issues, viz., the possibility of premature de-industrialization and premature spread of automation and labour-saving technology, become important.

Possibility of de-industrialization and adoption of modern technology also have implications

If countries of South Asia are taken for purposes of illustration, it can be seen that although the process of de-industrialization has not started, the share of manufacturing employment has stagnated at a much lower level compared to the peak share attained by the successful countries. Furthermore, in the current global context where competition based on cheap labour has become more intense and improving labour productivity has become much more important for achieving competitiveness, industrialization based on labour-intensive manufacturing is likely to hit the ceiling much earlier than has been the case.

The situation is likely to be aggravated by the availability and adoption of modern technology – often facilitated through distortions in relative factor prices – even in industries that are by nature more labour-intensive. Although the danger of large-scale automation in the wake of the fourth industrial revolution may be overblown, the possibility of technological progress reducing labour intensity and giving rise to capital deepening cannot be ignored.

The global context has also changed considerably with respect to the conditions in which labour is employed. Although workers continue to find themselves under pressure arising from the pursuit of competitiveness in the global supply chain, scrutiny of the terms and conditions of work is becoming more intense than has been the case. And that is making employers wary of investing in labour-intensive lines of production.

In addition, there is the danger of a race to the bottom

However, the above should not be taken to mean that the danger of a race to the bottom is gone completely. In fact, if the example of the ready-made garment industry in Bangladesh is any guide, it remains real, and may even aggravate. While elements of decent work relating to social protection and workers' rights remain far cry, even basic issues like protecting their real wages cannot be taken for granted. Workers in the industry face an unfriendly environment because of pressures arising from two sides. On the one hand, although there is a lot of discussion about the environment in which products are made, consumers often are not willing to pay a premium for compliance in places of work. This is starkly reflected in the decline in prices for the final products and the rigid position taken by brand retailers in bargaining for lowering prices. On the other hand, when suppliers face such pressures from the retailers, rather than taking a cut in their profit margin, they make every effort to squeeze workers through the wage mechanism.

Implications for strategies and policies

Need for a multi-pronged strategy

Given the importance of structural transformation and the pattern of growth in developing countries, an important question is why this is not happening at the desired pace and how the pace can be accelerated? Development strategies will need to address these questions. It is important to get away from growth fetishism and assume that high rate of economic growth will automatically solve the employment problem. Likewise, it is time to move away from the conventional thinking of labour market rigidity as the only barrier to employment growth.

A multi-pronged strategy would be needed to pursue the goal of productive employment through structural transformation. The primary focus should be on growth-induced employment so that jobs are created through the process of growth. A strategy for employment-intensive growth would involve the adoption of policies for promoting the growth of sectors that are by nature labour-intensive until surplus labour available in the economy is exhausted. It should be possible to identify such sectors by looking at the degree of employment intensity of various sectors and sub-sectors, and it would then be a matter of creating the right incentive structure for their growth.

The second part of the strategy would consist of a set of policies and programmes that can be conceptualized under the rubric of active labour market policies (ALMPs). Programmes aimed directly at boosting employment growth, e.g., through entrepreneurship development and special programmes for creating wage employment, as well as other programmes like skill development, retraining of workers to facilitate structural adjustment in an economy, and matching of workers with jobs would come under this broad package. If the experience of developed countries is any guide, employment growth is positively associated with government's expenditure on ALMPs.

Actions that would be required in the process of formulation and implementation of employment strategies and policies at the country level would include (i) setting of employment-related targets and goals (using an expanded framework over and above the SDG framework), (ii) identification of policy interventions and reforms that are needed to make economic growth more employment-friendly, (iii) formulation and implementation of active labour market policies and programmes, (iv) allocation of budgetary resources, (v) periodic assessment of the impact of various policy interventions and programmes, (vi) periodic monitoring of the situation in relation to the goals and targets set, and (vii) adjustments in policies and programmes based on the results obtained.

Implementation of employment policies: coordinating multiple actors in a multi-pronged strategy

Given the multi-pronged nature of the strategy and policies that are needed, it is natural that multiple actors will be involved in formulating and implementing them. Hence, a strong institutional mechanism is needed for managing the whole process. Coordination, monitoring, and evaluation of the effectiveness of the policies would be key to ensuring success of the effort.

In terms of framework, a balanced approach with focus on both demand and supply sides is desirable. As for the level at which coordination is done, it is important to assign the task to an organ of the government with a sufficient degree of responsibility and technical capacity in inter-ministerial coordination. Technical capacity to analyze possible employment implications of alternative sets of strategies and policies as well as to monitor the actual employment outcomes would be important. Starting from conceptual integration of the employment concern into the process of formulating strategies and policies, a series of employment-related questions and issues relevant for each ministry/department would need to be formulated so that the task of each of them can be outlined clearly. The task of coordination would become easier if the responsibilities of the respective agencies are clearly defined.

The system of monitoring can work better when there are clearly defined priorities and targets with work plans and budgets associated with them. Likewise, assessment and evaluation of the impact of policies on the employment outcomes can be easier when the expected outcomes are also clearly defined. However, temptation to have too many targets and too rigid work plans needs to be avoided. The policy implementation mechanism should not be burdened with too many targets and too rigid work plans.

Where employment policy implementation involves multiple levels, and formulation is done at the central level without involvement of the local-level agencies in charge of implementation, coordination issues may arise. This may be resolved by involving the implementers from the stage of formulation.

Availability of data needed for formulation as well as for monitoring the effectiveness of policies is an important issue because data relating to employment and labour markets are in short supply in many developing countries. Although the frequency of labour force surveys has improved in some countries, the situation is still far from ideal. Likewise, other sources of data, e.g., on key sectors like manufacturing and services are often inadequate and outdated. Application of the expanded framework for monitoring progress in attaining the employment goal suggested in this book will make considerable demand on data, and serious efforts will be needed to fill in the gaps.

The way ahead

A well-formulated policy with clear articulation of goals, targets, and strategies for achieving the targets is a first step in the whole cycle of formulation and implementation of employment policy. They, in turn, could be looked at from a medium- to long-term as well as short-term perspectives. It would be useful to start with medium- and long-term goals in broad terms and have them broken down to specific short-term goals and targets. For the former, a basic point of reference is provided by the employment-related targets and indicators of SDGs. But (as mentioned above) there are a number of limitations of the employment-related targets and indicators when looked at from the perspective of developing countries, and improvements can be made in the list. Suggestions have been provided in this book for an expanded framework, and they have been summarized above. It should be possible to use the suggested framework for formulating employment policies and for monitoring progress in attaining the overall goal of full employment at the level of individual countries.

Once global goals and targets are translated into country-level objectives and targets, strategies and policies may be formulated to attain them. Mechanisms for implementing the policies can start by breaking down the medium- and long-term goals into shorter-term targets of a specific nature, which, in turn, can be associated with implementation frameworks, budgetary allocation, and monitoring and evaluation of the performance. In this whole process, the country-specific context should be a major consideration, and the goals, targets as well as the associated implementation mechanisms should reflect such specificities. For example, in developing countries, structural transformation of the composition of employment should be a major element in the strategy for attaining the goal of full productive employment for all because the major challenge in such countries is to shift workers from employment characterized by low productivity to those with higher productivity. Likewise, a gradual insertion of the characteristics of formal employment into what is now informal employment could be another goal. Both of these are longer-term issues and can be addressed through a series of policies and action programmes. Once such action is identified, the implementation mechanism needed for pursuing them would also follow from them.

The support system for implementing employment policy will have to reflect the goals, targets, and strategies that are being pursued. A comprehensive system consisting of a broad array of instruments ranging from macroeconomic and sectoral policies to active labour market policies will have to be used. The institutional capacity as well as the coordination mechanism will have to be geared towards the functioning of such a support system. The key idea in that respect is mainstreaming of employment into the entire growth and development strategy and policymaking process.

Index

labour market outcomes 65; and wages
77–81
labour markets: adjustment to economic
downturns 93–7; country experiences
with respect to information 192–7;
and economic crises 91–7; and
fluctuations 88; instruments 5; job
creation hindered by rigidities in
150–6; lag in recovery of 97–103;
policies 2; resilience of 91; rigidity and
employment in India 153–6; risks 5;
and vulnerability 89
labour power 1
labour productivity 58–9
labour underutilization 62n16
Lee, E. 128n2
Lewis turning point 3, 9, 110–11, 118,
160, 210–11
Luddites 121

McKinsey report 124, 128n10
Mahatma Gandhi National Rural
Employment Guarantee Programme
(MGNREGP) 83
Mahatma Gandhi National Rural
Employment Guarantee Scheme
(MGNREGS) 156
Malaysia: automation and 124; informal
employment 52–3; manufacturing
employment 56; and manufacturing
sector 15, **16,** 17; share of manufacturing
in total employment in 118
manufacturing: *vs.* agriculture 11;
decrease in agriculture, and increase in
14, 15; and economic growth 10, 11;
employment in 56–7; growth elasticity
17; productivity growth in 11
market-oriented economies 144n6
migration: Bihar (India) 27–8, 33–4; and
domestic demand 23–4
Millennium Development Goals (MDGs)
148, 175; and economic growth
45; and employment goal 45–7;
employment indicators of 47
MOHRSS 177
Multifibre Agreement 135

Naastepad, C.W.M. 128n2
National Agricultural Labour
Commission 181
National Commission for Enterprises
in the Unorganized Sector (NCEUS)
84n14
National Economic Development and
Labour Council (NEDLAC) 178

National Employment Fund 199
national employment policies (NEPs) 169;
accountability system for monitoring and
evaluation of 198–205; accountability
system relating to employment policy
202–5; accountability systems in
practice 199–202; adjustment and
improvement 199; annual work plan
198; characteristics of implementation
mechanisms of 178–9; coordination
mechanisms employed at country level
179–87; coordination of implementation
of 179–91; employment policy financing
198–9; evaluation of 199; inspection
of 199; key indicators in national
development strategy 198; statistics and
reporting 199; strengths and weaknesses
of coordination mechanisms 187–91;
supervision of 199
National People's Congress 177
National Sample Survey Organisation 152
National Tripartite Committee 136–7
Nepal 37n20; employment elasticity 71;
and factor price distortion 24; GDP
growth 17; growth and employment
in tourism in 25–6, 34; growth in
manufacturing 17, 34; growth of
manufacturing employment in 120;
inflation and unemployment gap
44; share of manufacturing in GDP
and total employment in 119; and
structural transformation 10; and
surplus labour 9
New Growth Path 207n6
non-accelerating inflation rate of
unemployment (NAIRU) 4, 61n5;
described 43; and developed
economies 43; and developing
countries 43–4; measures of
estimates of 209; measures of open
unemployment of 209
non-farm activities: rural transformation,
in Bangladesh 28–33
"non-standard employment" 144n7

OECD 84n10; Employment Outlook
2006 84n9; estimates of NAIRU 43
Okun, Arthur 92
Okun's law 92, 106n5
"output effect" 111

Pakistan: employment elasticity 70; and
export demand elasticity 19; GDP
growth 17; growth in manufacturing 17;
growth of manufacturing employment